TRANSFORMING
HARRY

TRANSFORMING
HARRY

The Adaptation of *Harry Potter* in the Transmedia Age

Edited by
John Alberti and P. Andrew Miller

Wayne State University Press
Detroit

Library of Cataloging Control Number: 2017953972

ISBN 978-0-8143-4286-2 (paperback)
ISBN 978-0-8143-4491-0 (hardcover)
ISBN 978-0-8143-4287-9 (ebook)

Wayne State University Press
Leonard N. Simons Building
4809 Woodward Avenue
Detroit, Michigan 48201–1309

Visit us online at wsupress.wayne.edu

In memory of Danny Miller,
the Dumbledore of the NKU English Department

Contents

Acknowledgments

"I've always admired your courage, Harry, but sometimes you can be really thick," Hermione tells Harry in the final scene of the movie version of *Harry Potter and the Half Blood Prince*, after Harry tells his two best friends that he plans to finish the battle against Voldemort all on his own. "You don't really think you're going to be able to find all those horcruxes by yourself, do you? You need us, Harry." As in the wizarding world, so in Muggle academia. This essay collection relied on our own Dumbledore's Army of contributors, supporters, and fellow devotees of all things Hogwarts.

First, our thanks to the English department at Northern Kentucky University, and especially our friends and colleagues Dr. Jonathan S. Cullick and Dr. Emily Detmer-Goebel. As chairs of the department, they gave an enthusiastic green light to our idea of teaching a course called "Harry Potter on the Page and on the Screen" in the spring of 2012, as a way of commemorating the completion of the movie adaptations of J. K. Rowling's global literary sensation. Either singly or together, we have taught that course every spring since then to class after class of eager Potterheads, helping them to gain a deeper understanding of the complex nature of storytelling and adaptation. Ms. Marcia Johnson in the Media Collection department in Steely Library made sure we and our students always had access to DVD and Blu-ray versions of the movies, and Joe Wendeln and his staff in the College of Informatics made sure the technological Muggle magic of the George and Ellen Rieveschl Digitorium always worked smoothly.

We owe our deepest debt to Annie Martin, our acquisitions editor at Wayne State University Press. John has had the privilege and good fortune of working with Annie for over ten years, and she has offered genuine support and professional skill in shepherding the book from initial submission through the outside reviewing process and final editorial board approval. Our lively chats at various Wayne State conference book exhibits over the years have been sources of both motivation and wise advice.

Of course, the essay collection wouldn't exist at all without the creativity, insight, scholarly rigor, and commitment of all our contributors. Their patience and dedication over the long process of putting this collection together are the real magic behind this book. They have all responded to our suggestions for revision and our latest deadlines with good humor and good work, and we know their efforts will benefit scholars and serious fans of *Harry Potter* for years to come.

Just as this collection wouldn't exist without our contributors, the project never would have started without the inspiration and excitement provided by the students who have participated in our *Harry Potter* classes over the years, both at Northern Kentucky University and as part of study abroad classes we have led in the United Kingdom. What we thought would be a one-off course has become a regular part of our teaching and research lives, in part because of our own interest, but also because students demanded we continue to offer the course. The experience of discussing *Harry Potter* and the process of adaptation, as well as the various student projects related to what we now call transmedia *Harry Potter*, inform every aspect of our approach to this collection.

Finally, John would like to acknowledge his daughter and fellow Potterphile, Martha Dietsche-Alberti, as the true inspiration for this collection. John and Martha began reading and discussing *Harry Potter* together just before the turn of the century and would eagerly await the appearance of each new novel (John anxiously waiting for her to finish her reading in order to get caught up before the spoilers appeared), and then the arrival of each new movie. She was in elementary school when the journey began and a college graduate as the final movie appeared. What more appropriate tribute to this shared obsession could a fellow Ravenclaw offer than this scholarly labor of love.

Introduction

Harry Potter
and the Magical Screen

John Alberti and P. Andrew Miller

The eight film versions of the seven *Harry Potter* novels represent an unprecedented cultural event in the history of cinematic adaptation. The essays in *Transforming Harry: The Adaptation of Harry Potter in the Transmedia Age* explore the cultural, political, aesthetic, and pedagogical dimensions of this generation-defining event as a means of considering what the process of cinematic adaptation in the digital age tells us about popular culture in the twenty-first century.

The movie version of the first *Harry Potter* book, *Harry Potter and the Sorcerer's Stone*, premiered in 2001, in between publication of the fourth and fifth books of this global literary phenomenon.[1] As a result, the production and reception of both novel and movie series became intertwined with one another, creating multiple combinations of fans who accessed the series first through the books, first through the movies, and in various other combinations. The decision to cast three young, age-appropriate actors who would mature along with their fictional counterparts further represented a cross-pollination of the interpretive process, as readers began experiencing the newly emerging novels in terms of the visual imagination of their screen experiences.

At the same time, the adaptation, reception, and transformation of the *Harry Potter* narrative took place as digital technologies and the Internet were radically redefining all aspects of the media landscape, from the production and distribution of visual narratives to the very relationship between readers/viewers and cultural texts. As the boundaries between the producers and consumers of books and movies began to blur and fade, the process of "adaptation" began to include fan-based texts such as fan fiction and fan sites, mash-ups, GIFs, and other forms of "prosumer" activity, nowhere more so than in the fan culture that developed around the *Harry Potter* series on screens of various kinds.

The digital age has also raised our critical awareness of just how complex a cultural apparatus is contained within the seemingly simple term "the movies." More and more we recognize how the cinematic experience is (and really always has been) a radically multiscreen experience. Rather than relying on the textual stability evoked by the idea of the "movie version" of a novel, we want to explore how the mobility and interactivity of digital information challenges our basic definition of what a movie is. Just as significant for adaptation studies, a similar revolution is underway in literary studies, as we likewise come to appreciate how the reading experience is equally a multiscreen, interactive experience, taking place on tablets and smart phones, with the printed page now just one more (opaque and flammable) "screen."

The case of the *Harry Potter* series spans all of these screens in ways that are both unprecedented in the history of cinematic adaption and that speak directly to how the digital age radically challenges and expands our ideas about adaptation. The stories combine an atavistic nostalgia for a supposedly simpler era of media production, where characters use quill pens to write on parchment by firelight within the Gothic castle/school Hogwarts, with themes of transformation, adaptation, and the magical impermanence of the material world. Even though the plot of the novels spans the years from 1992–1998, with an epilogue set in 2017, the emerging digital world scarcely makes an appearance in the series, either in print or on screen. The Muggle technology that so fascinates the "pure blood" wizards remains for the most part stubbornly analog, from landline telephones to broadcast radio and television.

The movie versions, however, are themselves epitomes of digital blockbuster visual entertainment, incorporating computer-generated imagery and 3-D effects in part to evoke a sense of the magical world of *Harry Potter* for its viewers, in part to compete with a constantly evolving and technologized cinematic landscape, dominated by adaptations of equally fantastic comic book universes. But the adaptation of *Harry Potter* is not limited to movies based on the seven "canonical" novels. The larger culture of *Harry Potter* adaptation and reception itself exemplifies textuality in the digital age, encompassing a vast fan fiction community; an endlessly morphing variety of mash-ups and visual play (as represented by Katharine McCain's essay on GIF sets); and a continuing development of "new" *Potter* material by J. K. Rowling through the *Pottermore* web site (itself both an "original" *Potter* text and an extensive adaptation of Potterism) as well as her prominent Twitter presence, the new movie series *Fantastic Beasts and Where to Find Them* (a once "ancillary" *Potter* text now become part of the canon), and the two-part play *The Cursed Child*, focused on the children of the original Potter characters.

In short, as Maria Dicieanu argues in her essay, the case of the adaptation of the *Harry Potter* novels "from the page to the screen" is inseparable from the theoretical arguments over transmedia culture in the digital age and the extent to which the idea of transmedia either replaces or absorbs more conventional ideas about adaptation. As Henry Jenkins defines it, "Transmedia storytelling represents a process where integral elements of a fiction get dispersed systematically across multiple delivery channels for the purpose of creating a unified and coordinated entertainment experience. Ideally, each medium makes its own unique contribution to the unfolding of the story."[2] Again, the case of the *Harry Potter* series thematizes this debate, as the initial core audience and arguably most loyal fan base for the series remains the so-called millennial generation, whose acculturation into the world of wizards and owls paralleled the need to accommodate to an increasingly participatory and rapidly changing digital culture. Both throwback and throw forward, a textual experience rooted in the old-fashioned pleasures of curling up with a book that has easily encompassed the transmedia manifestations of theme parks and video games, the *Harry Potter* phenomena brings together—as does this collection—more traditional close reading and textual analysis with theoretical questions about just what we mean by the term "adaptation" in the digital age.

Perhaps the first and most vital question involves the very signifier "Harry Potter" itself. Just what do we mean, exactly, when we refer to "Harry Potter"? A character in a series of stories? The stories themselves? A complex subculture? A multivolume series composed of individual novels, "Harry Potter" shares with other literary and cinematic series the tension between reading these texts as separable units or as parts of an overarching whole. That *Harry Potter* would become a successful multivolume series was of course no guarantee from the start, and the openings of the first three novels in particular employ narrative (and cinematic) devices of summary and flashbacks that allowed new readers to access the frame story without necessarily having read any of the others. By the last books, however, such aids largely disappeared, and readers are expected to have been keeping up with the series.

The same recursive strategy can be seen with the first movie adaptations as well. Both *Harry Potter and the Sorcerer's Stone* (Chris Columbus 2001) and *Harry Potter and the Chamber of Secrets* (Chris Columbus 2002) relied on the repetition in story structure between these two novels, each involving Harry arriving at Hogwarts to go on a relatively self-contained quest, to create multiple entry points for beginners to either movie and the series itself. After Alfonso Cuarón's artistically ambitious third movie, *Harry Potter and the Prisoner of Azkaban* (2004), however, the movies came increasingly to depend on the prior knowledge of the other movies/novels that audiences would bring with them, an aspect of the movies very different from, say, the venerable James Bond franchise, and which resulted in some exasperated reviews by movie critics not versed or even that interested in the overarching Potter mythology, who nonetheless had to review each movie on the basis of its supposed intrinsic merits as an "individual" text.

The eight movie adaptations of the seven *Harry Potter* novels constitute another unique development in the history of movie adaptation as well, as the appearance of the movies overlapped the composition of the literary texts. When the movie *Harry Potter and the Sorcerer's Stone* opened (coincidentally but significantly just two months after 9/11), only four of the novels had appeared. The fifth, *Harry Potter and the Order of the Phoenix*, the longest book in the series and the most overtly political, appeared between the second and third movies. The final novel, *Harry Potter and the Deathly Hallows*, was published in July 2007, the same month as the movie version of *Order of the Phoenix* (David Yates) and a little over ten years after the first novel.

Just this happenstance of production and marketing itself complicates our understanding of adaptation, as J. K. Rowling's composition of the final Potter books occurred in the context of the cinematic adaptation and reception of her earlier works. Rowling worked closely as a consultant on the movies, even though the screenplays were all written by Steve Kloves, with the exception of *Order of the Phoenix*, written by Michael Goldenberg. This overlap continued with *Fantastic Beasts and Where to Find Them*, for which Rowling wrote the screenplay, as well as with *The Cursed Child*, written by Jack Thorne and based on a story by Thorne, Rowling, and play director John Tiffany. And as with all adaptations, the novel and film series have produced fans who have read only the novels, read both the novels and seen the movies, and have seen only the movies. Yet all three groups might unite around the collective signifier: fans of *Harry Potter*.

What many critics saw as the increasingly hermetic nature of the film series, the increasing unwillingness of the later movies to make any allowance for the newbie viewer, represents one crucial aspect of the *Harry Potter*

Eddie Redmayne as Newt Scamander in *Fantastic Beasts and Where to Find Them* (2016). Both an adaptation of an ancillary Hogwarts textbook that Rowling created as a charity project and an ambitious extension of the *Harry Potter* universe, *Fantastic Beasts* underscores the theoretical complexity of adaptation in the digital era.

series as a product of the age of democratized digital reproduction: how technology now allows for the easy multiple viewing of visual narratives on multiple screens. In terms of what we might call textual ontology, digitization erases the material differentiation among media, turning all narratives into code to be translated onto a screen in terms of visual imagery and auditory experiences, whether those images are letters on a Kindle or the multiple frames of a movie.

In terms of our practical experience of texts, the cutting-edge technology of digital culture has ironically made the old-fashioned book into a dominant reception model in the digital age. If episodic works such as the *Harry Potter* film series or a cable series such as *Breaking Bad* are becoming increasingly dense and self-referential in their transmission of narrative information, it is because digitization allows viewers to interact with visual narratives the way they traditionally have with books, watching them over and over, fixating on specific passages, and engaging with and adapting the texts. For contemporary viewers, the atavistic analog distinction between book reading as a domestic, familiar, and repeatable experience, and movie viewing as a fleeting, time-specific event, whether in a theater or on a pre-digital television schedule, is functionally obsolete.

For *Harry Potter* fans, the movies and the books have always been equally accessible, equally collectable. In terms of implications for adaptation studies, while the cultural distinction between "source" novel and "adapted" movie remains a relevant critical orientation for *Harry Potter* fans, and while the idea and ideal of "fidelity" also and equally remains an evaluative touchstone for them as well, the digitization of narrative produces a counter pressure against designating any particular narrative manifestation of *Harry Potter* as "original," "primary," or "definitive," especially when it comes to the diversity of what we have come to call fan culture.

All of these questions surrounding the complexity of the very idea of Harry Potter reflect an ongoing crisis in adaptation theory. As Thomas Leitch puts it in his trenchant essay, "Twelve Fallacies in Contemporary Adaptation Theory," "adaptation theory has remained tangential to the thrust of film study because it has never been undertaken with conviction and theoretical rigor."[3] The center of this crisis remains fixated on the concept of "fidelity," even though the demolition of this idea and ideal has become commonplace in discussions of adaptation theory, not the least in Leitch's essay, where it stands as fallacy number eight. In place of "fidelity," contemporary theorists are proposing new metaphorical models drawn from genetics and information theory, responding both to how the concept of fidelity underestimates the inherent complexity and instability of both written and cinematic texts and to the ways digital culture is transforming our understanding of textual interconnection itself. Robert Stam, for example, proposes an "intertextual" model of adaptation studies, one "not oriented by inchoate notions of 'fidelity' but rather by attention to 'transfers of creative energy.'"[4]

Even more radically, the cultural theorist Linda Hutcheon and the biologist Gary Bortolotti challenge "fidelity discourse" in adaptation studies by exploring a homology between biological and cultural notions of adaptation.[5] In this model, "sources" are rethought as "ancestors," and one purpose of critical investigation involves tracing the cultural lineage of a narrative idea through multiple vehicles in terms of the "success" of that idea measured by persistence, abundance, and diversity. Harry Potter, in this view, can be thought of as a kind of genotype, a narrative idea that adapts to differing cultural conditions and circumstances. While both Hutcheon and Bortolotti acknowledge that viewers and critics may still make aesthetic judgments about individual expressions, or phenotypes, of Harry Potter (such as the consensus among many film critics that *Harry Potter and the Prisoner of Azkaban* represents the most aesthetically interesting and satisfying of the *Potter* movies), the cultural success of Harry Potter as cultural idea is attested to by how well it has thrived in terms of persistence, abundance, and diversity.

The homology that Hutcheon and Bortolotti draw between biological and cultural manifestations of adaptation helps us adapt the concept of adaptation to the digital age by recognizing the mutability of individual textual and visual expressions of narrative ideas, but their focus on the metaphor of the "phenotype" still fixes the text, whether a book, movie, or work of fan fiction, as the source of meaning. The literary theorist N. Katherine Hayles, however, draws on information theory to introduce a distinction between information as a "thing" (as in the idea of the single, definable text) and information as an action (rooted in experience, the experience of information):

> In the choice between what information is and what it does, we can see the rival constellations of homeostasis and reflexivity beginning to take shape. Making information a thing allies it with homeostasis, for so defined, it can be transported into any medium and maintain a stable quantitative value, reinforcing the stability that homeostasis implies. Making information an action links it with reflexivity, for then its effect on the receiver must be taken into account, and measuring this effect sets up the potential for a reflexive spiral through an infinite regress of observers.[6]

This perspective explicitly introduces the question of reader/viewer/participant reception into the mix and points the way forward for our understanding of *Harry Potter* on the page and on the screen. The *Harry Potter* phenomenon not only complicates the idea of adaptation in terms of source and derivation, but the persistence, abundance, and diversity of *Harry Potter* fan culture suggests that reception *is* adaptation. From this view, interpretation is not a perspective on the text; in a fundamental sense it *is* the text, the only text we ever have access to.

What digital culture facilitates more than ever before is textual/visual production motivated by these individual interpretations/adaptations of these texts. It is an axiom now that digital culture and Web 2.0 are radically participatory cultures, with that participation ranging from comments sections to blogs to mashups, fan fiction, and fan videos. These multiple reactions/interpretations/adaptations of these texts function at the same time as both supplements to and constitutive parts of Harry Potter as a narrative idea. The result is a potential revolution in what we mean by reception and adaptation studies, moving beyond questionnaires and focus groups, beyond the idea of reception as commentary on a textual experience. Henry Jenkins's notion of participatory culture in the digital age, an idea built from earlier arguments carefully made by Janice Radway, Ian Eng, John Fiske, and others that media consumers were more than just passive receivers of ideological content, blurs the lines between reception and interpretation, making every act of reception an act of adaptation, a phenomenon captured in Liza Pott's essay, co-written with her students Emily Dallaire and Kelly Turner, about the culture of fandom as manifested in a study abroad experience.

After all, when we say that a certain cinematic adaptation is "unfaithful" to the original, we have always meant, whether we knew it or not, that the adaptation was unfaithful to our own interpretation of the original. The development of digital culture has not just meant that we have many more means to express and disseminate our personal interpretations/adaptations. The fact of digital fan culture—our knowledge and practice of participating in blogs, fan fiction, GIF production, Tumblr pages, mashups—conditions our reading experiences. We read knowing we can respond/adapt in this way. Readers in the age of cinema have long reported fantasizing the movie version of a novel as they read; in fact, this movie adaptation fantasy has perhaps become our default reading experience. In the digital age, this phenomenon has only multiplied in dimension, a version of Muggle magic that may be the most magical and irresistible part of the *Harry Potter* phenomenon.

For the contemporary writer, the digital age and the digital fan culture can be both a boon and a burden. Social media and fan sites can bring attention and success to a series or an author like Rowling. In fact, many publishers now require a webpage/blog/social media presence as part of an author's contract. This enables fans to find out more information about their favorite authors as well as their favorite characters. Rowling particularly uses this to her advantage to engage fans and to add details to the *Harry Potter* canon. For instance, her statement that the love of Dumbledore's life was Grindenwald was never in the original texts, but once Rowling stated it, it became canon. She is known for engaging her readers through Twitter, answering questions and providing tidbits of Potter lore. When many fans were outraged by the casting of a black actress as Hermione Granger for the play *Harry Potter and the Cursed Child*, Rowling reminded all with a tweet regarding the first book's initial description of Hermione: "Canon: brown eyes, frizzy hair and very clever. White skin was never specified. Rowling loves black Hermione."[7]

The internet has made the formation of fan cultures easier with fan sites both official and unofficial. Fan fiction has been around for decades, including the homoerotic category of "slash" fiction that began with Kirk/Spock stories.

Before the explosion of fan fiction on the internet, fanzines were a huge part of the fantasy and science fiction community, including award categories in the Hugo Awards. Moving on from the home-mimeographed zines of the analog era, fans set up websites and blogs to share reactions, reviews, and fan fiction. However, fan fiction can be problematic for the writer since it is technically a copyright violation. Successful authors know that fan fiction is being written about their characters and worlds but usually turn a blind eye towards it. If a fan lets an author know that there is a wonderful fan fiction story up on such a website, the author or publisher may be forced to send a cease and desist order to the webmaster and fans of such a site. Fans are seldom writing fanfic for personal financial gain, but more out of love of the characters and material, or in some case, like K/S, to take control of the narrative.

A prime example is the *Harry Potter Lexicon*.[8] Steve Vander Ark started the website in 1999 because he loved *Harry Potter*. Rowling had given it a fan site award and Warner Brothers admitted to using the site for reference as well. However, when he went to publish the encyclopedia with RDR Books in 2007, Rowling and Warner Brothers took him to court and received an injunction against the publication. Rowling argued that the physical publication of the *Lexicon* would harm her eventual plans to do an encyclopedia of her own, while Vander Ark and RDR claimed it fell into public domain. Rowling won the lawsuit, as a judge agreed that the *Lexicon* used her original work without enough added original commentary.[9]

Rowling has done much to secure and keep control of fan culture to some degree, especially with *Pottermore*. She has given an official place for fans to gather and be "sorted" into their houses. Where many authors have appendices and maps in their books, she has added such things to the *Harry Potter* world and canon through the *Pottermore* site, including Ilvermorny, the American wizarding school referenced in her script for *Fantastic Beasts and Where to Find Them*.[10]

Unlike some other series writers, Rowling does not seem to be tired of her creations yet. L. Frank Baum eventually grew tired of Oz, even sealing it off from our world at one point in the series. However, his readers and publishers wanted more Oz books and not other stories. Arthur Conan Doyle killed off Sherlock Holmes, though that didn't let him stop writing stories featuring the detective. (For a humorous take on the author that hates his characters, read Sharon McCrumb's *Bimbos of the Death Sun*.)[11] Successful authors often face the problem that fans are fans of a character or series and not the writer. Writers who do work-for-hire writing for franchise TV or movie series often find that while fans love their series books, those fans seldom cross over to buy the author's original works/stories, as Rowling found out when she wrote her non-Potter books. She also writes under the pseudonym of Robert Galbraith for her Cormoran Strike mystery novels. When she was revealed as the author, sales did take a bump, but the fandom for the series still doesn't match that of *Harry Potter*.

In looking at the *Harry Potter* phenomena, it is interesting to note not only how effectively the books were adapted into movies (and video games and theme parks) but how well Rowling has adapted to the digital culture and changing nature of fandom. She has been able to meet the demands of the fans and cause excitement about the series many years after the (almost) final book came out. As I write this, the two-part play *Harry Potter and the Cursed Child* has opened to massive box office success. Rowling has said that this is the last we will see of Harry from her. Time will tell.

From a creative writing approach, the *Harry Potter* series and its various adaptations show how the process of adaptation is part of the writing process itself. It is fairly easy to see the influences and sources that Rowling has used and adapted in writing the novels. The hero's journey is central to each novel and the overall story arc. She also adapts various folk and mythic traditions to create her world. For instance, Lupin and the other werewolves transform under the full moon and can create other werewolves with their bites, but they are certainly vulnerable to magic and there is no mention of needing silver (which is more of a Hollywood addition anyway). Her centaurs are adapted from the Greek myths, though she chose to make them all more like Chiron, the wise mentor to heroes, than the more common centaur of Greek mythology that pursued drink and women instead of knowledge.

Studying the adaptation from book to film, though, can help creative writing students to better understand the difference between plot and story. When looking at the fidelity of the adaptation, many think about fidelity to the plot, down to the last detail and floating ghost. What the writer of the adaptation must do is boil it down to the heart of the story instead of the details of the plot. The question of "what is the story about?" becomes a question of theme and conflict and character, more than a matter of what happens and then what happens and so on. Students realize that plot is still important and certain elements need to stay, but that capturing the essence of the story is the central idea of adaptation.

Structure of the Collection

The subtitle of this collection—*The Adaptation of Harry Potter in the Trans-media Age*—speaks to the multiple interpretive and theoretical implications of the *Harry Potter* novel and movie series in the digital era. The essays in the collection are grouped into two sections that approach the question of adapting *Harry Potter* at what might be called the micro and macro levels. The essays in the first section, "Adaptation, Fidelity, and Meaning," take as their starting places the question of "adaptation" in its traditional and still culturally dominant sense, as the translation of a coherent narrative from one distinct medium to another. They all engage critically with the persistent problematics of "fidelity" as a cultural value while approaching the *Harry Potter* film and novel series from a variety of perspectives: investigating how the *Harry Potter* series operates within contemporary global media marketing and the rapidly changing contours of popular culture; exploring the ethical implications of representing the moral choices faced by Harry in his battle against Voldemort; and providing a queer reading of how sexuality operates in the *Potter* movies.

Building off the fact that *Harry Potter* in both book and movie forms has been with us for a generation now, Andrew Howe, in "*Harry Potter* and the Culture of Tomorrow," looks back at the cultural reception of the series to begin a conversation about the long-term prospects for *Harry Potter* as a cultural touchstone. In particular, Howe asks whether and to what extent subsequent young adult book/movie sensations, from *Twilight* to *The Hunger Games*, have supplanted *Harry Potter* in the public imagination. Beginning with an overview of the evolution of attitudes toward and in some cases even backlash against the series since the appearance of *Harry Potter and the Deathly Hallows Part 2* in 2012, Howe traces the inevitably vexed trajectory of the cultural meaning of *Harry Potter* in the digital age, as the actors who embodied Harry, Hermione, and Ron onscreen have grown up and moved on to other artistic and political endeavors, and as J. K. Rowling herself has pursued a dual career, both as the author of the social satire *The Casual Vacancy* and the Cormoran Strike mystery series and as the continuing custodian and guiding genius of the *Harry Potter* universe, including writing the script for *Fantastic Beasts and Where to Find Them* (Peter Yates 2016) and collaborating on the two-part play *Harry Potter and the Cursed Child*.

If the prevailing conventional wisdom about movie adaptations holds that "novels are better than films," Cassandra Bausman in "'Elder' and Wiser: The Filmic *Harry Potter* and the Rejection of Power" considers how

Harry Potter and the Deathly Hallows, Part 2 deals with the central theme of the use and abuse of power.[12] Her thesis focuses on how the choices made by screenwriter Steve Kloves and director David Yates in creating the cinematic moment of Harry's destruction of the Elder Wand, the most powerful wand in the world and a kind of ultimate superweapon, conveys "Harry's ultimate rejection of power, aggression, and supremacy even more strongly than does the language of Rowling's texts."

As a result, Bausman's analysis is less rooted in passing an ultimate judgment on the overall success—let alone "fidelity"—of the movie adaptation than on considering the "political and pedagogical impact" of the narrative choices made and narrative strategies available to both Rowling and the movie makers. While arguing that the cinematic version of the "Battle of Hogwarts" favors spectacle and speed over narrative clarity and sacrifices a nuanced understanding of exactly why Voldemort is defeated in terms not just of battle tactics but the overall arc of Harry's moral development, she sees the quiet, visually intense gesture of Harry's breaking the wand and hurling it off the bridge leading to Hogwarts as an even more powerful statement of the overall political ethos of the series than even Rowling's "original" text.

In "Look . . . at . . . me . . . : Gaze Politics and Male Objectification in the *Harry Potter* movies," Vera Cuntz-Leng uses an updated version of the male gaze, Laura Mulvey's foundational concept of feminist film theory, to consider how gaze politics operates within the *Harry Potter* movies. Specifically, she builds off of Mulvey's revision of the original theory, a psychoanalytic analysis of how classical Hollywood movies objectify and fetishize women, to ask how male objectification changes our understanding of the dynamics of gender and sexuality in the Potter films. The title refers to Snape's dying request to Harry in *Harry Potter and the Deathly Hallows Part 1* and how the ways both Harry and Snape look at and are looked at by each other create ambiguities in terms of how viewers understand their gender and sexual identities and relationships.

Just as crucially, Cuntz-Leng embeds her argument in a consideration of how in "an age of transmedia narratives and transmedia adaptation," a "significant increase of the possibilities of active participation in the process of meaning-making of texts must be taken into account." In considering the fluid operation of multiple gazes in the *Harry Potter* movies, Cuntz-Leng points out how the decoupling of the audience gaze from the "restrictive perspective" of Harry encountered in the written narrative allows "the possibility for a character like Severus Snape to become more complex, more attractive, and in the end more desirable for viewers of all genders."

The essays in the second section, "Transmedia Adaptations," all take what the media theorist Henry Jenkins describes as the "convergence culture" of the digital era as a given. While those artifacts and experiences we refer to as "books" and "movies" continue to exist and retain powerful cultural capital and meaning, they function as part of what Stam referred to as "transfers of creative energy" within a media ecosystem that includes fan fiction, mashups, video games, theme parks, tourist venues, and a multitude of screens. Within this flow of "information [as] an action," as Hayles puts it, the focus is on "reflexivity," on the interplay and interchangeability of writers/readers/fans/producers/consumers. The textual experience of the book still matters, as does authorial authority. Indeed, the use of the term "canon" to refer to the "original" texts that fan fiction then reinvents and reimagines if anything elevates the signifier of "J.K. Rowling" to divine status, signaling an atavistic desire for interpretive stability within the reflexive swirl of convergence culture. While the essays in this section explore an equally diverse set of subjects, from online meme and GIF cultures, to Rowling as transmedia visionary, to fieldwork involving fan culture and study abroad programs, they all represent examples of what Stam means in his call for an "intertextual" approach to adaptation studies.

In "*Harry Potter*, Henry Jenkins, and the Visionary J. K. Rowling," Maria Dicieanu directly engages the question of whether to regard the *Harry Potter* phenomena as an example of "old school" adaptation between the traditional media of books and movies or as one of the first instances of what media theorist Henry Jenkins describes as a "transmedia" project. In his work, Jenkins distinguishes between traditional adaptation and franchising, with the former involving a source text and adaptations derived from it, even if in multiple media, and the latter entailing transmedia narratives that from the beginning are conceived as involving various platforms, no one of which is the sole origin or source. Herself adapting and modifying Jenkins's work, Dicieanu argues that J. K. Rowling's approach to creating *Harry Potter*, occurring as it did at the dawn of the Internet age, reveals an intuitively transmedia understanding of the possibilities of the *Harry Potter* universe on Rowling's part.

As Dicieanu traces in detail the multiple media incarnations of *Harry Potter* since the appearance of the first novel, from fan fiction to ancillary texts such as *Quidditch Through the Ages*, from the creation of *Pottermore* to theme parks and video games as well as eight full-length movies, she demonstrates how all along Rowling acted as the transmedia "visionary" of the title. In particular, Rowling has been especially receptive and innovative in responding to and engaging with the increasingly participatory fan communities that Jenkins has argued defines digital and online media cultures.

As *Harry Potter* fans create community through the internet, they also have been using internet forms to react to and analyze the books and their film adaptations. Katharine McCain explores the use of GIF-sets by the fan community in the essay "Epoximise!: The Renegotiation of Film and Literature Through *Harry Potter* GIF sets." GIF sets are a series of GIFs that combine animated visual scenes combined with text. Fans use GIF sets for a variety of functions, including entertainment and passing on information other fans would find interesting. McCain examines how these GIF sets have become a new form of fan fiction in the ways that both GIF sets and prose fan fiction engage in an analysis of the canonical texts and also transform them. For one, fans are using GIF sets to fix what they see as flaws in the movie adaptations of the novels. Through using GIFS from other movies and scenes, fans can repair the damage that they feel the movies have done to the written text. Likewise, fans use GIFs from other media sources in order to create new scenes they wish had happened, including slash fic about Harry and Draco, and to create Alternate Universes, just like textual fan fiction. The GIF sets are another means for fans to engage, change, and comment on *Harry Potter* texts, both films and novels.

In her essay "*Harry Potter* and the Surprising Venue of Literary Critique," Michelle Markey Butler examines how fans use internet memes to engage in the same inquiries that literary critics employ when looking at texts. She starts with examples of memes dealing with plot, character, and world building before moving on to more complex memes that engage in comparative analysis. Butler gives examples of how memes point out differences and often criticize the adaptations of the books into the movies, particularly Dumbledore's reaction when Harry's name emerges from the Goblet of Fire. Lastly, she examines how fans compare *Harry Potter* to other fantasy works and iconic characters. For instance, fans use memes to criticize female characterization in YA novels by comparing Hermione and Katniss (from *Hunger Games*) with Bella of *Twilight*. Butler argues that through the use of graphics and concise written text, memes and meme makers engage with the texts in the same way that literary critics do.

For *Harry Potter* fans, gathering places exist in both the digital and physical world. Liza Potts, Kelly Turner, and Emily Dallaire explore the places in Britain that help create participatory memory for Harry Potter fans in their essay, "Taking Tea at Elephant House: How Potterheads Researched *Harry Potter* During a Fandom-Focused Study Abroad." Potts was the instructor for the course and, using theoretical texts on collective memory and participatory culture, she designed a research-based course focusing on "sacred" places for *Harry Potter* fans. Turner and Dallaire were the student researchers who visited the physical places during the study abroad class as scholar fans, looking at each place as first a fan and then a scholar. They focus on the places that allowed fans to participate with the space, such as the Elephant House coffee shop in Edinburgh, where Rowling famously worked on the novel that would launch an empire.

In both form and content, this final essay in the collection perhaps best embodies the underlying concept that all reception is adaptation. As the essay traces the theoretical growth of students beginning to apply concepts from memory studies and participatory culture to their fan experiences, Potts, Turner, and Dallaire use a Q-and-A format and the user-generated narrative platform Storify to present their findings experientially and chronologically. This web-influenced approach to scholarly analysis reflects how our understanding of both reception and interpretation, the experience of what we traditionally refer to as "primary" and "secondary" literature, is being reshaped in the digital age.

A mythic traditional narrative that has flourished in the radical flux of the digital age; a series hailed for connecting and reconnecting young readers to the pleasures of print text that has become one of the most successful movie franchises in cinema history; a pop culture phenomenon that continues to acquire new generations of fans. *Harry Potter* has become a definitive text in the transmedia age, and it continues to serve as a focal point for discussions, debates, and theorizing about what we mean by reception and adaptation. Books and movies, "the page" and on "the screen," in the end describe not only two particular modes of textual reception; they challenge us to ask what isn't a screen in the age of digital reproduction. That these interpretive questions continue to grow as focal points for the critical investigation of adaptation underlines the connection between the revolutionary upheaval of the transmedia age and our continuing fascination with the magical world J. K. Rowling summoned into being twenty years ago.

Notes

1. The title of the original British edition of the first novel, *Harry Potter and the Philosopher's Stone*, was changed to *Harry Potter and the Sorcerer's Stone* for the American edition, over concerns the term "philosopher's stone" was not familiar to American readers. Both titles were used for the movie versions in various markets around the world.

2. "Transmedia 202: Further Reflections," *Confessions of an ACA—Fan, the Official Weblog of Henry Jenkins*, August 1, 2011, http://henryjenkins.org/2011/08/defining_transmedia_further_re.html.

3. Thomas Leitch, "Twelve Fallacies in Contemporary Adaptation Theory," *Criticism* 45.2 (2003), 149.

4. Robert Stam, "Introduction: The Theory and Practice of Adaptation," in *Literature and Film: A Guide to the Theory and Practice of Film Adaptation*, ed. Robert Stam and Alessandra Raengo (Malden, MA: Blackwell Publishing, 2005), 46.

5. Gary R Bortolotti, and Linda Hutcheon, "On the Origin of Adaptations: Rethinking Fidelity Discourse and 'Success'—Biologically," *New Literary History* 38.3 (2007): 444.

6. N. Katherine Hayles, *How We Became Posthuman: Virtual Bodies in Cybernetics, Literature, and Informatics* (Chicago: University of Chicago Press, 1999), 56–57.

7. J. K. Rowling, Twitter post, December 21, 2015, 5:41 a.m., https://twitter.com/jk_rowling/status/678888094339366914?lang=en.

8. *The Harry Potter Lexicon*, www.hp-lexicon.org.

9. John Eligon, "Rowling Wins Lawsuit Against Potter Lexicon," The *New York Times*, September 8, 2008, www.nytimes.com/2008/09/09/nyregion/09potter.html.

10. J. K. Rowling, "Ilvermorny School of Witchcraft and Wizardry, *Pottermore*, www.pottermore.com/writing-by-jk-rowling/ilvermorny.

11. Sharyn McCrumb, *Bimbos of the Death Sun* (New York: Ballantine Books, 1996).

12. Leitch, "Twelve Fallacies," 154.

Part One

Adaptation, Fidelity, and Meaning

1

Harry Potter and the Popular Culture of Tomorrow

Andrew Howe

On July 21, 2007, J. K. Rowling released the final installment in her landmark *Harry Potter* heptalogy, cementing a position of importance in young adult literature and millennial culture. Indeed, the world she created in the early 1990s and exposed to the reading public in 1997 had, by 2007, transformed into an empire featuring movies, action figures, and the whole range of other artifacts that typically accompany tremendously popular texts that capture the imagination of a global audience. Rowling's popularity had grown to extend into different parts of society, both popular and elite. When Richard Dawkins announces that he's writing a book debunking your text and later recants, re-posting numerous positive articles on his website, you know you've arrived.[1]

Harry Potter has also proven fertile for academics who are also fans, who can annually get their fix at conferences dedicated solely to Rowling's fictional world. These conferences have been held in Chicago, southern California, Canterbury, Wales, and many other locations. The names given to them—Terminus, Potterwatch, Pottermania, DiaCon Alley, Ascendio, LeakyCon, and Infinitus—are indicative of the desire to bridge scholarship with popular culture and, in particular, fandom. An extreme manifestation of the hybridization between the academic and the fan (known as "aca-fan") has been encouraged by several of these conferences, which have invited participants to attend dressed up as their favorite characters (cos-play joining fan fiction as two ways in which fans can interact with the text on a more personal level). The most common location for these conferences has been Orlando, Florida, largely due to the existence of the *Wizarding World of Harry Potter* theme park, a part of Universal's "Islands of Adventure," which opened to the public in 2010, followed by analogues in Osaka, Japan (opened in 2014), and Universal City, California (opened in 2016). In addition to reading the books and watching the movies, fans can now experience Potter-themed roller coasters and other attractions and visit life-sized models of both Hogwarts and Hogsmeade. Naturally, they can also shop at a number of Potter-themed establishments within the park, choosing from hundreds of Potter-associated products.

The success of the *Harry Potter* franchise is undeniable, with well over 450 million book copies sold and with the original book in the series spending a full decade (1998–2008) on the *New York Times* Bestseller List.[2] Indeed, at one point (in 2000), *Potter* books occupied the top three places on that list, and the series' dominance led to first a separate children's book list and a further sub-division for children's series in order to free up spots for newer texts.[3]

A look at the worldwide box office gross for the eight film adaptations indicates the immense popularity of the series above and beyond those who read the books. Released in November 2001, *Harry Potter and the Sorcerer's Stone* (2001) grossed over $975 million USD at the worldwide box office; ten years later, *Harry Potter and the Deathly Hallows: Part II* (2011) surpassed the billion-dollar mark, at the time ranking third in all-time box office receipts, behind *Avatar* (2009) and *Titanic* (1997). Certainly, the decision to split *Deathly Hallows* into two films was facilitated by the franchise's continuing popularity even after seven books and six previous films. On average, the *Potter* films grossed well over $900 million worldwide. The fact that the first and last films were the two highest grossing in the franchise stands as a testament to the sustained popularity over the course of a decade.

However, inevitably over time there have been other popular books and film series that have arisen, and new developments that have impacted the continuing reception of Potter, leading one to speculate about the placement of this text in the canon of popular culture in twenty, fifty, or a hundred years. In the ten-year period since the publication of *Harry Potter and the Deathly Hallows*, one can already perceive shifts in the popular landscape of Potter as the original books and film adaptations recede further and further into the past. Although they are still beloved, these texts are increasingly outdated in an era rich in popular culture and media saturation, including other para-canonical *Potter* works that have been subsequently released.

The following events have all played a part in the incrementally changing face of the Potter universe: the disclosure that popular character Albus
Dumbledore was gay; the ascendancy of other popular young adult literature series, such as Stephenie Meyer's *The Twilight Saga* and Suzanne Collins's *The Hunger Games*, as well as the success of the films adapted from
these books; accusations of commercialism in regard to the decision to
break *Harry Potter and the Deathly Hallows* into two separate films, a move
that was largely viewed as driven by studio greed rather than artistic sensi-
bility; accusations of elitism over the initial decision not to publicly release
Tales of Beedle the Bard, and to release short stories solely to members of
Rowling's website, *Pottermore*; the perceived shortcomings, in both popular
and critical spheres, of Rowling publications outside of the Potter world; the
graduation of Daniel Radcliffe and Emma Watson from child stars to more
adult figures, in particular with Radcliffe's appearance in the play *Equus*
and Watson's high-profile status as an icon of global feminism; and finally,
the reception of the play *Harry Potter and the Cursed Child* and the first of
five cinematic adaptations of *Fantastic Beasts and Where to Find Them*. This
chapter examines the inevitable transformation of *Harry Potter* the cultural
juggernaut of the millennial period to *Harry Potter* the product of post-
millennial nostalgia.

Three months after the publication of *Harry Potter and the Deathly Hallows*, Rowling appeared at Carnegie Hall to read excerpts from the book
to a group of several thousand lucky winners of a contest sponsored by
Scholastic, the American publisher of the series. Partway through the event,
Rowling outed Albus Dumbeldore as gay. This revelation was greeted by a
prolonged standing ovation, and news quickly spread around the world.[4]
The reaction in the media and the court of public opinion was swift and
divided, and the blogosphere went into overdrive. In some ways, the revelation made as big a splash as the coming out of many famous real life
individuals, which by that point had become almost routine a decade after
television personality and comedian Ellen Degeneres had come out on her
own terms.

Naturally, there was a return to the text, as readers sought to find clues
they had previously missed: much of this renewed focus was turned upon
Dumbeldore's relationship with Gellert Grindelwald. Andrew Sullivan
of *The Atlantic* posted on his blog: "Let's run the gay-check, shall we? No
known female companion ever. Brilliant in school. Befriends a despised
classmate. Childhood crush on another boy."[5] Others were even more
tongue-in-cheek in reading tea leaves from the past, such as those who

focused upon descriptions of Fawkes, Dumbledore's Phoenix, as "flaming,"[6] and those who employed the phrase "don't ask, don't spell."[7] Taking a cue from wordplay in *Harry Potter and the Chamber of Secrets*, Andrew Slack, as reported in an article in the *Los Angeles Times*, noted that "Albus Dumbledore" is an anagram for "Male bods rule, bud."[8] The cynical and, in some cases, homophobic humor didn't stop there, impacting even those who indicated that they simply did not care. As Edward Rothstein quoted in his *New York Times* article, one commentator noted, "Oh, who cares? The whole bloody lot of them were gay as far as I'm concerned. All those hours of movies and not a single car chase, shootout or kung fu fight."[9] However, not too surprisingly, public opinion largely polarized into two camps: those who supported and those who did not support Dumbledore's outing.

Many applauded Rowling's decision to both create a gay character in a book for youth and then publicly out him.[10] Those in this group generally focused upon how this revelation fit into the larger framework of tolerance found throughout the Potter canon, most notably in the textual rejection of bias against those of mixed blood heritage (Mudbloods). However, despite widespread acceptance of Dumbledore's homosexuality, there were detractors who found themselves, at least on this one particular topic, in a strange alliance of conservative Christians, politically active gays, and literary critics. For conservative Christian groups, this episode only served to further fuel a fire that had been burning since the success of the initial book. To the laundry list of other criticisms, including the fact that these novels hinged upon magic, drew attention away from God, and encouraged rebelliousness against authority, one could now add an embrace of homosexuality. Soon after Rowling's announcement, Roberta Combs, president of the Christian Coalition of America, stated: "It's very disappointing that the author would have to make one of the characters gay. It's not a good example for our children, who really like the books and the movies. I think it encourages homosexuality."[11] Some went even further, such as pastor and radio host Kevin Swanson, who in late 2015, between advocating for the execution of homosexuals and organizing a GOP conference ahead of the 2016 Iowa presidential caucus, invited America to "repent of *Harry Potter* . . . Repent that Dumbledore emerged as a homosexual mentor for Harry Potter."[12]

Joining in the criticism of Rowling were many gay commentators, who viewed Dumbledore's outing as "too little, too late." Certainly, Rowling didn't do herself any favors with her quote following the standing ovation:

"If I had known this would have made you this happy, I would have announced it years ago."[13] This quote seemed to indicate that her decision was more about popularity than conscience. Furthermore, others questioned the timing of the announcement, at a point when no more books were forthcoming and most of the sales had been made, although it is important to note that, at the time of the revelation, there were still three more films to come.[14]

Finally, some felt as if this announcement was a public relations concession made to gay readers following the marriage of Nymphadora Tonks and Remus Lupin. These two characters had both gained queer followings in previous books, Lupin most likely for his medically-marginalized turn in *Prisoner of Azkaban*, reminiscent of how those with AIDS were treated in the 1980s and thereafter. Rowling herself made this connection, stating that, "His being a werewolf is really a metaphor for people's reactions to illness and disability."[15] As Adam Shecter noted: "I wish Dumbledore could have been a model of possibility for queer and questioning youth."[16]

Rounding out the coalition of those skeptical of Rowling's revelation were critics, literary and otherwise, who cried foul regarding her introducing non-canonical information and expecting people to take it at face value. An example of such a critic was Edward Rothstein, who in a *New York Times* opinion piece noted that although he continued to admire the series for its clear lines between good and evil, tolerance and intolerance, he viewed the revelation to be manipulative in that it further crowded Rowling's world with another marginalized protagonist: "Her heroes are the hybrids, the misfits, those of mixed blood, all bearing scars of loss and love: the half-giant Hagrid, the mudblood Hermione (whose parents were not wizards), the poverty-stricken Ron, the orphaned Harry. Perhaps speaking of Dumbeldore as gay was just a matter of creating another diverse rebel against orthodoxy."[17]

Although in no discernible way did this episode detract from Rowling's popularity, it illustrates the manner in which topical controversies often follow in the wake of an extremely successful text and in particular how, when that text becomes part of a culturally mediated past, the process of revision and reinterpretation begins. In essence, when a textual journey is complete, the text itself is no longer as important as the political discussions that it engenders and that migrate and evolve over time.

It is predictable that, upon completion, a popular work will at some point be replaced by another tale with contemporary cultural resonance that exists at the forefront of collective consciousness. That has certainly transpired since the 2007 publication of *Harry Potter and the Deathly Hallows* and the final film adaptation four years later, most notably with the ascendancy of the *The Twilight Saga* and *The Hunger Games* franchises, as well as other popular young adult fare such as the *Divergent* trilogy. Following the conclusion of *Harry Potter*, Stephenie Meyer replaced Rowling as the queen of young adult fiction, although she in turn was replaced by Suzanne Collins and Veronica Roth. When it came to giant, global book launches and multimillion-dollar film openings, Bella Swan and Katniss Everdeen soon eclipsed *Harry Potter*. Although not as successful as Rowling in cultivating a diversity of audiences, Meyer's tale of vampiric pubescent angst and Collins's allegory of privation and rebellion have served to cast a shadow over their predecessor. Such a phenomenon is not new; no matter how large a tidal wave of support a cultural text might enjoy, it is eventually bound to wash up against a high enough mountain of familiarity and, over time, be replaced by another wave.

What is interesting about *Harry Potter* and *The Twilight Saga* is that they both resonate with a tradition of societal fear extending back into the nineteenth century, and beyond (really, back to the Trial of Socrates): the fear of a cultural sway with the youth population that cannot be controlled. Due to its focus upon vampires and werewolves, in addition to inheriting the mantle of a billion dollar franchise, *The Twilight Saga* also acquired the wrath and ire of the Christian right, despite Meyer's works existing as thinly veiled metaphors promoting abstinence.[18] In the United States, vampirism has long been portrayed in terms of class and excess, often of a distinctly European flavor. These associations, combined with the occult symbolism that often accompanies such tales, resulted in this series being treated as the heir apparent to *Harry Potter*, the *du jour* threat to youth. The fact that *The Hunger Games* and *Divergent* are set in the future, and largely stay away from issues involving familiar and problematic elements of the supernatural, perhaps allowed them to avoid this external cultural baggage.

What is ironic about the transference of bogeyman status from Rowling to Meyer is that both involve the increasingly archaic artifact that is the book. To a large extent, the twentieth century has seen the mediums of film and, particularly, music fulfill this function. Since World War II, Elvis Presley, the Beatles, Nirvana, and Madonna have, in different moments and in different ways, been the focus of those decrying the hold that popular culture has over the youth. Books haven't figured so much in this regard since the erosion of the Hays Code in Hollywood during the 1950s and subsequent relaxation of standards by the FCC (Federal Communications Commission) and other regulatory agencies.[19] Indeed, the focus upon "dangerous books" in the past forty years has largely involved those written in previous eras brought into the modern classroom, such as the perennial angst over the inclusion of Mark Twain's *The Adventures of Huckleberry Finn* in secondary curricula.

The popularity of the *Harry Potter* books among youth was thus notable for disrupting the trend of declining non-mandatory reading, something that even the most strident of Rowling's detractors could not deny. The replacement of another book series in the form of *The Twilight Saga* thus served to doubly undermine the position of *Harry Potter*. If the new cultural bogeyman had come from another medium, Rowling would have continued to be marked as the lone prophet of "dangerous" teen literacy wandering the post-literate wasteland. With the ascendancy of Meyer and now Collins, Rowling is just one of several who have helped to partially reacquaint youth with the joys of reading, even if it constitutes a small blip in the general trend that shows literature holds a diminishing purchase on the imagination of youth.

One aspect of how perceptions change over time is unique to the film adaptations: the maturation of child actors. This problem is usually only manifest in television, especially in shows that run for multiple seasons and feature child actors who age a lot more quickly than do their characters, such as Isaac Hempstead Wright (Bran Stark) in HBO's *Game of Thrones*. The lag between Rowling's books and the film adaptations, however, led to credibility problems involving the perceived age of characters on film and actors in real life. The casting of the central three characters in the film version of *Harry Potter and the Sorcerer's Stone* was so successful that the actors were retained throughout all eight films. Initially, the difference in age between the actors and the characters they portrayed was not an issue, but the fact that it took ten Hollywood years to cover the seven-year story arc caused some problems. Fortunately, the more extreme examples—e.g. Matthew Lewis (Neville Longbottom) appearing to grow over a foot between two of the films, and Tom Felton's (Draco Malfoy) voice dropping several octaves—did not involve the core three stars.

The lion's share of the controversy, however, surrounded Daniel Radcliffe and Emma Watson, who play Harry Potter and Hermione Granger, respectively. Radcliffe signaled his departure from being known solely for playing the bespectacled teen wizard when he agreed to play the tortured teen stablehand in *Equus*, which ran from February to June 2007. At the age of seventeen, Radcliffe appeared nude and participated in a frank sex scene. To a certain extent, the fallout over Radcliffe's appearance in this role overshadowed much of the lead up to the publication of *Harry Potter and the Deathly Hallows* and the film version of *Harry Potter and the Order of the Phoenix* later that year. It is interesting to note that the headlines, several of which included "Harry Potter Strips" and "Harry Potter Goes Nude,"[20] elided Radcliffe's identity as the one who disrobes, suggesting something fundamental about the titanic nature of this cultural product and the inability of those encapsulated within it to exert significant powers of self-definition. During the same year, Radcliffe also starred in the Australian film *December Boys* (Rod Hardy 2007), which included a scene in which the character he plays loses his virginity, following Rupert Grint (who plays Ron Weasley), who also experienced sexual awakening in *Driving Lessons* (Jeremy Brock 2006).

Even though she steered clear of potentially controversial roles during her run as Hermione Granger, Emma Watson didn't have to wait long after her eighteenth birthday before being anointed by the media as a sex symbol. In Watson's own words:

> It was pretty tough turning 18. I realized that overnight I'd become fair game. I had a party in town and the pavements were knee-deep with photographers trying to get a shot of me looking drunk, which wasn't going to happen . . . The sickest part was when one photographer lay down on the floor to get a shot up my skirt. The night it was legal for them to do it, they did it. I woke up the next day and felt completely violated by it all.[21]

After completing work on the final film, Watson quickly transformed herself into a model and fashionista of note, embracing a more adult image that, in many ways, was not congruent with the fictional character that many had come to love. By the film *Deathly Hallows: Part 2*, the gulf between Watson's twenty-one-year-old public image and her seventeen-year-old Potter character created a tension evidenced in both critical and popular reactions to a scene where a jealous Ron imagines sensual interplay between Harry and Hermione. Despite being portrayed as dream imagery and with the nude Hermione clearly computer-generated, the scene was criticized from several different quarters. Some focused upon the contrived nature of the scene, noting that it in essence rewrote the intent of Rowling's initial written scene and capitalized upon Radcliffe and Watson's growing status as sex symbols. As Stuart Heritage of *The Guardian* noted, this plot development may have in part been influenced by the success of the much sexier *The Twilight Saga*: "Next to the Twilight series, with its endless middle-distance stares and emo-pop soundtrack and, crucially, the fact that none of the principal male leads seem to understand what a shirt is for, Harry Potter runs the risk of looking a little staid."[22] Others pointed to the inappropriateness of such a scene in a film aimed at young adults. As Charlotte Martin noted in an opinion piece for *The Sun*: "Last time we saw the wee lad he was waving his wand to cast spells at Hogwarts. But now his wand is out for a very different reason—in a love scene scheduled for new flick *Harry Potter and The Deathly Hallows*. . . . Fans may be intrigued by celebs baring all but there are some stars we never want to see in that way."[23]

Although the emergence of real life sexuality in contrast to a relative textual innocence drew the most attention as the child actors matured, that was not the only factor in their maturation. As they embraced adulthood and left Potter behind, and due to their bankable status, Radcliffe, Watson, and also Grint were approached for other roles, most of which were set in the real world and without the veneer of young adult fantasy, although Watson's success as Belle in *Beauty and the Beast* indicated that a return to fantasy was certainly possible.[24] Following *Deathly Hallows, Part 2*,[25] Emma Watson received critical acclaim and awards for her supporting role in the coming-of-age film *The Perks of Being a Wallflower*.[26] A year later, she played herself in the post-apocalyptic comedy *This is the End*, her violent and foul-mouthed turn generating humor in response to the role's distance from a character more similar to Hermione.[27]

Daniel Radcliffe branched out even more. In addition to starring in several horror films, Radcliffe also starred as a young Allen Ginsberg in the film *Kill Your Darlings*.[28] Playing the controversial Beat poet was just another step in Radcliffe's self-redefinition following his graduation from the Potter franchise, culminating in his most recent turn in *Swiss Army Man*, a film in which he plays a corpse.[29]

A final aspect of actor biography cannot be overlooked, and that is Emma Watson's work to promote global feminism. It can never be known the degree to which the character traits of Hermione Granger, as written by J. K. Rowling, influenced the actor chosen to play her in the film adaptations. Certainly, Granger has a courage and sense of social justice that has been embraced by Watson. However, perhaps the films merely provided a platform for the expression of what would have been present in Watson even if someone else had been cast. Regardless, in only a few short years after the final *Potter* film Watson has

Emma Watson in a very non-Hermione role in the comedy-apocalypse film *This Is the End* (2013).

Daniel Radcliffe sheds his teen wizard image by playing Allen Ginsberg in *Kill Your Darlings* (2013).

become a global icon for gender equality, serving as a goodwill ambassador for the United Nations Entity for Gender Equality and Empowerment of Women.[30] In September 2014, she helped launch, and became the primary spokesperson for, the U.N. initiative HeForShe, which seeks to educate and encourage men to advocate for women's rights. In launching HeForShe, Watson delivered an address to the United Nations during a meeting at its New York building. Her speech garnered worldwide attention and acclaim.[31]

However, Watson's speech was not without its detractors, who again came from very diverse perspectives. Naturally, there was a bit of a backlash from fundamentalist quarters. Legions of internet trolls took to blogs and internet bulletin boards to voice their displeasure with Watson, ranging from those simply disagreeing with her that gender inequality was as large a problem as she indicated all the way to those making death threats and even threatening to release nude photos of her.[32] Other criticisms came from elsewhere, including those who faulted Watson for her position of privilege, claiming that although she admitted aspects of her upbringing gave her an advantage growing up, she still was clueless as to her subject positionality.[33] People in this camp viewed HeForShe as yet another example of a gender initiative pushed by a white westerner who did not, and could not, understand the full sweep of issues facing both global men and women of color.

Finally, yet another criticism came in the form of the gender binary implied by HeForShe. Amy McCarthy notes that, "there is nothing feminist about a campaign that reinforces a gender binary that is harmful to people whose gender identities don't fit into such tidy boxes. When we reinforce the idea that only people who neatly fit the gender binary are worthy of being protected and supported, we erase and exclude the people who are at most risk of patriarchal violence and oppression."[34] McCarthy goes on to note how Watson's race, sexual identification, and income have colored her life experiences, and thus her perspective. McCarthy concludes that the blind spots evident in those pushing the campaign are re-inscribed in the campaign itself:

> When Watson speaks of equal pay, she's talking about the white women who make 78% of their white male counterparts, not the 46% gap that Latina women face in the workplace. When we discuss sex work, we don't talk about the transgender women who rely on the industry to survive. Put simply, the discussion that He For She and Emma Watson are having fails to invite the people whose voices need to be heard most at the table.

There may be some truth to these accusations, and certainly a campaign such as HeForShe is less likely to take hold in the most patriarchal of societies, where it is needed the most. The amount of pushback that Watson received was surprising, however, given the unimpeachable, core goal of the campaign, that of "gender equality politically, culturally, socially, economically."[35] The backlash was perhaps a testament to the difficulty in making the transition from actor typecast as entertainer to a political figure with a more substantial message, a transformation that was all the more challenging because Watson suffered from being a child actor who was rapidly caparisoned by the media as a sex commodity towards the end of her run as Hermione Granger.

Another aspect of the changing perception of *Harry Potter* as the series moves into the realm of nostalgia has been Rowling's difficulty in moving beyond the Potter universe, which is arguably due more to the expectations of her readers than her skill in working outside of the fictional world that made her famous. Rowling's first post-Potter novel, *The Casual Vacancy* (2012), sold well, although the critical and popular response was decidedly mixed. The title of Jan Moir's article for *Daily Mail*—"Where's the Magic in This Tale of Middle-class Monsters?"—encapsulates the two core critiques levied against this novel: that it was not *Harry Potter*, and that it pushed a blatant political agenda.[36] Regarding the former critique, Rowling never stood a chance with those who were disappointed about her move into adult fare and the situating of her narrative in the real world. Even though Rowling had long indicated that she would not write another Potter book, her readers were already conditioned to expect certain fantasy conventions.[37] A tale focused upon the rotten underbelly of a small British town simply would not do. In relation to the latter critique, Rowling did infuse her narrative with pungent social criticism, situating *The Casual Vacancy* in the same vein as *Peyton Place* (1956) and other works pulling back the curtain on a seemingly functional community that is in fact divided deeply by class warfare.

Charges of elitism had been levied against Rowling a few years earlier with *The Tales of Beedle the Bard*, of which initially only seven copies were made available in 2007, although the sales of one copy that Rowling auctioned on Amazon for nearly £2 million went to charity, as did proceeds of the general book sale a year later.[38] Unlike with this short work, however, with *The Casual Vacancy* audience expectation was working against her, as those conditioned to expect light or escapist fare found the socially motivated plot to be elitist, depressing, and/or preachy. The linking of the narrative specifically to real-world British social problems made the novel feel

Terri Weedon (Keeley Forsyth), a drug addict and prostitute in the miniseries adaptation of J. K. Rowling's *The Casual Vacancy* (2012).

more culturally determined, and thus, unlike the *Potter* books, it could not effortlessly cross national lines. Still, despite the mixed success of the book, there was praise for Rowling's foray into social commentary. *The Casual Vacancy* sold well enough to rate a miniseries (adapted by Sarah Phelps), which although well reviewed did not gain widespread attention, particularly in the United States, where it was released to mixed reviews by its stateside distributor, HBO.[39]

Rowling's sophomore post-Potter effort, *The Cuckoo's Calling* (2013), was much better received although not without its own controversy. The first of three novels (to date) following private detective Cormoran Strike, *The Cuckoo's Calling* was written under the pseudonym Robert Galbraith. The book did not sell well initially, but following leaks that Rowling was the author, it immediately became the bestselling book on Amazon.[40] Exactly how Rowling's involvement was discovered is disputed, although she did file a lawsuit against Chris Gossage, a partner at Russells Solicitors, a law firm that in the past had represented Rowling and knew her *nom de plume*.[41] The fact that the lawsuit was quickly dropped when the law firm made a donation to a veteran's organization bears note, particularly in that the fictional centerpiece of the novel is himself a veteran of the Afghan War. Whether or not the author's revelation and subsequent lawsuit was a publicity stunt, *The Cuckoo's Calling*, and its two successors, were critical and popular successes, optioned by the BBC to serve as the basis of a forthcoming television series.[42] Rowling's 2013 success in another genre appeared to move her further away from Potter, although in reality the seeds had already been sown for her return. On July 30, 2016, the two-part play *Harry Potter and the*

Cursed Child debuted in London's West End to showings sold out months in advance, mixed reviews, and a record eleven Olivier award nominations.[43] Three months later, the first of five planned films based on *Fantastic Beasts and Where To Find Them* was released.[44] Popular and critical opinions of this film were largely positive, and it won an Academy Award—for Best Costume Design—the first of any of the *Potter* films.[45] Regardless of why Rowling returned to her *Potter* roots—whether due to a lack of success in other endeavors or in order to express storylines she had not been able to fit into her original narrative—these para-canonical *Potter* texts are sure to supplant the originals in cultural immediacy while simultaneously deepening the nostalgia felt for those works.

Finally, it is interesting to note the relative success of the *Harry Potter* films relative to other films from popular fantasy series, only some of which are based upon books. Although box office receipts represent a distinctly flawed bellwether of a book series' cultural penetration due to reasons such as inflation and cinematic re-releases, it is nevertheless instructive to note *Harry Potter*'s placement among other cultural luminaries constituting a "series" (at least three films). Although there were seven books, the final installment (*Deathly Hallows*) was split into two films by Warner Bros, a move that initiated a trend—also seen with *The Twilight Saga*, *The Hobbit*, and *The Hunger Games*—that many feel compromises aesthetic integrity for increased profit.[46] None of this criticism was directed at Rowling, probably given her long-standing and well-documented philanthropic efforts, including donating the proceeds from the novellas *Fantastic Beasts and Where to Find Them* (2001) and *Quidditch Through the Ages* (2001) to the British charity Comic Relief. As of Spring 2016, the average box office gross of the eight Potter films was $966 million USD. Seven of the eight films appear on lists of the Top 50 worldwide box office grossers, and the only one that is not on that list (*Prisoner of Azkaban*) is 57th[47] Below is a list of a dozen popular film series that have all averaged over $500 million USD, with the number of films and average box office gross noted for each:

The Lord of the Rings (3 films): $988
The Hobbit (3 films): $977
Harry Potter (8 films): $966
Star Wars (7 films): $948 ($862 in first release dollars)
Transformers (4 films): $943
Pirates of the Caribbean (4 films): $930
Jurassic Park (4 films): $924

Spider-Man (5 films): $793 ($832 for the Sam Raimi trilogy)
Marvel Cinematic Universe (13 films): $757 ($1,462 for the two
    ensemble *Avengers* films)
The Hunger Games (4 films): $726
The Twilight Saga (5 films): $661
Batman (8 films): $565 ($820 for the Nolan trilogy)[48]

Obviously, the *Harry Potter* films did quite well, topped only by films within the J. R. R. Tolkien world. It is interesting to note that, with only two exceptions, all of the series listed above have a film (or multiples) that were released after *Deathly Hallows: Part 2* in July of 2011, testament to *Potter*'s continued popularity despite numerous subsequent challengers. Both *Harry Potter* and *Pirates of the Caribbean*, one of the other series with no films released subsequent to 2011, have films scheduled for release in the next year. Apparently, studios like proven winners, especially those guaranteed to flirt with a billion-dollar box office take. The other series with no recent film is *The Lord of the Rings*. The fact that this series continues to sit atop this list, despite the last film having been released well over a decade ago, indicates how much of a singularity it truly represented. Then again, this series benefitted from decades of fan interest and cultural relevance from the books (published in 1954–1955) prior to its 2001–2003 cinematic run.

    Indeed, an examination of this list indicates two models of success. The *Harry Potter* series is joined by *Jurassic Park*, *The Hunger Games*, and *The Twilight Saga* as film series that succeeded immediately following the books upon which they were based. For them, the films were built upon waves of current support, although built to last for years, or, in the case of *Jurassic Park*, in a reboot a generation later. The majority of the series on the list, however, benefitted from years of fandom based upon source books, comic books, television shows, or (in the case of *Pirates of the Caribbean*) a theme park ride! The success of *Star Wars* is an outlier in that there was no prior source text whatsoever. In one sense, given the recent additions to this list, *Harry Potter* is now just one of many big box office juggernauts. However, given the series' placement upon this list and the immediate success of the films only a few short years after the book's ascendancy, the books and the films partner to suggest a level of cultural penetration that is still potent, despite the fact that other cultural texts have appeared, and will continue to appear, on center stage.

    Rowling is still popular, as evidenced by the massive interest generated by the continued success of the *Potter* brand, from the construction of theme parks through the short stories that she occasionally releases on her website *Pottermore*, and most recently with the tremendous success of *Harry Potter and the Cursed Child* and the film version of *Fantastic Beasts and Where to Find Them*. When it comes to her book sales and the box office revenue from the film adaptations, the series continues to compare favorably to other, more recent, globally popular texts. However, on another level, *Harry Potter* will never be quite the same, no matter how fully Rowling returns to her fantastical roots. She has moved in other directions, as have the filmmakers and, most notably, the actors associated with the success of the film adaptations. Rowling's fictional world will continue to exert a tremendous purchase upon the hearts and minds of those who grew up with her stories, increasingly within the realm of nostalgia.

Of course, a sustained move back into this fictional world will no doubt serve to combine nostalgia for the original tales with a fandom revitalized by these new narratives. Only time will tell how future generations, living in a post-literate world of hyper-digital immediacy, will be exposed to these stories, which they will no doubt be prodded to experience for themselves. The children of tomorrow may listen when their elders extol the wonders of *Harry Potter*, and proceed to either read the books or watch the films, or ignore both in favor of newer texts. It is unclear to what extent Harry Potter the cultural text will continue to occupy a position of primacy as future events modify the way we view the past, and future texts with more contemporary cultural currency ascend to the position of popular aesthetic monoliths.

Notes

1. Richard Dawkins, "Why Everyone Should Read Harry Potter," *Richard Dawkins Foundation for Reason & Science*, September 9, 2014. https://richard dawkins.net/2014/09/why-everyone-should-read-harry-potter/.

2. "J. K. Rowling by the Numbers," *USA Today*, September 25, 2012, www .usatoday.com/story/life/books/2012/09/25/j-k-rowling-harry-potter-the-casual-vacancy/1582921/.

3. Dwight Garner, "Ten Years Later, Harry Potter Vanishes from the Best-Seller List," *The New York Times*, May 1, 2008, http://artsbeat.blogs .nytimes.com/2008/05/01/ten-years-later-harry-potter-vanishes-from-the-best-seller-list/?_r=1.

4. Hanna Siegel, "Rowling Lets Dumbledore Out of the Closet," *ABC News,* October 20, 2007, http://abcnews.go.com/Entertainment/story?id=3755544.

5. Andrew Sullivan, "Dumbledore!" *The Daily Dish,* October 20, 2007. www.theatlantic.com/daily-dish/archive/2007/10/dumbledore/224374/.

6. Deborah Netburn, "Seven Clues That 'Potter's' Dumbledore Was Gay," *Los Angeles Times,* October 23, 2007, www.latimes.com/entertainment/movies /la-et-showbiz7-23oct23-story.html.

7. Chauncey Mabe, "Don't Ask, Don't Spell," *Sun Sentinel,* October 23, 2007, www.sun-sentinel.com/sfl-mtblog-2007-10-dont_ask_dont_spell_1-story.html.

8. Netburn, "Seven Clues."

9. Edward Rothstein, "Is Dumbledore Gay? Depends on Definitions of 'Is' and 'Gay,'" *New York Times,* October 29, 2007, www.nytimes.com/2007/10/29/ arts/29conn.html.

10. Mark Harris, "Dumbledore's Outing: Why it Matters," *Entertainment Weekly,* October 30, 2007, www.ew.com/article/2007/10/30/dumbledores-outing-why-it-matters.

11. "JK Rowling Under Fire from US Bible Belt After Outing Dumbledore as Gay," *Daily Mail,* October 28, 2007, www.dailymail.co.uk/news/article-490261/ JK-Rowling-US-Bible-belt-outing-Dumbledore-gay.html.

12. Sophia Tesfaye, "Repent that Dumbledore Emerged as a Homosexual Mentor for Harry Potter," *Salon,* November 9, 2015, www.salon.com/2015/11/09/ repent_that_dumbledore_emerged_as_a_homosexual_mentor_for_harry_ potter_inside_the_bizarre_anti_gay_conference_featuring_ted_cruz_mike_ huckabee_bobby_jindal/.

13. EdwardTLC, "J. K. Rowling at Carnegie Hall Reveals Dumbledore is Gay," *The Leaky-Cauldron.org,* October 20, 2007, www.the-leaky-cauldron. org/2007/10/20/j-k-rowling-at-carnegie-hall-reveals-dumbledore-is-gay-neville-marries-hannah-abbott-and-scores-more/.

14. Emily Asher-Perrin, "Albus Dumbledore Didn't Come Out at the Right Time (According to Everyone)," *Tor,* September 26, 2013, www.tor.com/ 2013/09/26/banned-books-week-harry-potter-jk-rowling-dumbledore-gay-icon/.

15. Lindsey Fraser, *Conversations with J. K. Rowling* (New York: Scholastic Press, 2001), 40.

16. Adam Shecter, "Seeking an LGBTQ Middle-Grade Blockbuster," *School Library Journal,* May 14, 2014, www.slj.com/2014/05/diversity/seeking-an-lgbtq-middle-grade-blockbuster/.

17. Rothstein, "Is Dumbledore Gay?"

18. Laura Leonard, "The Trouble with *Twilight,*" *Christianity Today,* February 19, 2010.

19. Bob Mondello, "Remembering Hollywood's Hays Code, 40 Years On," *NPR,* August 8, 2008, www.npr.org/templates/story/story.php?storyId= 93301189.

20. Milosh Marinovich, "Harry Potter Goes Nude!" *CBS News,* July 28, 2006, www.cbsnews.com/news/harry-potter-goes-nude/.

21. Louise Gannon, "I Find Being Sexy Embarrassing, Reveals Emma Watson," *MailOnline,* February 6, 2009, www.dailymail.co.uk/home/moslive/article-1127838/I-sexy-embarrassing-reveals-Emma-Watson.html.

22. Stuart Heritage, "Harry Potter Enters the Twilight Zone," *The Guardian,* December 8, 2009, www.theguardian.com/film/filmblog/2009/dec/08/harry-potter-twilight.

23. Charlotte Martin, "Nudes that make you go ewww," *The Irish Sun,* December 8, 2009, www.thesun.ie/irishsol/homepage/woman/2761965/The-worst-celebrity-nude-scenesWorst-naked-film-scenesMost-weird-nude-scenesNudeNakedtoplesssex-scenesstrange-sex-scenes.html.

24. Directed by Bill Condon (Disney, 2017).

25. *Harry Potter and the Deathly Hallows, Part 2,* directed by David Yates (Warner Bros, 2011).

26. Directed by Stephen Chbosky (Summit/Lionsgate, 2013).

27. Directed by Even Goldberg and Seth Rogen (Sony Pictures, 2013).

28. Directed by John Krokidas (Sony Pictures, 2013).

29. Directed by The Daniels (A24, 2016).

30. "UN Women announces Emma Watson as Goodwill Ambassador," *UN Women,* July 8, 2014, www.unwomen.org/en/news/stories/2014/7/un-women-announces-emma-watson-as-goodwill-ambassador.

31. Rachel Moss, "Emma Watson Calls on Men to Fight for Gender Equality in Powerful UN Speech," *The Huffington Post,* September 22, 2014, www.huffingtonpost.co.uk/2014/09/22/emma-watson-un-speech-feminsim-equality_n_5859580.html.

32. Cavan Sieczkowski, "Emma Watson Says Nude Photo Leak Threat After Gender Equality Speech a 'Wake-Up Call,'" *The Huffington Post,* March 9, 2015, www.huffingtonpost.com/2015/03/09/emma-watson-nude-photo-leak-threat_n_6832066.html.

33. Zeba Blay, "Emma Watson Gives Smart Answer When Asked if She's A 'White Feminist,'" *The Huffington Post,* October 12, 2015, www.huffingtonpost.com/entry/emma-watson-gives-smart-answer-when-asked-if-shes-a-white-feminist_us_561bea68e4b0dbb8000f4ea9.

34. Amy McCarthy, "Sorry Privileged White Ladies, But Emma Watson Isn't a 'Game Changer' for Feminism," *XO Jane,* September 24, 2014, www.xojane.com/issues/emma-watson-he-for-she.

35. Eileen Sutton, "How Emma Watson Continues to Deal with HeForShe Death Threats," *Racked,* March 9, 2015, www.racked.com/2015/3/9/8175609/emma-watson-heforshe-death-threats.

36. Jan Moir, "Where's the Magic in this Tale of Middle-Class Monsters?" *Daily Mail,* September 26, 2012, www.dailymail.co.uk/news/article-2209165/J-K-Rowlings-The-Casual-Vacancy-review-Wheres-magic-tale-middle-class-monsters.html.

37. Kelly West, "Will Harry Potter 8 Ever Happen? Here's What J. K. Rowling Says," *Cinema Blend,* www.cinemablend.com/celebrity/Harry-Potter-8-Ever-Happen-Here-What-J-K-Rowling-Says-71246.html.

38. Gary Cleland, "Amazon Admits to Record Harry Potter Bid," *The Telegraph,* December 7, 2014, www.telegraph.co.uk/news/uknews/3669918/Amazon-admits-to-record-Harry-Potter-bid.html.

39. Alessandra Stanley, "Review: 'The Casual Vacancy,' Based on J. K. Rowling's Novel, on HBO," *The New York Times,* April 28, 2015, www.nytimes.com/2015/04/29/arts/television/review-the-casual-vacancy-based-on-j-k-rowlings-novel-on-hbo.html.

40. Liz Bury, "Cuckoo's Calling by JK Rowling: Did you Know?" *The Guardian,* July 15, 2013, www.theguardian.com/books/2013/jul/15/cuckoos-calling-jk-rowling-did-you-know.

41. "JK Rowling Law Firm Pays Damages Over Pseudonym Leak," *BBC News,* July 31, 2013, www.bbc.com/news/entertainment-arts-23515054.

42. "Robert Galbraith's Cormoran Strike Novels to be Adapted for Major New BBC Drama Series," *BBC,* December 10, 2014, www.bbc.co.uk/mediacentre/latestnews/2014/cormoran-strike.

43. Sarah Begley, "The Magic is Gone but Harry Will Never Die," *Time,* August 12, 2016, http://time.com/4445149/harry-potter-cursed-child-jk-rowling/.

44. Sandra Gonzalez, "J. K. Rowling Says There Will Be Five 'Fantastic Beasts' Movies," *CNN,* October 20, 2016, www.cnn.com/2016/10/13/entertainment/fantastic-beasts-five-movies/.

45. Ramin Setoodeh, " 'Fantastic Beasts' Becomes First 'Harry Potter' Movie to Win an Oscar," *Variety,* February 26, 2017, http://variety.com/2017/film/news/fantastic-beast-first-harry-potter-oscar-1201997179/.

46. Matt Stinger, "Split Decision: How Breaking Movies in Half is Ruining Hollywood Blockbusters," *Screen Crush,* November 21, 2014, http://screencrush.com/splitting-movies-into-parts-1-and-2/.

47. "All Time Box Office," *Box Office Mojo,* September 28, 2016, www.boxofficemojo.com/alltime/world/.

48. "All Time Box Office."

2

"Elder" and Wiser

The Filmic *Harry Potter* and the Rejection of Power

Cassandra Bausman

When moviegoers around the globe packed theater seats in record numbers to see how J. K. Rowling's culture-shaping epic would translate to the big screen in the franchise's final installment, the series' final climactic battle between good and evil was an outcome well-known to many who had followed the exploits of the humble boy wizard and his journey into maturity. Yet, Steve Kloves's sensitive adaptation of the film's final moments in *Harry Potter and the Deathly Hallows, Part 2* deviates from Rowling's text in ways that, while seemingly slight, are in fact highly significant in coloring the construction of Harry's heroic identity and his last step into manhood.

While the values of love, friendship, and community are an explicit and recurrent message of the *Potter* stories, the final screenplay renders Harry's ultimate rejection of power, aggression, and supremacy even more strongly than does the language of Rowling's novels. Finding himself in uncontested possession of the wizarding world's most powerful weapon—the invincible Elder Wand—Harry breaks it to bits and hurls it into a gorge in a wordless action, with no more ceremony than an exhausted half-smile shared among friends. An interesting and arresting aesthetic choice, Harry's ultimate and unequivocal rejection of power carries even stronger sociopolitical implications. This chapter investigates this defining moment of Harry's heroism, exploring the ideological implications of Kloves's rendering and its political and pedagogical impact so central to the enduring legacy that is the global Potter phenomenon.

More than escapist fantasy, in a final adventure that finds Harry wrestling with his obligations not only as a wizard but as a man, the filmic *Harry Potter* confronts many of the complex ethical questions its story merits, thoughtfully addressing the nature of leadership and heroism, of evil and ascendency, and their inherent interplay with power and privilege. The fantastic films that emerge from our tent-pole movie culture often force interior struggle, ethical debate, and even character development to take a backseat to external razzmatazz, but the *Potter* saga culminates in a finale as emotionally and ethically intense as it is visually grand. Even in adaption, the *Potter* series retains its ability to operate as a deeply moral fantasy. Begun with a shaggy-haired boy sleeping in a cupboard under the stairs and concluding with a young man who proves the salvation of his world, the *Potter* story distinguishes itself with its particular brand of heroism: its emphasis upon individual choice; on self-sacrifice and the use of power to protect and defend; on the preference to disarm rather than murder; to act, above all, from love. All resolute markers of the series' eponymous hero's identity, the Potterverse undercuts the idea that chosen-one fantasies must function, by default, as reductive power fantasies. In so blatantly discarding the Elder Wand, an "unbeatable" wand of inestimable power, the filmic Harry gives a clear answer—significantly here, a clear refutation—to a more traditional hero's problematic relationship to power and its temptations.

Redefining heroism and reconfiguring the conventional quest to culminate in a rejection of power rather than an ascension to it, Harry's complexly positioned heroism is nowhere more clearly rendered than in Kloves's especially poignant, brief yet effective adaption of the final battle's culmination. More than a mere magical MacGuffin, the Elder Wand becomes a means of addressing complex questions and offering resolution to embattled themes. Book seven and, like it, the eighth film were always destined to end with a last great confrontation between Harry and Voldemort, a final battle between the forces of Good and Evil writ large, and, though book and film represent the last stand-off in the Battle of Hogwarts with considerable differences, the film's translation of Harry's heroic journey adeptly preserves the powerful message of his indelible coming-of-age story and the ethics underlying its fantasy.

There is a wealth of critical and scholarly interest in the *Potter* phenomenon, and many texts have given serious consideration to social and political issues raised in and by Rowling's works. Lest one consider this critical work as indulgent, scholarly vainglory, Rowling has characterized her own books as political statements with a clear social conscience, describing her series as "a prolonged argument for tolerance, a prolonged plea for an end to bigotry," something she thinks "is a very healthy message to pass on to young people," especially accompanying the lesson that "you should question authority and you should not assume that the establishment or the press tells you all of the truth."[1] In her view, her books throughout "preach against . . . bigotry, violence, struggles for power no matter what"[2] and invite sustained dialogue with such weighty themes. Indeed, Rowling has also said that she has specifically written for "obsessives," academic or otherwise, who would mine every nugget of her texts for meaning and subject them to extreme scrutiny, the reading experience designed to reward critical attention.[3]

Collections like Giselle Anatol's *Reading Harry Potter* and Elizabeth Heilman's *Critical Perspectives on Harry Potter* have captured the broad scope of a resultant interdisciplinary interest while Nancy Reagin's *Harry Potter and History*, Neumann and Nexon's *Harry Potter and International Relations*, Thomas and Snyder's *The Law and Harry Potter*, and Bethanny Barratt's *The Politics of Harry Potter* offer more specialized investigations.[4] And yet, while disciplinary or methodological approach may vary greatly, all of these texts share similar arguments in their understanding of *why* the Potterverse is deserving of study—and it lies not in the creativity or popularity of the fiction alone, but rather in its reverberations with the real.

As Elizabeth Heilman explains the importance of taking the wizarding world seriously, these works contain not only "powerful, thought-provoking literary themes" but also "portrayals of social and cultural normalcy."[5] The *Potter* stories "serve as a powerful form of social text" and thus "deserve serious critical attention" and demand to be read critically.[6] Inasmuch as the *Harry Potter* megatext has become a contemporary classic, a dominant, common cultural touchstone, we must recognize that the "narrative story, images, and lessons of the books are infiltrating the lives and imaginations of readers and consumers of related products," and understand, too, that the resultant internalization is not passive or inconsequential, no passing fiction or fancy.[7] As Giselle Anatol echoes, the *Potter* series is an incredibly significant formative narrative, and as such necessitates "exploration and study rather than rejection as simply pulp, pop culture, or the latest fad."[8] Just as "neglecting the potency of the novels" or discounting their cultural weight "as childhood trivia" is a dangerous dismissal, the *Potter* books, as can be argued of the corpus of children's literature generally, "reflect and/or comment upon the cultural assumptions and ideological tensions of contemporary society" and can affect the "intellectual social development of today's children and tomorrow's adults."[9] Such fictions can be understood as a "powerful tool for inculcating social roles and behaviors, moral guides, desires, and fears,"[10] and to understand the power and appeal of such texts, we must also understand that "literature and cultural products can simultaneously represent, reproduce, and transform cultural, political, and institutional norms."[11]

As Nancy Reagin elegantly points out, the wizarding world, just like many of its characters, "is a half-blooded one" because of its vital connection to the real; "its roots go deep into Muggle history, the history that Professor Binns does not teach his pupils," although it certainly undergirds their world as much as the reader's own.[12] Though a fantasy, Rowling's works are deeply attuned to our immediate world, her conflicts an exploration of shared anxieties and a reflection of our mutual heritage. Rowling's is yet a "world built of magic and history," and exploring the fictions' implications, "seeing how the wizarding world grew from our own helps us enjoy it"—and understand it—"all the more."[13] As Lana Whited confirms in *Harry Potter and The Ivory Tower*, books "must conjure a real world or one that parallels the real world in intriguing ways," their stories and language reflecting culture and cultural values.[14] Indeed, as the forward to *Harry Potter and Politics* underscores, the *Potter* world "is a complete vision that includes a class system, the politics of identity, love and hate, good and evil, sin and redemption, and rivalry and power struggles," the fantasy ever-relevant to the modern condition, the "parables and allegories" Rowling employs riddled with contemporary political importance.[15]

Furthermore, while some scholars find it most useful to position *Potter* as a metaphorical lens for considering past history and/or as a barometer of the contemporary moment, other scholars, perhaps most singly philosophers, as evidenced in Carrie-Ann Biondi's *Imagining Better: Philosophical Issues in* Harry Potter and David Baggett and Shawn Klein's *Harry Potter and Philosophy*,[16] find the fantasy an ideal means of addressing more universal, less temporally-circumscribed ethical and moral questions in an approach that values *Potter* less for its ability to draw specific corollaries or concrete analogues and more for providing readers with the open-ended opportunity and the critical tools necessary to examine what they "make of themselves and their world."[17] A broad, metaphysical approach that transcends, like classic literature must, any particularly circumscribed place and time to speak anew and renewably to all ages, the "once upon a time" trope of fantasy un-paradoxically both future-oriented and embedded in past history, the moral imagination central to Rowling's fantasies "teaches us how to be truly human" and "how to live rightly with other humans."[18] Indeed, in their article "What Would Harry Do?," Lana Whited and Katherine Grimes take on conservative Christian detractors to demonstrate that the *Potter* books are centrally about providing "examples of moral and ethical decision-making" for young readers.[19] Finding *Potter* "an effective illustration" of the dominant theories on children's moral reasoning, Harry's adventures require readers to evaluate the decisions and actions of the characters in the narrative, provoking discussion of moral conflict and modeling moral decision-making via the characters who inhabit Rowling's magical and Muggle worlds.[20]

As Biondi reminds us, "the best fantasy literature calls us to face the human condition" and affords us with an opportunity to "attain better understandings of ourselves," something the importance Rowling places on choice and the cultivation of one's character certainly emphasizes.[21] Travis Prinzi in *Harry Potter and Imagination* particularly gets to the heart of the work of the moral imagination in *Potter*, demonstrating the extent to which Rowling is clearly writing morality tales, as he argues that the *Potter* stories "do more than lay down ethical lessons to be put into action," and actually "get to the very soul of the human being and teach what it means to be a moral human."[22]

With these grand themes at play in the *Potter* zeitgeist, this chapter's interest in the politically and ethically-valenced dynamics of Harry's heroism are in good company. However, where most of these scholarly works use the *Potter* texts to explore an external concept—political, philosophical, theological, theoretical, psychological, sociological—textual explication is less the focus, with many scholars invoking *Potter* as a tool, a pedagogical entry point serving an instructive, introductory purpose, a means to an end which sees the fiction used as a conduit to understanding that displaces the analysis away from the text itself. In literary studies that is less the case, but such works also tend to focus any engagement with power on structures of authority or on social systems writ large, with responses either organized around lines of race, class, species, wealth, and gender or invested in a critical investigation of institutions (the government; practices of house elves and slavery or the related subjugation of other social castes or non-human magical creatures; the sorting hat and school house assignations or other social hierarchies; the prison system; the media, legal and justice systems; modes of interrogation, surveillance, communication, etc.) that made Voldemort's rise and return possible. Typically, when considering power, in other words, scholars have been more focused on the world Harry moves through, the systems he encounters, the opponents he faces, or the more ambiguous friends he makes than on Harry's heroic arc or any particularly crystalized revelatory textual moments.

Indeed, as this chapter is built around one illustrative moment—the fate of the Elder Wand and its implications for the *Potter* story's heroic ethics and politics—it's important to note that such an analytical approach is only appropriate, or perhaps even possible, because of its unique basis in medium adaptation. It is the act of comparing the final film with the final novel that makes the importance, the iconicity, of Harry's association with the Elder Wand particularly poignant and its import so particularly visible.

The filmic translations of the *Potter* novels make us see the original work anew. After all, an adaptation is, in essence, a significant act of textual interpretation. Considering the transmedia *Potter* story collectively underscores how multi-faceted it is; investigating a particular element, or seeking a definitive essence, when approached through the lens of adaptation, reveals how the *Potter* story encourages and resists easy or singular interpretation. Thus, the work of analyzing a cinematic adaptation, the cinematic means employed to make interior lives visible and to compress and condense complexly constructed themes, must not be couched in terms of faithfulness to source material alone. Adaptation, as Walter Benjamin notes, is fundamentally a kind of translation, and no translation or interpretation would be "possible if in its ultimate essence it strove for likeness to the original. For in its afterlife . . . the original undergoes a change."[23] Adaptation is about determining the essence of a textual experience, about then determining an alternative means of delivering and disseminating that experience in a new mode; it is about the spirit more than the letter of the adapted text. As Benjamin would say, an adaptation's success lies in locating the "intended effect" of a text and producing, in transmutation, "the echo of the original."[24] As the *Potter* story echoes loudly through popular culture, the *Potter* films foreground acts of interpretation, modeling what they uphold as vital, critical, interpretive socio-political work.

In the case of the Elder Wand, and all it represents to the wider *Potter* story particularly, we should remember the lessons of adaptation and translation theory: that translation is "not a rendering of some fixed nontextual meaning to be copied or paraphrased or reproduced; rather, it is an engagement with the original text that makes us see that text in different ways."[25] The films, in this sense, themselves enter into a debate on the meanings of the novels, the *Potter* films engaging with Rowling's original, reinventing it, revisioning it and allowing viewers to participate in its meaning afresh.[26] Part of a vibrant transmedia tapestry that will only continue to grow with the *Potter* brand, the cinematic adaptations function as an important location for creative and critical explorations of what and how Rowling's works continue to mean in complex multiplicity. Thus, the film adaptations afford opportunities for intriguing interpretive work, particularly where psychological and emotional realism and thematic resonance is privileged over textual accuracy, as in the case of the iconic centrality of the Elder Wand.

Director David Yates and screenwriter Steve Kloves's adaptation of Harry's rejection of the Elder Wand and the power it represents is just such a significant interpretive decision. Serving to both compress and clarify Rowling's ongoing epic themes and their interplay with moral recommendations, the final scene that sees the snapping of the Elder Wand is a finely distilled visual essence that stands as the last word—or, more accurately and significantly, image—of Harry's particular mode of heroism and the values undergirding his heroic journey.

The Chosen One and the Power of Choice

In order to fully understand the weight of the series' finale, it is important to first recognize that Harry's story has long been marked by a critical interest in and an intersection of power and choice. The summative moment in which Harry determines the fate of the Elder Wand is but the last word on recursive elements Rowling develops and deepens alongside her hero's growth in maturity across the series. As the boy wizard, progressing through his school years, must naturally grow into his powers as a wizard and, as our protagonist, into his identity and responsibilities as a heroic figure, this may seem a natural, uninspired thematic concern. Yet, the mutually constitutive relationship between the two becomes essential philosophical bedrock for the *Potter* series.

The second volume, importantly, sees the early strong emergence of this theme of power and choice explicitly, as Harry negotiates the strange magic of the Sorting Hat, a device whose power over students' destinies and role as detector of personalities is a ready emblem of free-will, choice, and destiny in the Potterverse. In *Harry Potter and The Chamber of Secrets*, as Harry has already begun to struggle with his connection to Voldemort and his "Chosen One" identity, his own choices are shown to reign supreme. At the adventure's close—always the moment for dispensing wisdom and cementing morals—Dumbledore offers a sage gloss of the hat's omnipotence which empowers Harry. As Dumbledore reassures the child Harry, tortured by his

Slytherin-skewing associations, the power of Harry's own decisions are not to be underestimated, particularly by himself.

"It only put me in Gryffindor," said Harry in a defeated voice, "because I asked not to go into Slytherin . . ." "*Exactly*," said Dumbledore, beaming once more. "Which makes you very different from Tom Riddle. It is our choices, Harry, that show us what we truly are, far more than our abilities."[27]

Harry's choices here, interestingly, are given considerable power: over his own destiny and also over the narrative. While Harry may have thought to contend with a destiny prepared for him at birth, as The Chosen One, The Boy Who Lived, or even as a potential Heir of Slytherin, Dumbledore's statements suggest that, instead, Harry's journey is one he must make for himself, his identity ever in-process and yet undetermined. As Rowling herself has said, in commentary originally published on her official website, "Destiny is a name often given in retrospect to choices that had dramatic consequences," a statement issued to directly acknowledge the extent to which her novels were crafted to explore numerous, nuanced examples of characters making choices, both large and small, that bear surprising impact on the narrative in challenge to any sense of closed inevitability in her take on the chosen-one heroic tradition. Despite the air of destiny, even prophecy, that surrounds Harry, Rowling proves as interested in challenging any uncritical assumption of "chosen one" certainty and innate exceptionalism as she is in reproducing a comfortable, familiar heroic narrative.

Harry Potter and the Order of the Phoenix, then, which centrally concerns prophecy—about Harry's future, and also about the threat that leads to Voldemort's attack in his infancy—makes especially sure to question the function of prophecy. In an elaboration upon the lesson of the Sorting Hat, the fifth volume emphatically insists that prophecies require human action and interpretation to have meaning. As Dumbledore again underscores to Harry and his readership, it was Voldemort's choices that shaped past events, as it must be Harry's choices that will shape the future.

Indeed, Harry's interactions with Voldemort, both in direct confrontation and in contending with the long shadow his legacy has cast, often mutually highlight the antagonists' similarities and the difference individual choice makes. These encounters repeatedly imbue individual choice with power, demonstrating that it is Harry's choices which separate him from Voldemort, and these choices which mark Harry as good, as hero. While Harry's connection to Voldemort is considerable—indeed, much of the final volume is motivated by Harry's realization that a piece of Voldemort lives within him, and that his death will be required to break Voldemort's power and tether to life—their points of contrast garner significant attention at every turn, and they have little to do with biography.

As we learn through flashback, before accepting his place at Hogwarts, Tom Riddle already found pleasure in cruelty, using his magic to manipulate and dominate, to cause pain and to punish. Once enrolled in the school and sorted into Slytherin House, the home of cunning witches and wizards willing to venture anything necessary to achieve their ambitious aims, his obsession with power only grows. As one analysis summarizes his nature, "Born into rejection and isolation, finding his only sense of self in his ability to control others, power gives Voldemort meaning." Thus, it might be said that "Voldemort's evil is that he consistently chooses power, at any cost."[28] Harry, however, in spite of similarities to Voldemort, consistently chooses otherwise. And, just as is true of his nemesis, it is this patent rejection of power that gives him *his* unique power. It is those differences which save him from Voldemort's attempted possession at the Ministry, and the series' cultivation of Harry's courage, the essential goodness of his character, often revolves around his ability to choose to act for good, to act from love, a motivator fundamentally inconceivable to Voldemort.

Indeed, for those already interested in playing the comparison game, the cinematic adaptations of the *Potter* story have similarly viewed choice as a central theme and have been careful to stress it to audiences, highlighting Harry's inner struggle well before the final film. In the filmic transposition of *The Order of the Phoenix*, for example (the only script Steve Kloves did not pen), screenwriter Michael Goldenberg adds two new significant sentences to a vital conversation between Sirius and Harry at Grimmauld Place in which Harry confesses concerns about "becoming bad" to his godfather. While Goldenberg opens the loaded exchange with reassurance in the form of one of Rowling's repurposed lines, "The world isn't split into good people and Death Eaters," the conversation continues off-book as Sirius continues, "We've got both dark and light inside of us. What matters is the part we choose to act on. That's who we really are." While not drawn explicitly from the novel, this conversation is an excellent example of the cinematic adaptation's ability to economically address its themes and encapsulate its moral messages. Here, this expanded scene effectively highlights two central themes of Rowling's series in asserting that good and evil are not easy, simple binaries, but rather entwined in a close and complex relationship, and again validating the idea that the exercise of free will is the greatest indicator of a character's moral worth. However, in a further fascinating example of cinematic interpretation and the choices that shape a narrative's meaning, *The Order of the Phoenix* also makes significant narrative shifts that detract from Rowling's exploration of the morality of choice and its centrality to her epic. In the fifth film, the adaptation paradoxically chooses to remove Neville from the prophecy plot, a significant lapse, as Rowling's critical investigation of the power of prophecy depends upon the fact that Voldemort identifies Harry as the Chosen One over Neville, when the prophecy may have indicated either boy as a threat. This elision is significant, as Rowling's novel uses this revelation to not only again draw parallels between the two sets of characters, but to further emphasize that it is Voldemort's choices that mark him as immoral, just as it is Harry's choices that make him moral. However, as we will soon see, future entries into the *Potter* story—both on the page and on the screen—make this same point abundantly clear.

Thus, as the sixth entry into the saga is the beginning of the ending, the calm before the storm, *Harry Potter and the Half-Blood Prince* must cement Harry's character, and particularly these aspects of choice and corresponding morality. As Emily Asher-Perrin notes, this is the story in which Harry's morals solidify, and, importantly, his heroism emerges "not through his valiant deeds, but through his character," less through dramatic actions than quiet decisions.[29] No longer concerned with fitting in, Harry defends his off-color supporters, managing his grief and keeping his friends close, no longer the angst-ridden, scream-prone, moody teen of *The Order of the Phoenix*. A marked maturation, this is the Harry, as Asher-Perrin succinctly puts it, "who will defeat Voldemort."

Indeed, while Harry's interactions with Dumbledore across the series increasingly take on the flavor of a disciple groomed for a pre-destined fate in defeating the Dark Lord, Dumbledore, against the appearance that Harry's adventures play out as they were predetermined to do, also consistently works against either eponymous hero or audience reading or reflecting on Harry's experiences as a too-easy, secured and fated narrative, opting instead to focus on his choices and the development of his moral character. Clearly displaying much affection for the "Potter boy" over the course of his education at Hogwarts, Dumbledore cares for Harry-as-individual as well as Harry-as-hero, and he repeatedly frames him as such. The rhetoric deployed in the Headmaster's moralizing of each story's meaning underscores Harry as both plot function and person, his character and choices always shown to have bearing and a weighty impact upon events. In spite of his role as didactic narrative authority, Dumbledore is also simultaneously the voice of an unorthodox resistance to that kind of closed narrative framework.

Rather than teaching Harry that he is destined through prophecy and historic repetition/predetermination to face Voldemort, Dumbledore instead strives to teach the importance of choice and free will, continuously reinforcing their significance from within his traditional role and summative discourse as mentor and guide. As Harry ultimately reflects in preparing for the final stage of his journey, "he understood at last what Dumbledore had been trying to tell him. It was, he thought, the difference between being dragged into the arena to face a battle to the death and walking into the arena with your head held high." While some might say "there was little to choose between the two ways . . . Dumbledore knew, and so do I . . . and so did my parents," Harry realizes, with a fierce rush of pride, "that there was all the difference in the world." [30] As this moment particularly encapsulates, with a Harry who is resolved to face and destroy his enemy, choice, and what it reveals of one's character, is a surpassingly important theme in the series. Here, Harry acknowledges that one cannot always determine one's options or choose the circumstances, but, despite such a seemingly un-empowered position, he is far from a pawn: he always has a choice in how he will face his challenges, even extending to how he may choose to live his life or meet his death. Harry's attitude, the personal ethics and moral compass of his heroism in meeting his battles, and what, similarly, makes him powerful, is made explicit context in his heroic journey. Beyond a focus on plot and the set pieces of his fantastic adventures, the *Potter* story relentlessly refocuses the narrative on Harry's decisions, on the "hows" of his heroism more than the "whats" of his exploits and achievements, and only more so as it hurtles to its epic conclusion.

Indeed, the culmination of the "special lessons" Dumbledore gives Harry across the duration of the sixth novel emphasizes Harry's heroic trajectory and, again, hangs its viability on his character, on his innate goodness, his nobility, morality, and protective spirit, on his ability, and his choices—especially significant in the face of increasing adversity—to resiliently retain them. After discussing Voldemort's Horcruxes and the task Harry has ahead of him, Dumbledore attempts to make this clear to Harry (as well as communicate this unconventionally-defined heroism to readers who have always followed him) in preparation for the important beats of the final confrontation and anticipated resolution. As Dumbledore pronounces, in terms which highlight the values in conflict as much as the figures:

> "It will take uncommon skill and power to kill a wizard like Voldemort even without his Horcruxes." "But I haven't got uncommon skill and

power," said Harry before he could stop himself. "Yes, you have," said Dumbledore firmly. "You have a power that Voldemort has never had. You can—" "I know!" said Harry impatiently. "I can love!" "Yes, Harry, you can love," said Dumbledore. "Which, given everything that has happened to you, is a great and remarkable thing. You are still too young to understand how unusual you are, Harry." "So when the prophecy says that I'll have 'power the Dark Lord knows not,' it just means—love?" asked Harry, feeling a little let down.[31]

While love has always been an important theme in the *Potter* stories, this formulation is particularly noteworthy, as love is so closely and explicitly equated with power. Here, love is almost figured (if to Harry's dismay) as his super-power. Further underscoring Harry's capacity for love, Dumbledore reminds Harry that, despite his links to the Dark Lord and his "privileged insight into Voldemort's world," he has "never been seduced by the Dark Arts, never, even for a second, shown the slightest desire to become one of Voldemort's followers!"[32] Harry's indignant explosion, "Of course I haven't! He killed my mum and dad!" only secures Dumbledore's point: "You are protected, in short, by your ability to love! . . . The only protection that can possibly work against the lure of power like Voldemort's! In spite of all the temptation you have endured, all the suffering, you remain pure of heart."[33] This elaboration on the power of love and its significance to Harry's future as heroic Chosen One is an important complement to Dumbledore's previous statement about the nature of Harry's heroic identity and positioning. Love is not only a powerful weapon in Harry's arsenal, but a powerful protection, a powerful defense.

This is an important formulation, as this power is set against that of Voldemort's traditional, terrifying brand. Love, the power the Dark Lord knows not, is Harry's power, both his greatest protection and a considerable defensive weapon. Furthermore, as we see in Harry's favoring of the "Expelliarmus" spell and his abilities with shield charms and the Patronus (all his skill, in general, with Defense Against the Dark Arts), his greatest power is often framed as protective in nature. Indeed, his desire to protect, to do for the good of others, is a hallmark of his identity. Occasionally mocked as "a saving people thing," whether derided in the flight of the seven potters, celebrated in the Tri-Wizard Tournament, or used against him in Sirius's faux-capture, the deployment of Harry's heroism—his choices in how he uses his power—espouse protective, defensive, unselfish principles.

Indeed, the dramatic abjuration of the Elder Wand, which we'll explore later as the final, cumulative cementation of these values, is itself but a masterful elaboration upon Harry's earliest climactic test at the close of his first adventure. In *Harry Potter and the Sorcerer's Stone*, Harry is able to use the Mirror of Erised to find the philosopher's stone, an alchemical artefact Voldemort covets in his quest to return to power and attain immortality. Only one who could find the stone, with no wish to use it or claim it for themselves, would have been so able. As Dumbledore reminds Harry, "when you stared into a mirror that reflected your heart's desire . . . it showed you only the way to thwart Lord Voldemort, and not immortality or riches. Harry, have you any idea how few wizards could have seen what you saw in that mirror?"[34] His is an incredibly pure-hearted, selfless spirit, a rare worldview that eschews power or self-aggrandizement in favor of a greater communal good. Indeed, as Dumbledore adds extra commentary—"Voldemort should have known then what he was dealing with, but he did not!"—we get important foreshadowing via the astute, ever-winking mentor.[35] While Harry (and his readers) may not yet see the significance of the stone's test, this reminder of Harry's first heroic outing comes as Dumbledore endeavors to shape the important factors of his last great battle, and is thus hugely resonant. Demonstrated in the case of the retrieval of the philosopher's stone in his first year and echoed in his duel with Voldemort in his last, Harry paradoxically and poignantly finds his greatest power unleashed in the refusal to seek or consolidate power within himself. In this neat poetry of the series, Rowling's ethics of power rings clear.

Indeed, these final lessons of Dumbledore's are especially important as this penultimate chapter of Harry's journey is interwoven with insight into Voldemort's character and explorations into his past. Via Pensieve, we see Voldemort directly deny the importance of such "powers" and perspectives, as he tells Dumbledore how he has "pushed the boundaries of magic further, perhaps, than they have ever been pushed . . . but nothing I have seen in the world has supported your famous pronouncements that love is more powerful than my kind of magic."[36] What we must understand here is that Voldemort's magic, his "kind of magic," is fundamentally not that of Dumbledore's, nor Harry's. Similarly, his kind of power is not, and will not be, Harry's. Just as Harry rejects Draco's invitation to stick with him and make the right sort of friends on his first day in Hogwarts, electing to take Luna to a Slug Club dinner, as he has no wish to use the philosopher's stone for his own ends, nor keep use of the Elder Wand, Harry's growth into his power, into his heroic identity and into maturity, is, repeatedly, a rejection of traditional power. It is a rejection of power as understood by Voldemort, as customarily understood and recognized by society broadly, and critically embodied in the kind of "might is right" rule of the ministry. Yet, in addition to rejection, it is also an important redefinition of power, a re-prioritizing and reconfiguring such that power can also mean love, can mean protection and selflessness or willing sacrifice.

Hallows and Horcruxes

As *Harry Potter and the Deathly Hallows* dawns, there is then no more time left to grow up, and no pretending that someone else holds the answers. With Dumbledore's death, Harry must draw upon his own resources and act on his own. While his mentor left some hints and instructions, Harry must step out from beneath his shadow, must leave the relatively safe confines of the school and, at last, fully make his own choices. It's a rocky transition, which leaves some critics, (including Ron and Hermione) complaining of slow pacing, as Harry finds his footing and direction alone (in the woods), but it is an important transition nonetheless, as it is these experiences that prepare Harry for the final face off with Voldemort and determine the battle's stakes and the conditions governing it. Chief among the difficult and painful choices Harry must make in the last stages of his hero's journey concerns the Deathly Hallows, and, paramount amongst these powerful items, the Elder Wand.

One of the most significant turning points in the plot of *Deathly Hallows* hinges upon Harry's decision to continue the search for the Horcruxes—the dispersed parts of Voldemort's fragmented soul secreted into protected magical artefacts—or to pursue the Hallows, the three magical objects said to make their possessor master of Death (an unbeatable wand, a stone that can bring back the dead, and a cloak that can hide the wearer from Death). Ultimately, Harry choses to carry out his mission to destroy Voldemort's Horcruxes, to weaken his enemy rather than claim the Hallows in an attempt to strengthen or defend himself. Yet it is a difficult decision, and one fundamental to the ethics of his heroism.

Once Harry, Ron, and Hermione learn about the Hallows, piecing together that in Harry's heirloom invisibility cloak and Marvolo Gaunt's ring-cum-Snitch they are already in possession of two of the three relics, and, further realizing that Voldemort is himself seeking the Elder Wand as the means to attain a foolproof supremacy and surefire defeat of Harry, Harry can't help but wonder if the trick to his survival may lie in pitting Hallows against Horcruxes. Increasingly obsessed by their allure, in spite of Hermione's attempts to keep him focused on Dumbledore's directive to destroy Horcruxes, Harry is drawn by the possibility that the Hallows might keep him safe from Voldemort and grant his defeat, that the Hallows may in fact be his rightful answer to Voldemort's Horcruxes, a supernatural way of clinging to life and of enhancing his power. Understandably driven by the desire to stay alive, to have a fighting chance against an unimaginable evil, the prospect of the Hallows represents the point in Harry's quest where he grasps at his mortality and newly prioritizes self-interest. This difficult moment of transition adds impact to his eventual sacrifice, but his choice also significantly colors the timbre of his resilient opposition to Voldemort. As the Hallows would seem to offer salvation, they serve to show what Harry must give up, what he must eschew in making difficult, right choices.

The Elder Wand, of course, is the crux of this contest. Hailed as an "unbeatable wand," the Elder Wand, also known as "The Deathstick" and the "Wand of Destiny," is the most powerful wand in existence. Said to have been crafted by Death himself, made for "a combative man" who "asked for a wand more powerful than any in existence: a wand that must always win duels for its owner," the wand possesses a bloody history.[37] After killing a rival wizard, and drunkenly boasting of the wand's powers, its original owner was soon murdered, beginning a chain of possession that eccentric Hallows quester Xenophilious Lovegood describes as a "bloody trail . . . splattered across the pages of Wizarding history,"[38] the powerful wand passing through various owners, usually by violent means, all "killed by their successors in a lust for power."[39] In time, the legend of the wand grew to include the assumption that murder is necessary to attain mastery of the Elder Wand, although famed wandmaker Garrick Ollivander confides that the association, more than a requirement, is "simply due to the fact that it is such a desirable object and arouses such passions in wizards."[40] Yet, this wand—"immensely powerful, dangerous in the wrong hands"—also behaves differently from other wands in its lack of loyalty and own preference for power, as Rowling has clarified its particularly nefarious nature.[41] As Rowling glosses the sinister temperament of her super-weapon,

> The Elder Wand is simply the most ruthless of wands in that it will only take into consideration strength. One would expect a certain amount of loyalty from one's wand, [that] it has developed an affinity with you that it won't give up easily. . . . However, the Elder Wand knows no loyalty

except to strength. It's completely unsentimental. It will only go where the power is. So if you win, then you've won the wand. You don't need to kill with it. But . . . almost inevitably, it attracts wizards who are prepared to kill and who will kill. And it also attracts wizards like Voldemort who confuse being prepared to murder with strength.[42]

Embodying the conceit that "might is right," the wand represents the aspects of power and invincibility common to the Hallows as a whole, "the tent pole, as it were, of the entire edifice."[43] Associated with power, and distinctly, with its most negative connotations and interpretations, the Elder Wand is yet a tempting artifact (indeed, the Golden Trio debate its potential and moral use in spite of what seem clear lessons of its lore. As Ron wistfully emphasizes, the comfort and potential of "*an unbeatable wand, Hermione*" is not easily abandoned).

Indeed, the association of wands with power and, particularly, the exercise and indication of it, can be seen in the very fabric of Rowling's Wizarding World. In this world, not all magical creatures are equal, a harsh truth exemplified by the fact that magical creatures other than humans are denied wands and, further, are presumed guilty of a crime should they be found in possession of one (an anxiety we see played out in reference to gnomes, giants, centaurs, and house elves). The denial of wands is a clear symbol of disenfranchisement and the disempowered. Similarly, the series' later installments introduce the concept of the "wandless" in a further elaboration of a problematic social hierarchy that privileges not just wizards, but certain kinds of wizards. By the end of *The Deathly Hallows*, the Muggle-born have been increasingly excluded from the wizarding community, their social status aligning them with the sub-human as they, too, are denied wands, their own stripped from them, their knowledge and abilities denounced and recoded as "stolen." Denied access to power, denied use of it on the same terms as wizards (or, later, on the same terms as wizards with the 'right' social and genetic background), and denied agency and participation, the possession of a wand is an important marker of power; the loss or lack of one signaling the absence of it. Wands, clearly, are highly symbolic of power at every turn, from Harry's first exhilarating experience in Ollivander's to the dark appeal of the Deathstick, and Rowling's dissemination of them builds a world in which the basis of authority and power is thus noted as problematically regressive and hierarchal. The Elder Wand is a consistent thread in this critical, morally corrupt framework, a condensation and amplification of this theme as the series concludes.

Wands are indeed very much the symbol of a wizard's power, the tool through which their power is channeled, their will implemented upon the world, and, as such, they take on immense thematic importance in Harry's final outing. The importance of wand-as-weapon builds throughout *The Deathly Hallows*: when Harry's trusty holly wand breaks in an explosive escape, the sinking feeling that dominates the aftermath of its loss feeds into a sustained reflection that reveals how much Harry had been counting on his wand and "the protection of the twin cores" it offered from Voldemort. Previously thwarting Voldemort in the cemetery and protecting him again in the Battle of the Seven Potters, where the wand turned in his hand, unbidden, to shoot golden sparks at a circling Voldemort, Harry can't help but feel he's lost a valuable and all too rare asset, fears which are only compounded by the knowledge that Voldemort, too, seeks a new wand that would be unaffected by the bond between his and Harry's wands. Similarly, these tensions are particularly poignant as they come on the heels of a disturbing scene in which Harry witnesses his parents' murders from Voldemort's perspective, the Dark Lord mocking Lily and James for not having their weapons—their wands—at close hand in their home, the Dark Lord's surprised glee emphasizing their vulnerability and the level of cruelty in the betrayal of their trust and security.

Following the torture of Ollivander and the killing of Gregorovitch and Grindewald in search of the Elder Wand, the thought of Voldemort with an unbeatable wand, an even more effective means of killing and achieving his ends, is scaffolded to elicit maximum horror. Thus, that Harry is required to knowingly turn away from pursuit of the Elder Wand in order to continue to chip away at Voldemort's tethers to life, that he must leave the wand to Voldemort's hands and watch (psychically) as he secures it, is doubly cruel.

Indeed, the first part of the film adaptation brilliantly chooses to close on Voldemort taking possession of the Elder Wand. Robbed from Dumbledore's desecrated tomb and raised triumphantly to the ever-darkening sky, the cinematic story constricts on the Elder Wand in an intense visceral visual. As lightning crackles, everything is charged: we should be very afraid; darkness is gathering, and there seems little hope; such is the power and import of the Wand. Thus, Harry's determination to abandon his quest for the Hallows, understanding, at last, that they will not keep him alive, nor is he meant to live, is an important test of his ability to resist temptation and reassert a moral compass that has always been guided by his selfless bravery and fierce protection of what he loves.

Indeed, while the wand is most central to the thematic work of the Hallows, the temptation of the Hallows also extends to, and plays out in, Harry's further interaction with the Resurrection Stone and its reconfiguration of power lines and intersection with choice. As Harry walks to his death in the Forbidden Forest, a notably "different brand of bravery than his usual Gryffindor bravado," he wishes someone knew where he was and what he planned—wishes, essentially, to have this ultimate choice taken from him, to be stopped from sacrificing himself or to die in battle, from action instead of this excruciating surrender.[44] However, rather than turn to the resurrective Hallow as a means of cheating death, Harry's use of the Stone affords him the reassurance necessary to submit to death, an incredibly important and poignant choice on which the resolution of the series hinges. The wraiths the Stone conjures are protective, but only in so far as to enable his sacrifice.

Similarly, the act of Harry's submission to death is a willing and conscious surrender, but it is notably not framed as a moment of powerlessness. Although Voldemort takes it thusly, much as he also wrongly interpreted Dumbeldore's death, Harry's surrender is a mark of great strength of character, a realization of his selfless heroism that transcends Voldemort's egocentric understanding and enables a brighter, collective future. Making the ultimate choice to destroy the power of his enemy and the threat of Voldemort rather than seek to possess the power of the Hallows for himself ultimately establishes Harry as *more* powerful than Voldemort and enables his defeat. (For those fuzzy on plot, Voldemort's killing curse destroys not Harry, but the Horcrux he bore, the Horcrux Voldemort never meant to make, grafted to Harry as an infant as the result of his parents' murder.) In sacrificing himself, Harry is resurrected, his willing martyrdom extending a powerful protective charm, like his mother before him, to those he willingly gave his life to protect.

Indeed, the quieter solitary confrontation with Voldemort in the Forbidden Forest, a battle waged largely inside Harry's own head, is poignant foreshadowing of the resonant ethics that will repeat in the grand finale of pitched battle at Hogwarts. Just as he will have no interest in using or keeping the wand, Harry also chooses to deliberately lose the Resurrection Stone, dropping it in the wild tangle of the Forest. Knowing that his friends and family are inside him, in his heart and with him "always," lets him release the Hallow. Like the wand whose power he later eschews in favor of love, sacrifice, and protection, with his enlightened perspective Harry can similarly have no good further use for the Stone. Understanding this kind of love, its relationship to grief and loss, he embodies "the power the Dark Lord knows not" and achieves the ability to let go in another mark of maturity and further step in becoming master of death.

While a rejection of power or a refusal to use it for selfish means seems clearly established by Harry's self-sacrificial choice in the Forest, Hallows and Horcruxes yet intersect climactically in the Battle of Hogwarts. Coming face to face with Voldemort in the Great Hall of Hogwarts, Harry is seemingly faced with impossible odds. Voldemort possesses the Elder Wand and believes himself its master; yet, Harry realizes that full mastery and control of the wand belong to him. As Harry explains to his nemesis in front of an awed audience, Dumbledore not only asked Snape, a double agent, to kill him and thus nullify the wand's power, but was also first disarmed by Draco Malfoy—who Harry recently bested—in an unforeseen consequence of devoting his last act to shielding Harry rather than defending himself. Pointing out these mistakes, and exhibiting the values that underlie them, Harry encourages Voldemort to feel remorse, seeking to save what's left of his soul even at the last, but Voldemort rejects such a choice and refuses to believe Harry. Shouting the killing curse as Harry calls on him to disarm, the spells collide, and the Elder Wand flies into the air, arcing into Harry's hand and directing Voldemort's killing curse back at its caster. Voldemort falls to the ground, dead, his spell rebounded. A surprise turn of events that comes down to convoluted wandlore, the ethics and politics of the tale's morality are nonetheless a clear through-line. In the finale, evil destroys itself, the good triumphing while the bad ruin themselves, murder producing only death and destruction in return.[45]

The Elder Wand's role in this revelation is significant, thematically even more so than logistically. Indeed, as indicator of its significance and its centrality to Harry's last heroic chapter, Rowling revealed in an interview that the first working title for *Harry Potter and the Deathly Hallows* was, in fact, *Harry Potter and the Elder Wand*.[46] As Harry's last, best, hope, shouted to the rafters, is a spell to disarm, this staging of his final performance demonstrates that death and violence, the campaign of fear waged by Voldemort and his quest to consolidate and privilege power, is not Harry's way. As Dumbledore explains the moment, this final confrontation, this battle between "good" and "evil," is fundamentally a clash of values, an understanding particularly articulated in Harry's speech outlining all that Voldemort had overlooked or failed to comprehend. As Dumbledore clarifies the Elder Wand's role in this framework, "Voldemort, instead of asking himself what quality it was in you that had made your wand so strong, what gift you possessed that he did not, naturally set out to find the one wand that, they said, would beat any other."[47] The Wand "became an obsession," Voldemort believing "that the Elder Wand removes his last weakness and makes him truly invincible."[48] Instead, because of Voldemort's narrow understanding of power, because of his reliance on tools rather than character traits, because of his dismissal of Harry's moral qualities as limitations instead of strengths, the Elder Wand paradoxically reveals his weaknesses. Knowing that "that which Voldemort does not value, he takes no trouble to comprehend," it is clear that what Harry represents and champions is indeed "a power beyond his reach," the strength of which he has "never grasped."[49] Voldemort's definition of power—dependent upon strength, dominance, selfishness, and the willingness to privilege ends over means—is dramatically undercut, and the qualities Harry exhibits effortlessly prevail. As he is egalitarian, selfless, devoted to family and friendship, loyal, noble, and ruled by love (which Voldemort holds in contempt and sees only as weakness), the wand is revealed as tool more than solution, the qualities and experiences of the wizard more important.

Indeed, the construction of their last battle is itself thematically significant, its framing speaking to the series' moral underpinnings as well as to the needs of genre and plot. An interesting rendering of a final "battle," in this last confrontation, all Harry "really does," tellingly, "is talk and throw a disarming charm."[50] In an ultimate demonstration that power is not what or where Voldemort understands it to be, Harry's final battle relies upon the re-balancing of an equation. Verbally warning Voldemort that his Horcruxes are destroyed, that no one else in the battle can fall (protected by Harry's willingness to give his life to stop their execution), Harry insists that he knows many things Voldemort does not and that the corrupted Riddle should listen before making a final mistake. Voldemort, sneering, supposes that Harry must think he has a more powerful weapon or knows more of magic. First deemed impossible, with Voldemort's destruction, Harry demonstrates that both are true. His unconventional heroism, his rejection of power and his unwillingness to resort to the kind of "strength" Voldemort respects, and his unconventional weapon—love, his ability to choose to act from love against all odds and obstacles—holds the true power. Voldemort's plans—his conception of power and what makes one powerful—are revealed as fatally flawed, for Harry, paradoxically, becomes the true master of the Deathly Hallows, Elder Wand included.

Unsurprisingly, the significance of identifying Harry Potter as the true master of the Deathly Hallows is a particularly important development

Not the Elder Wand's true master, Voldemort is bested, undone, with the proof that the wizarding world's most powerful weapon is not within his control, nor is it his ticket to victory.

for a thematic understanding of his journey's navigation of what makes one powerful. Indeed, Harry's ability to resist the temptation of the Hallows, and, in so doing, to truly understand their purpose and master their safe use, represents a significant statement about the nature of power and Harry's ability to negotiate its fraught use, even more so as it is one test Dumbledore himself failed. As Harry has matured, he has needed to distinguish himself from various father figures throughout the series, navigating the arrogance of his father, James, and the action-prone, daredevil orientation of Sirius Black, and it is no accident that the final volumes are consumed with damaging revelations and an ultimate reconciliation with Dumbledore's flaws. The Hallows, ever symbolic, are also the crucible for the exploration of these concerns. Calling the Hallows "real, and dangerous, a lure for fools," Dumbledore admits to having long kept silent on the relics' existence for fear that Harry might make his same mistakes.[51] As Rowling delves into his backstory, we learn that Dumbledore, like Voldemort, once sought the Hallows as a means of power. The revelations of Dumbledore's past reveal that, "as a very young man . . . power was [Dumbledore's] weakness and temptation," the quest for the Hallows a symbol of the folly and regret of his youthful ambitions.[52] Once involved with Grindelwald, a forerunner of the Dark Lord, the two wizards naively planned to use the Hallows "for the greater good" in their ascendency to world domination. The wand, they believed, would give direct power—"The unbeatable wand, the weapon" that would immediately grant and lead to it. In the Resurrection Stone, Grindelwald saw an army of Inferi, while Dumbledore would resurrect his family to free himself of the burden of caring for his sister, attempting to "lift . . . all responsibility from [his] shoulders." And, lastly, the cloak eluded their selfish vision in allowing the user to protect others besides themselves, a use they did not, in their self-interest, value. As Dumbledore confesses to Harry, in his selfishness, in his understanding of power, he was thus unworthy to unite the Hallows. Although he did ultimately claim the wand, recovering it from Grindelwald, who followed a dark path Dumbledore narrowly evaded, Harry's headmaster recognizes he was fit only to possess this least of the Hallows because he took it to save others from its power. He did not care enough about the cloak in its less-flashy protective values to have it work as it does for Harry, who used it to hide friends and keep them safe, and who cast it aside to embrace his own death. And, unlike Harry who used the stone to enable his own bravery and self-sacrifice, facing death to protect others, Dumbledore wanted to use the stone to disturb people who were already at rest, a selfish pursuit that led to his poisoning and death.

It is, as Dumbledore clarifies, Harry's difference in all these areas that makes him a worthy possessor of the Hallows:

> Maybe a man in a million could unite the Hallows, Harry. I was fit only to possess the meanest one of them, the least extraordinary. I was fit to own the Elder Wand, and not to boast of it, and not to kill with it. I was permitted to tame and to use it, because I took it, not for gain, but to save others from it. But the Cloak, I took out of vain curiosity, and so it could never have worked for me as it works for you, its true owner. The stone I would have used in an attempt to drag back those who are at peace, rather than to enable my self-sacrifice, as you did. You are the worthy possessor of the Hallows.[53]

As the philosopher's stone exemplified early on, the revealed lesson is that only the person who would use the artefacts for unselfish means could truly possess the Hallows. It took Dumbledore the death of his sister to change his attitude toward power; in his shame, he no longer sought it for himself, or sought power in the same way again. While he had previously felt that "power gives us the right to rule,"[54] he "learned that [he] was not to be trusted with power," [55] and learned, likely, to re-conceptualize his definition of power.

As these revelations make clear, Harry is a special hero, unique in the values he repeatedly espouses, the temptations which never tantalize him, and the priorities he holds clear. Only in surrendering, in not seeking the Hallows, does he gain them and understand their power, and, as Dumbledore surmises, therein lies a clear message about the nature of power itself and how its mantle falls upon Harry: "It is a curious thing, Harry, but perhaps those who are best suited to power are those who have never sought it. Those who, like you, have leadership thrust upon them, and take up the mantle because they must, and find to their own surprise that they wear it well." [56] In this, the message of Harry's heroism finds clear definition: he is a Chosen One hero because of the choices he made for himself, the savior of the wizarding world because of his selflessness and sacrifice, a powerful wizard because his understanding of power rejects and revises its traditional terms.

Due/al Fates and a Phenomenon's Finale

For all the importance of the Elder Wand and its central, inviolable role in the ethical stakes involved in Harry's relationship to power, in the novel and film this infamous "deathstick" meets two separate fates. In the seventh novel, Harry, after restoring his own broken wand, returns the inestimably powerful wand to Dumbledore's tomb, in hopes that it will never again be mastered, its power broken and rendered impotent:

> "I'm putting the Elder Wand," he told Dumbledore, who was watching him with enormous affection and admiration, "back where it came from. It can stay there. If I die a natural death like Ignotus, its power will be broken, won't it? The previous master will never have to be defeated. That'll be the end of it." Dumbledore nodded. They smiled at each other. "Are you sure?" said Ron. There was the faintest trace of longing in his voice as he looked at the Elder Wand. "I think Harry's right," said Hermione quietly. "That wand's more trouble than it's worth," said Harry. "And quite honestly . . . I've had enough trouble for a lifetime." [57]

In this decision, Harry recognizes absolute power as dangerous and demonstrates the ability to say no to too much of it. His wish to break the pattern of the Elder Wand and to lay it to rest again in Dumbledore's tomb proves his worthiness in possessing the Hallows; he knew when to use them, how to use them correctly, and now, also, when to let go.

In the final film, the message is much the same, but Harry's rejection of the Wand is a nonverbal exclamation point. Relative to many film adaptations, the *Potter* films minimally diverge from their source text. Little of the plot is sacrificed, little artistically altered unless to achieve either expediency or "something more cinematic."[58] The films often excel, for example, in showing rather than telling, dispelling with exposition and distilling essential information into visuals. Harry's refusal to claim use of the Elder Wand is just such a perfect visual distillation of the essence of the *Potter* story.

Of course, adaptive decisions are not always a triumph—there is much lost, for instance, in the final moments of the film's Battle of Hogwarts. The visuals and the spectacle of the Battle are appropriately grand, but there are disappointing misses in the adaptation's beats that undercut vital thematic work. Harry's final confrontation with Voldemort is shot as a one-on-one battle, without the theatrics and audience of the novel. In an odd articulation of the final action, Voldemort pursues Harry through the castle, spewing magic-tentacles until Harry plunges them both into a seeming suicidal tandem dive from a tower. Grounded and alone in the shattered courtyard, they duel wordlessly, their spells locked as lightning between them, powerfully and dually channeled until Voldemort's is pushed back onto himself, and he slowly dissipates like so much flaking ash. In the words of one critical reviewer, "any subtlety was utterly forgone in exchange for big booms and lots of CGI," the whole fight rather accurately summed up by Mark Kermode, the UK's "leading film critic," as "two people hitting each other with fireworks until one falls over."[59]

Cinematic instead of poignant, the film's choices were seemingly dictated by an anticipated audience's conditioned expectations of the level of special-effect-expenditure deemed necessary to signal an appropriately impactful "final battle," and it is a shame to see these aspects of the adaptation come at the expense of many of Rowling's richly developed themes, particularly in their unconventionality. As Tor.com's Asher-Perrin succinctly summarizes what is lost in adaptation: "There is no show . . . in front of the school, no point where Harry tells Voldemort to work for remorse, not a word about the many mistakes the Dark Lord made with the Elder Wand and Dumbledore's plans. There's no real showdown. It just ends with some loud noises and a lot of thoughtless action."[60]

The film's deviations and omissions relative to the book cause major alterations. The more Hollywood-style heroic arc, ensuring Harry develops into the Chosen One who actively defeats Voldemort, ignores the overarching themes of the power of love, the acceptance of death, and the value of communicative discussion and nonaggression. Indeed, the "showdown" we receive on screen is much more traditional, an unfortunate choice that elides the import of Harry's refusal to play Voldemort's game, and Harry's, as well as Rowling's, unwillingness to navigate toward easy, heroic conclusions for his character. The conversation between Voldemort and Harry is vital: asserting his values and pointing out the many errors of Voldemort's ways is an important moment demonstrating Harry's maturity; it underscores his growth, his ability to see beyond the desires that elevate him over Voldemort and prove, again, his utter difference from the dark wizard whose soul he shared. The omitted dialogue not only explicitly cemented those values, but also risks concealing the important fact of Harry's unorthodox "Expelliarmus" spell choice. Indeed, the film's Voldemort may die confused as to how he was defeated, which is so very much not the point.

His very death, even, in its important corporality, is undercut by the adaptation. Given that Voldemort has spent his entire life trying to ensure that he cannot die, Voldemort's dead body is the ultimate proof that no one can escape death, and a mute testimony to his misunderstanding of the Deathly Hallows and his failure to establish a life of true meaning. Rowling is careful to make his mortality and mundanity clear, to give him no "special" death. When Voldemort's body hits the floor, the wizarding community sees him as no different from themselves in death; his search for immortality, his grand claims, schemes, and hubris have amounted to nothing, his defeat revealing him as the petty, ignorant, and self-obsessed wizard Tom Riddle, his power, always false, ultimately broken.

However, the bold decision to snap the Elder Wand goes a long way towards recuperating much of what is lost in the Battle's other deviations. Whereas many of the novel's vital scenes explicating Harry's complex relationship to power and the Hallows don't translate, perhaps sacrificed to the risk of bogging the film down, Kloves and Yates instead placed their bets on a single, dramatic final scene. Relying on cinematic narrative techniques to convey the gravity of Harry's decision, underscore its ethical stakes, and impress viewers with its thematic importance—situated, as it is, as the trio's final moment at Hogwarts and the culmination of Harry's heroic journey—the film, in its conclusion, rests on a notable adaptive change that visually encapsulates the critical work of the novel and honors its politics.

Departing dramatically from the novel's decision to allow the Elder Wand to fall passively out of power, the film is significantly more decisive. As Harry explains the circumstances of his possession in the film, he asserts clear ownership and then takes clear, resolute and absolute action:

Holding the Wand, Harry: It's mine

Ron: What should we do with it?

Hermione: We?

Ron: I'm just saying, that's the Elder Wand. Most powerful wand in the world. With that, we'd be invincible.

Harry stares down at the thing in his hand, then brings it across his body to test it. Cut to Hermione, who exchanges an incredulous look with Ron. Harry snaps it and, turning, hurls the shattered pieces into the gorge. Ron and Hermione stand, still shocked, but with a dawning sort of approval, a shared understanding of what Harry's done, and why. Harry nods in weariness, but also with a lifted weight, and steps down and away from edge. It's like a giant breath of relief, drawn amidst the ruins of the school which built them. Harry turns with a pleased half smile; pride at his choice, his word-less action. All three come together, Ron smiling now, too, in a sort of stunned disbelief at the way everything turned out, at their survival and unlikely triumph. It's just dawning, what these three little ones managed, the enormity of their journey and its resolution. The trio hold hands, exhausted, their togetherness cemented again, in not quite victory, because it's not that easy or clean, but in a certain tired but shining triumph nonetheless. The battle is won.

This altered conclusion neatly recuperates and encapsulates the essence of the moral message explored via the Elder Wand. Inasmuch as the books are about power and the temptations of power, particularly as the volumes advance, Harry's adventures are not about claiming or gaining power, but about destroying and rejecting it. In this, Harry proves an important hero: he is, in Dumbledore's words, a remarkable boy, "brave" and "wonderful," and yet also, determinedly unremarkable; still "Harry. Just Harry," as he was as an eleven-year-old boy, new to his identity as a wizard, let alone one of fame and fate.[61] While novel and film present the moment of the Wand's

Harry, weary but self-assured, prepares to snap the Elder Wand in the battle's aftermath.

negation differently, both are about understanding that seizing power is not what gives it. Both are a rejection of the wand's power and of the kind of power and attitudes about power that it represents.

A concern with choice and power run throughout the *Potter* books, and, woven especially tightly at story's end, this conflict is perfectly encapsulated in one visual: Harry snapping the Elder Wand. This final moment of the Battle of Hogwarts is also the final word on this thematic issue, as well as the final word on Harry's heroic journey; thus, its strong rendering is particularly charged with cementing its politics. A symbol of power and control, Harry's interactions with the Elder Wand afford a more nuanced consideration of evil—what defines and perpetuates it—than those embodied in more conventional opposition to the Dark Lords of fantasy. As a tool, the wand reflects the opportunity all people have for the exercise of free will and choice and the ability to make morally correct or incorrect decisions. Yet, it also demonstrates how the exercise of unbridled power and desire to dominate is the antithesis of free will and free choice as well as the route to destruction.

As Ron quotes an old bit of wizarding lore, "Wand of elder, never prosper," Rowling's politics are laid bare.[62] Like "The Tale of the Three Brothers" morality tale she crafts to provide origin and backstory for the Elder Wand, hers is a moral fantasy, a power fantasy only inasmuch as it is intent on exploring the implications and workings of power and the responsibilities of those who wield it. Much as Harry and Ron's discussions concerning the potential use of the wand similarly enact the age-old debate about ends versus means, Kloves's screenplay resolves such a contest particularly clearly. Rather than merely setting the wizarding world's most powerful weapon aside, or keeping it safe as a respected artefact removed from use as the novel describes, at the film's close, Harry completely rejects any purpose and any temptation the wand might offer. His action reads as poignant argument: no good can come of the exercise of an evil means; power must be destroyed and disarmed, not preserved for oneself, no matter the intention. In this, Rowling's narrative resists recapitulating the more frequently presented belief that righteous violence can redeem us, even ennoble us. Undercutting the myth of violence many heroic epics are prone to, Harry demonstrates, as Dumbledore often counseled and died demonstrating, as Voldemort died unable or unwilling to learn, that violence neither redeems nor enlightens nor empowers.

As a Chosen One hero, Harry proves remarkably sensitive to the responsibilities and difficulties of that position; similarly, it is more than incidental that Harry's heroic path invites a consideration of the powerless, the disenfranchised, the oppressed, and groups who are unfairly discriminated against. He understands his position of privilege and power, yet constantly and consistently interrogates his role within it. A particularly self-conscious hero, the design of the Elder Wand raises moral questions and embodies the truth he learns by story's end: that a rejection of power is a necessary part of rejecting others' powers over oneself, as well as a rejection of having power over others. In this, Harry's example is not only that of a positive role model to young adults everywhere, but a prescient portrait of complex, conflicted heroism and ethical responsibility in the twenty-first century, for his leadership might be said to lie in modeling or teaching the oppressed how to fight back against oppression without becoming oppressors themselves.

Notably, these politically-laced ideas clash with many ideologies that still dominate society; in this sense, Harry's quest takes on a new dimension of political and social meaning. It is no accident that the series' characters grow up with its themes and events or that the conclusive battle culminates with their ascension to adulthood. *Harry Potter* is imbued with moral instruction for a global generation's responsibilities as citizens, for all that some literary scholars question the viability of children's or young adult literature's capacity to challenge the status quo and doubt its ability to empower young readers rather than emphasize their relative position of powerlessness within the world and its institutions. While Roberta Seelinger Trites identifies that, as seems true in the case of *Harry Potter*, "the crux of" adolescent literature "resides in the issue of power,"[63] she also discouragingly feels that YA literature limits the adolescent's power and, in so doing, destroys the "adolescent reader's potential power."[64] As Trites points out, the *Potter* stories are limited in their structure, as an adolescent never proclaims a major theme; such is the province of "the textually-constructed adult," (usually Dumbledore, even dead-Dumbledore, serving as the source of all wisdom), and thus the young adult is denied ownership over them.

In the final chapter, however, Harry does take on this role, explaining the novel's (and, at its conclusion, the series') themes to Voldemort, and to the entire Great Hall filled with an observant audience, which tacitly includes his story's readers. His story is his own. Furthermore, the film certainly belies Trites's assessment: The snapping of the Elder Wand is obviously Harry's choice and Harry's message, a defiant conclusion empowering adolescents to make powerful choices themselves. In the film's finale, none but the trio stand united on the bridge as Hogwarts dwindles into the distance. In this sense, over returning the wand to Dumbledore's tomb, and seeking his approval in making such a choice, the film may be even more effective than the novel in its ability to affirm its audience's individual sense of power and agency. Indeed, while Kloves includes a moving tribute to Rowling's stunning literary accomplishments, as on-screen Dumbledore winkingly asserts that "words are, in my not so humble opinion, our most inexhaustible source of magic," the films, while different, exert equal power.

Furthermore, as Rowling has proved a prominent figure in social justice work in addition to inspiring dovetailing millennial attitudes, her kind of power has proven especially necessary in the real world as well as in fictional representation. As the *Potter* stories champion the value of an individual's choice, no matter how small, Rowling affirms the same, asserting "we do not need magic to change the world. We carry all the power we need inside ourselves already. We have the power to imagine better."[65] Indeed, to see the relevance of Potter's message, we have only to consider how prescient is the emphasis on love, its framing as a power, the only power that can save us, and its echoes in many contemporary messages such as the emphatic language of Lin-Manuel Miranda's emotional tribute to the Orlando nightclub shootings in his Tony Award acceptance speech and President Obama's statement on the same tragedy, and in responses to vitriolic Trumpian politics and policies and the divisions they otherwise encourage.

It is precisely these dimensions of the politics of the *Potter* series and the values it unwaveringly champions that are particularly underscored in the adapted screenplay's deliberate and powerful final diversions. Redefining heroism and reconfiguring the conventional quest to culminate in a rejection of power rather than an ascension to it, Harry's complexly positioned heroism is nowhere better encapsulated than in the device of the Elder Wand, and perhaps nowhere more clearly rendered than in Kloves's remarkably poignant adaptation.

Notes

1. John Granger, *Harry Potter's Bookshelf: The Great Books Behind the Hogwarts Adventures* (New York: Berkley, 2009), 159.

2. Ibid., 150.

3. Ibid.

4. Giselle Liza Anatol, ed., *Reading Harry Potter: Critical Essays* (Santa Barbara: Praeger, 2003); Elizabeth E. Heilman, ed., *Critical Perspectives on Harry Potter* (London/New York: Routledge, 2003); Nancy Ruth Reagin, ed., *Harry Potter and History* (Hoboken: Wiley, 2011); Daniel B. Nexon and Iver B. Neuman, eds, *Harry Potter and International Relations* (New York: Rowman and Littlefield, 2006); Jeffrey E. Thomas and Franklin G. Snyder, eds, *The Law and*

Harry Potter (Durham: Carolina Academic Press, 2010); Bethany Barratt, *The Politics of Harry Potter* (New York: Palgrave MacMillan, 2012).

5. Heilman, *Critical Perspectives*, 2.

6. Ibid.

7. Heilman, *Critical Perspectives*, 2.

8. Anatol, *Reading Harry Potter*, xv.

9. Ibid.

10. Ibid.

11. Heilman, *Critical Perspectives*, 2.

12. Reagin, *Harry Potter and History*, 4.

13. Ibid.

14. Lana A. Whited, ed., *The Ivory Tower and Harry Potter: Perspectives on a Literary Phenomenon* (Columbia: University of Missouri Press, 2004), 9.

15. Reagin, *Harry Potter and History*, x.

16. Carrie-Ann Biondi, ed., *Imagining Better: Philosophical Issues in* Harry Potter, *Reason Papers* 34.1 (June 2102); David Baggett and Shawn Klein, eds, *Harry Potter and Philosophy: If Aristotle Ran Hogwarts* (Chicago: Open Court, 2004).

17. Biondi, *Imagining Better*, 5.

18. Travis Prinzi, "Don't Occupy Gringotts: *Harry Potter*, Social Upheaval, and the Moral Imagination," *Reason Papers* 34.1 (June 2012): 16.

19. Lana A. Whited and M. Katherine Grimes, "What Would Harry Do? J. K. Rowling and Lawrence Kohlberg's Theories of Moral Development," in *The Ivory Tower and Harry Potter*, 183.

20. Whited and Grimes, 206.

21. Biondi, *Imagining Better*, 6.

22. Travis Prinzi, *Harry Potter and Imagination: The Way Between Two Worlds* (Cheshire, CT: Zossima Press, 2008).

23. Walter Benjamin, "The Task of the Translator," in *Illuminations: Essays and Reflections* (New York: Schocken Books, 1985), 73.

24. Ibid., 76.

25. Linda Hutcheon, *A Theory of Adaptation* (New York: Routledge, 2006), 139.

26. Phillip Nel, "Lost in Translation?" in *Critical Perspectives on Harry Potter*, ed. Elizabeth E. Heilman, 287–88.

27. J. K. Rowling, *Harry Potter and the Chamber of Secrets* (New York: Scholastic, 1998), 333.

28. Casper Ter Kulie, "What Can Harry Potter Teach Us About Evil in Our World Today," *On Being*, Saturday, January 31, 2015, www.onbeing.org/blog/what-can-harry-potter-teach-us-about-evil-in-our-world-today/7244.

29. Emily Asher-Perrin, "The Anxiety of Power and the Love of Wise Men," *Tor.com*, June 30, 2011, www.tor.com/2011/06/30/the-anxiety-of-power-and-the-love-of-wise-men-harry-potter-and-the-half-blood-prince/.

30. J. K. Rowling, *Harry Potter and the Half-Blood Prince* (New York: Scholastic, 2005), 512.

31. Ibid, 509.

32. Ibid., 510.

33. Ibid.

34. Ibid.

35. Ibid.

36. Rowling, *Half-Blood Prince*, 443.

37. J. K. Rowling, *Harry Potter and the Deathly Hallows* (New York: Scholastic), 2007, 261.

38. Ibid., 351.

39. "Elder Wand," *Harry Potter Wiki*, September 27, 2016, http://harrypotter.wikia.com/wiki/Elder_Wand.

40. Rowling, *Deathly Hallows*, 425.

41. Rowling, *Deathly Hallows*, 425.Ibid.

42. J. K. Rowling, "PotterCast Interviews J. K. Rowling, Part Two," by Melissa Anelli, John Noe, and Sue Upton, *PotterCast #131* podcast, December 24, 2007.

43. "Elder Wand," *Harry Potter Wiki*, September 27, 2016, http://harrypotter.wikia.com/wiki/Elder_Wand.

44. Emily Asher-Perrin, "The Harry Potter Reread: *The Deathly Hallows*, Chapters 33 and 34," *Tor.com*, May 12, 2016, www.tor.com/2016/05/12/the-harry-potter-reread-the-deathly-hallows-chapters-33-and-34/.

45. Liz Bourke, "They Are Coming: Harry Potter and the Deathly Hallows," *Tor.com*, July 5, 2011, www.tor.com/2011/07/05/harry-potter-and-the-deathly-hallows/.

46. J. K. Rowling, "J. K. Rowling Web Chat Transcript," *The Leaky Cauldron*, July 30, 2007, www.the-leaky-cauldron.org/2007/07/30/j-k-rowling-web-chat-transcript/.

47. Rowling, *Deathly Hallows*, 608.

48. Ibid.

49. Ibid., 599.

50. Emily Asher-Perrin, "The Harry Potter Reread: *The Deathly Hallows*, Chapters 35 and 36," *Tor.com*, May 20, 2016, http://www.tor.com/2016/05/20/the-harry-potter-reread-the-deathly-hallows-chapters-35-and-36/.

51. Rowling, *Deathly Hallows*, 602.

52. Ibid., 605.

53. Ibid., 605.

54. Ibid., 309.

55. Ibid., 605.

56. Ibid.

57. Ibid., 147–50.

58. Emily Asher-Perrin, "Rewatching the *Harry Potter and the Deathly Hallows: Part 1* Film," *Tor.com*, June 2, 2016, www.tor.com/2016/06/02/rewatching-the-harry-potter-and-the-deathly-hallows-part-1-film/.

59. Mark Kermode, "5 Live Review: *Harry Potter and the Deathly Hallows—Part 1*," *BBC*, November 23, 2010, www.bbc.co.uk/blogs/markkermode/2010/11/5_live_review_2.html.

60. Emily Asher-Perrin, "Rewatching the *Harry Potter and the Deathly Hallows: Part 2* Film," *Tor.com*, June 9, 2016, www.tor.com/2016/06/09/rewatching-the-harry-potter-and-the-deathly-hallows-part-2-film/.

61. Rowling, *Deathly Hallows*, 597.

62. Ibid., 356.

63. Roberta Seelinger Trites, "The Harry Potter Novels as a Test Case for Adolescent Literature," *Style* 35.3 (2001): 473.

64. Ibid., 480.

65. J. K. Rowling, Very *Good Lives: The Fringe Benefits of Failure and the Importance of Imagination* (New York: Little, Brown and Company, 2015).

3

Look . . . at . . . me . . .

Gaze Politics and Male Objectification in the *Harry Potter* Movies

Vera Cuntz-Leng

Introduction

In her influential and controversial essay "Visual Pleasure and Narrative Cinema," Laura Mulvey discusses Classical Hollywood cinema in terms of the dramaturgy of gazes that shape the audience's experience of a film.[1] The spectators adopt the male coded gaze by looking through the eyes of the protagonist (the camera, respectively). As a result, Mulvey argues that female characters on screen are put into the position of passive and desired objects of the male gaze (with the active position solely attributed to the male gender). Mulvey's work has been further explored by feminist film theory, masculinity studies, postcolonial studies, and queer studies. In recent years, Mulvey's concept of the gendered gaze has been replaced by more open and more flexible conceptions of identification and spectatorship that allow the inclusion of multiple perspectives based on class,[2] ethnicity (oppositional gaze,[3] imperial gaze[4]), and sexual orientation (queer looks,[5] gay gaze[6]). Nevertheless, one has to keep in mind that while independent cinema and other media like television, music videos, and social media may have helped to construct alternative ways of looking, "the basic formula for generating visual pleasure may not have shifted significantly" in mainstream cinema.[7] However, in an age of transmedia narratives and transmedia adaptation that is paralleled by a significant increase of the possibilities of active participation in the process of meaning-making of texts (e.g., through gaming or fan practices such as the writing of fan fiction), the multiplicity of possible points of entry in a text, and therefore the multiperspectivity of gazes in both audio-visual media and written texts, must be taken into account. In the end, these developments have consequences for the gaze politics that operate in more classic media forms like literature and film. Especially with literature and film, both adaptation and transmediality teach us that the (imagined) boundaries between images and words have become permeable.

Following the ideas of Mulvey, Neale, and Halberstam, among others, the aim of this chapter will be the exploration of gaze politics as a primarily film-specific device in the *Harry Potter* movie adaptations.[8] Gaze politics are meaningful regarding their distribution of power, their gendered quality, and the queerness in/for the *Harry Potter* story. This may be perceivable in a tendency towards male objectification and in a lack of consistency in the gendered gazes that a heteronormative condition of the films would (possibly) have required. Through close reading and a hermeneutic approach to film analysis, emblematic sequences in the film saga will be discussed in terms of the dramaturgy of gazes, with a particular focus on Hermione Granger and Severus Snape in relation to the character of Harry Potter. The goal of this chapter is to identify landmark moments of female empowerment and "to-be-looked-at-ness" for males on screen, which may come at the expense of the desirability of female characters and a loss of power for some male characters. This distortion of established power relations questions the still prevailing reinforcement of heteronormative codes in Hollywood. I will discuss how the gendered condition of gaze politics in film may be queer(ed) and operates, in the case of Harry Potter, on a continuum that challenges the monolithic binary concepts of subject and object, male and female.

Gaze Politics and Hollywood Cinema

"Visual Pleasure and Narrative Cinema," an essay that is strongly influenced by the ideas of Sigmund Freud and Jacques Lacan, is one of the key texts for both early feminist film theory and psychoanalytical approaches to film studies. Mulvey chose Classic Hollywood cinema as her prime example to describe the cinematic apparatus as inherently male and patriarchal. The films discussed by Mulvey depend "on a sexual and gendered economy of looking, watching and identifying" that is still at the core of mainstream cinema.[9] According to Mulvey, camera and cast provide the spectator with the subject position of the male protagonist. The identification with the protagonist gives the spectator the satisfying illusion of omnipotence, since the protagonist, as surrogate of the spectator, controls the events on screen. Mulvey points out that the male actor thus does not become the object of the spectator's gaze but is perceived instead as an idealized mirror image of the viewer. David N. Rodowick concludes: "Mulvey discusses the male star as an object of the look but denies him the function of an erotic object. Because Mulvey conceives the look to be essentially active in its aims, identification with the male protagonist is only considered from a point of view that associates it with a sense of omnipotence and narrative control. She makes no differentiation between identification and object choice in which sexual aims may be directed towards the male figure."[10] With this understanding of gaze politics in cinema as both gendered and sexualized, the activated look is always male, whereas female characters on screen operate as iconic objects of that gaze. In consequence, the pleasure of looking (at women) in the cinema can be differentiated into two modes—it can be either fetishistic or voyeuristic.[11] John Ellis describes these two modes in a straightforward manner: "The voyeuristic look is curious, inquiring, demanding to know. The fetishistic gaze is captivated by what it sees, does not wish to inquire further, to see more, to find out."[12]

In her follow-up essay "Afterthoughts," Mulvey reacted to the vast corpus of criticism towards her essay, which was not so much concerned with the general concept of voyeuristic and fetishistic pleasure in movies, but more with the role of the female viewer. As a solution to the dilemma of female identification in the cinema and the exclusiveness of the male point-of-view, Mulvey suggests a cross-gender-identification with the (mandatory) male protagonist in order to give the female viewer access to the illusion of the same satisfying power over the women on screen. The female spectator "may find herself secretly, unconsciously almost, enjoying the freedom of action and control over the diegetic world that identification with a hero provides."[13] But this comes at a price, because through "a simple adoption of the masculine position in relation to the cinematic sign, the female spectator is given two options: the masochism of over-identification or the narcissism entailed in becoming one's own object of desire."[14]

Mulvey's assumptions about female spectatorship can be connected to the concept of the masquerade as described by psychoanalyst Joan Rivière in 1928 and further explored by Mary Ann Doane in terms of its relevance for film studies.[15] Also referring to Freud, Doane connects theories of femininity with the cinema and concludes that cinema is "writing in images of the woman but not for her."[16] Doane agrees with Mulvey that the "cinematic inscription of a sexual differentiation in modes of looking" is at work.[17] However, Doane suggests that female spectatorship is also marked by women's "sexual mobility," defining the female spectator as a possible transvestite.[18] This assumption already implies a queer quality of spectatorship in general, although Doane fails to expand her ideas to queer studies.

But is it not possible to imagine an activated female gaze as well as male objectification? Wouldn't it make sense to think of spectatorship less in terms of a gender binary or a strict heteronormative flow of desire? Queer theory enables us to understand the process of identification and the pleasure in female looking at male-centered mainstream programs (e.g., Hollywood films) as queer in itself. In other words, to understand spectatorship only as a binary of looking/to-be-looked-at, subject/object, and male/female is shortsighted. Instead, gender, the pleasure in looking at the movies, identification, and the reception process must be understood more as a continuum of options, because films offer various points of entry and opportunities for heteronormative, transvestite, and queer gazing.

Whereas Mulvey insisted that only female bodies are objectified in the cinema, Neale identified various examples of male bodies on display (e.g., *Spartacus* [1960]). Interestingly, the look towards the male body is not necessarily marked as feminine: "We are offered the spectacle of male bodies, but bodies unmarked as objects of erotic display. There is no trace of an acknowledgement or recognition of those bodies as displayed solely for the gaze of the spectator. They are on display, certainly, but there is no cultural or cinematic convention which would allow the male body to be presented in the way that Dietrich so often is in Sternberg's films. We see male bodies stylised and fragmented by close-ups, but our look is not direct, it is heavily mediated by the looks of the characters involved. And those looks are marked not by desire, but rather by fear, or hatred, or aggression."[19]

Neale also argues that the male viewer may gain an autoerotic pleasure from identification with idealized males on screen. In a similar vein, Paul Willemen assumes that the cinematic male body as object of the protagonist's and spectator's looks is not marked as an object of heterosexual desire but must rather be understood as a repressed homosexual look.[20] Because of the denial of queerness in a heterosexual and patriarchal society, Neale states that it may be possible to look at male bodies, but this gaze cannot be marked explicitly as erotic.[21] Paradoxically, the effect of this repression is that "male homosexuality is constantly present as an undercurrent, as a potentially troubling aspect of many films and genres, but one that is dealt with obliquely, symptomatically."[22] Neither Neale nor Willemen explicitly consider males as objects of an activated female heterosexual gaze.

In a more recent book, J. Jack Halberstam analyzes the success of the melodrama *Boys Don't Cry* (2000) and argues that "the seduction of mainstream viewers by this decidedly queer and unconventional narrative must be ascribed to the film's ability to construct and sustain a transgender gaze."[23] I would argue, however, that a movie series like *Harry Potter*, though on the surface not much concerned with sexual desire, is able to provide a rich semiotic field for all kinds of identifications, meanings, and desires. Mainstream cinema has become very much aware of the fact that camera, dramaturgy, mise-en-scène, on the one hand, and individual spectatorship on the other hand is quite variable and demands different points of entry and self-inclusion. Therefore, Hollywood movies can, and indeed must, include various modes of desire-laden gazes in order to succeed with a heterogeneous audience.

Gazing at "the girl next to Krum"

Female characters have rarely become icons in the *Harry Potter* movies in the way Mulvey understands the term. This may be, in comparison to the examples chosen by Mulvey (e.g., Marlene Dietrich in Josef von Sternberg's *Morocco* [1930]), because women in general have less screen time in films of the fantasy genre. There are far fewer prominent female characters in the saga compared to male characters,[24] although the *Harry Potter* franchise has been praised for its depiction of females.[25] Hermione's entrance at the Yule ball in *Harry Potter and the Goblet of Fire*, which initiates her transformation from an ugly duckling into a beautiful swan, is one of the rare occasions where the film experiments with classic Hollywood cinematic conventions regarding gaze politics.

In the Yule ball scene, Harry and Ron come into the entrance hall and meet their partners for the ball, the sisters Parvati and Padma Patil. At first, we follow Harry's gaze to his friend Ron, who is leaving and entering the Great Hall with Padma; then his gaze moves to his crush Cho Chang, who is with her boyfriend, Cedric Diggory. In the reverse-shot, we see Harry smiling at her with longing. But then, in the next shot, the camera doesn't return to Cho to further highlight Harry's desire for her. Instead, we suddenly perceive Hermione lurking from behind a pillar, checking if the time

When Hermione descends the stairs (in *Harry Potter and the Goblet of Fire*, 2005), she becomes the object of both Parvati's and Harry's gazes.

is right for her appearance. It is obvious that this part of the narrative is actually not directed by Harry's gaze, as he most likely still observes Cho. The viewer is for a moment freed from Harry's focus, only bound to the omnipotent camera, unaware of whose gaze he or she has been adopting. This liberation from the protagonist's gaze signifies a shift in classic forms of storytelling. That the gaze in this sequence is not restricted by Harry's interior monologue, as it is in the books, emphasizes the quality of film (as/ and transmedia adaptation) to offer its audience multiple points of view.

A resolution to the question of whose gaze has been adopted comes in the next shot: "She looks beautiful," says Parvati in awe.[26] Harry is filmed from the back—an awkward perspective on the protagonist. He needs a moment to understand that Parvati is actually not referring to Cho, and then he turns around. Parvati's desiring gaze towards Hermione, who is slowly descending the stairs in a stunning pink and purple silk dress, is transferred back to Harry. We see both Harry and Parvati, in the same frame, looking at Hermione, which signifies a simultaneous presence of two differently gendered positionalities of desire.[27] When Harry is in charge of the look again, Hermione's body is shown in fragmented close-ups, more intimate, more personal, because he knows her much better than Parvati does. Although Harry is in awe at what he sees, his gaze is not primarily laden with sexual desire (as is Parvati's or later Ron's jealous gaze), because Harry's desire for Cho has been counter-balanced prior to Hermione's appearance. Harry's gaze towards Hermione is one of wonder and astonishment. Hermione recognizes Harry; she's actively looking back but not going to or with him. Victor Krum enters the frame, redirects her attention, and breaks Hermione's eye contact with Harry. One last wave good-bye to the adoring audience of Harry and Parvati, and off she is with the third man. She leaves the frame with a Marlene Dietrich-like smile that highlights her awareness of her own beautiful transformation rather than her potential unease with the situation.

In the Yule ball sequence, Hermione is recognized as feminine for the first time since her confrontation with the troll in the bathroom in *Harry Potter and the Sorcerer's Stone*, which marked an important turning point in her relationship to Harry and Ron. The Yule ball sequence marks yet another such turning point, because Hermione becomes noticeably gendered, her transition to adulthood—from child-friend to possible love-interest— highlighted in that moment. In Elizabeth E. Heilman's words, Hermione is "transformed like Cinderella, and, like many tomboys in teen novels, into a 'princess.' She becomes physically acceptable."[28] Heilman analyzes this as an anti-feminist move in the story, because Hermione has to follow current concepts of beauty and has to please a male audience. However, if we assume that Hermione is in charge of the situation and—in a way similar to Dietrich's character of Amy Jolly in *Morocco*—the desirability of her character is not bound to a certain gender or sexual orientation, it does not necessarily reinforce heteronormativity, and Hermione's passivity is not an inevitable consequence. As Eliza Dresang argues, from the perspective of radical-libertarian feminism, "females have the right to do whatever they want to with their bodies."[29] Choice and free will are perhaps the most important thematic staples of the *Harry Potter* saga. Dumbledore tells Harry: "It is our choices, Harry, that show what we truly are, far more than our abilities."[30] If Hermione shows us anything, it is the power of the masquerade. As a smart postfeminist heroine, Hermione knows how to play certain roles. She easily switches between nerd and prom queen.[31] And therefore, Hermione's transformation at the Yule ball shows us that physical beauty and desirability are deliberate choices. And so is gender.

The Yule ball scene has been described by Ximena Gallardo and Jason Smith as a "formal introduction into heterosexuality."[32] It is an event requiring the performance of heteronormativity.[33] This takes on an interesting dimension in the case of Harry's other sidekick, Ron, who is dressed for the ball in robes that look feminine and out-of-date. ("I look like my great aunt Tessie," Ron observes.)[34] We see Ron's feminized body side-by-side with Harry, through a mirror, signifying Ron's lack of male hegemonic power, in opposition to both Harry and Krum. Ron is being looked at, objectified. The mask of womanliness that may be empowering to Hermione is weakening Ron at the same time. He did not choose his outfit by himself; instead, his mother sent the robe. Ron appears unfit to accompany Hermione to the ball. In contrast to Donaldson and Heilman's claim that "Ron decides when to romance Hermione," a close reading of the power relations in the Yule ball sequence signifies quite the opposite.[35]

Gazing at "greasy black hair, a hooked nose, and sallow skin"

Another object of Harry's (constant) gazing is his potions teacher, Severus Snape. Camera movements, mise-en-scène, and editing suggest that the relationship between the protagonist and Snape is special from the very beginning. The staging of gaze politics is essential for this configuration

During the sorting hat ceremony (in *Harry Potter and the Sorcerer's Stone*, 2001), Harry becomes the bearer of the look and Snape the object of his gaze.

and no other relation between characters on screen in the series possesses a similar intensity in its erotic effect.

The first meeting of Harry and Snape takes place in the Great Hall during the sorting hat ceremony. At first, the camera captures the Hogwarts staff from Harry's perspective, in full and long shots. When Harry finally becomes aware of Snape's presence, the framing changes to medium shots and close-ups, edited in a shot-reverse-shot mode. It becomes quite clear that Harry's undivided attention is fixed on Snape, which is odd since no other student is looking in this direction. The interaction between Snape and Harry is a secondary site, because the essential events of the ceremony obviously take place at a different location. Harry's focus on Snape during an event as incisive as the hat ceremony emphasizes their interaction to an extent that the recipient cannot (yet) make sense of. Film history provides us with various examples of the melodrama with a similar art of montage.

Snape responds to this act of being looked at by initially gazing back at Harry. However, Harry's role as protagonist and "bearer of the look" is accentuated, since he continues to gaze at Snape even when addressed by Ron. Although Snape is a teacher and an adult, the sequence suggests Snape's inferiority: He cannot stand Harry's gaze and finally turns away, while Harry continues to look at him intently. In a Mulveyean sense, Snape becomes the object of Harry's gaze; Snape remains silent and becomes the image. His turning away signals Snape's inability to activate the gaze himself in order to switch their power relations. As the camera follows Harry's gaze axis, it moves away from the spectacle of the hat ceremony. Snape becomes the spectacle. There is a queer quality to this objectivization of a male character and the exposure of a curious and voyeuristic male look.

A comparison of first encounters between other movie characters, to a similar melodramatic effect, can be useful in understanding the erotic quality of the dramaturgy of gazes in the sorting hat sequence. *Gone with the Wind* (1939) features both a powerful female protagonist and a depiction of the male as spectacle.[36] Scarlett O'Hara and Rhett Butler meet for the first time at the Twelve Oaks party, also in a festive setting and at a secondary site that becomes important only through the gazes of the two characters. Scarlett is going upstairs to take a nap with the other women, while the inscrutable Rhett stands at the bottom of the stairs, watching her. All other events take a back seat. The protagonists' eyes are nevertheless drawn to the object of (future) desire, as if by chance, and linger there—Scarlett becomes aware of being looked at, but she straightaway refuses to accept a passive role, actively looking back. She asks her friend—in a manner comparable to the way Harry asks Percy about Snape, "Cathleen, who's that? . . . That man looking at us and smiling. The nasty, dark one. . . . He looks as if . . . as if he knows what I look like without my shimmy."[37] There is a dangerous eroticism implied in her words and their glances. The extreme high angle view of Rhett, placing him in a subordinate position, as well as Scarlett's refusal to interrupt the gaze signal the heroine's rebellion against a subordinate role that the conventions of classic Hollywood cinema would demand. The protagonist Scarlett is in charge of the gaze, and it is actually Rhett who becomes an object of (forbidden and dangerous) desire. This corresponds with the further course of the narrative, in which Scarlett is characterized by a continuous transgression of conventional norms of gender and class (e.g., working in Tara). Eventually, she is doomed for consistently breaking out of her pre-determined role as an object of desire for the male gaze and instead imposing that role on Rhett, whereas Rhett's tragedy lies in his own lack of hegemonic masculinity since he can never control Scarlett—not even with his gaze.

It is striking that the sorting hat ceremony's dramaturgy of gazes in *Harry Potter and the Sorcerer's Stone* mirrors conventions that the audience is familiar with from film history. We learn that the relationship between Snape and Harry is based on power, and an inherent homoeroticism is implied. The significance of this first encounter is further emphasized by another sequence in the film, confirming Snape's status as an object of Harry's gaze. Strolling around Hogwarts at night, hidden by his invisibility cloak, Harry discovers Snape and Quirrell. Harry witnesses an argument between the two teachers, but its specific content is not revealed to him. Through his own physical invisibility, Harry succeeds in yielding to the voyeuristic pleasure of seeing without consequences—comparable to the audience in the darkened room of the cinema. Snape, however, becomes aware of the gaze; he turns around to look back at Harry but cannot see him. He almost breaks the fourth wall when he stretches out his hand to get ahold of the intruder (the audience). But he fails to get hold of the spectator and involuntarily remains exposed to the gaze, and likewise his attempt at self-empowerment fails.

Even in *Harry Potter and the Chamber of Secrets*, a film in which Snape is mainly unimportant to the plot, Snape's passive role as an object of the gaze is emphasized. In a digressive moment, the course of the narrative is interrupted by the spectacular appearance of Gilderoy Lockhart and Snape in the dueling club sequence. When Snape enters the stage, he is exposed to the voyeuristic pleasures of Harry, his friends, and of course the audience.

Like Marilyn Monroe in *River of No Return* (1954) or Dietrich in *Der blaue Engel* (1930) and *Morocco*, the appearance of a (female) character onstage in a film doubles their fetishization. The desire of the audience in the cinema is reflected by the intradiegetic desire of the spectators attending the dueling club. That the inherent eroticism of the sequence is exaggerated by Lockhart for comic effect (e.g., theatrically throwing his cloak to his moaning female fans) all the more underlines its erotic vigor. Harry's eventual need to enter the stage himself to fight against Draco is an unpleasant switching of positions that questions his dominance for a brief moment and signifies the fluidity and ambiguity of categories like passive/active and object/subject. In other words: How can we be sure that it's Scarlett looking at Rhett and not Rhett looking at her?

Snape's exposure to a doubled audience is recapitulated in the Boggart sequence in *Harry Potter and the Prisoner of Azkaban*. Again, a comic effect is used to disguise the actual erotic effect of the spectacular male body on stage. As Neville Longbottom's biggest fear, the Boggart exits the wardrobe in Snape's outer appearance: dressed all in black, bearing a sinister physiognomy, featuring Alan Rickman's elegant, cat-like moves. Through a quick Riddiculus spell, Snape is transformed into Neville's grandmother, wearing a skirt, crazy hat, and a purse. Similar to other examples of cross-dressing from film history—*Some Like It Hot* (1959), *Tootsie* (1982), and *Mrs. Doubtfire* (1993)—this drag number in *Harry Potter and the Prisoner of Azkaban* mainly serves as confirmation and reinforcement of conventional male identity (e.g., Harry's).[38] If understood as a transformation from one social gender to another, drag usually operates on three levels: as guarantor of humor, as a diffusion of heterosexual tensions, and as a potential indicator of queer desire. Instead of dismantling conventional images of males, drag signifies that heterosexual masculinity may also form a kind of mask, under which feminine, homosexual, or masochistic forms of desire proliferate.[39]

The most striking power struggle involving gazes between Harry and Snape takes place in the Occlumency lessons in *Harry Potter and the Order of the Phoenix*. As ordered by headmaster Dumbledore, Snape tries to teach Harry the ability to control his mind (Occlumency) in order to arm himself against Voldemort's mental attacks (Legilimency).[40] By means of Legilimency, Snape literally moves beyond eye contact to access the innermost integrity of his student's mind. In a Platonic sense, Legilimency can be understood as the ideal and most unadulterated form of learning, because no detour through textbooks or the spoken word is necessary—the spirit of mentor and student are magically linked. But Snape is angry, impatient, and desperate to humiliate Harry in order to eventually achieve power over the gaze. Harry does not learn how to defend himself but experiences instead the violent rebellion of his teacher against a subordinate status.

"I will attempt to penetrate your mind. You will attempt to resist."[41] In *Harry Potter and the Order of the Phoenix*, the penetration of Harry's mind becomes a metaphor for (involuntary) sexual penetration and the loss of his virginity. The expression of Harry's sweaty face is defined by anxious expectation; his shirt is darkened with moisture. In the two Occlumency sequences of the movie, the dynamic and strong intimacy between Harry and Snape is produced by aggressive camera work and rapid cuts that contrast, in particular, with the quiet, almost static camera in the same film's kissing scene with Cho.

Briefly, Snape succeeds in mastering Harry and becomes the bearer of the gaze. But already in the second lesson, Harry succeeds in reversing the intruding gaze, actively pushing back and entering his teacher's memories. In comparison to the book, in which Harry is not able to penetrate Snape's mind directly, but secretly watches his intimate memories in the Pensieve, the more dynamic and immediate interaction between Snape and Harry emphasizes the erotic quality of Occlumency. Harry's re-conquest of the gaze unmasks Snape's weakness and reinforces his status as object. In his worst memory, which Harry witnesses, we learn that it is precisely this lack of power and the curse of objectification that Snape fears the most, because this is basically what the Marauders did to him when he was still a child. Because of Harry, Snape experiences the trauma of his schooldays for a second time, and the Occlumency lessons have to come to an end for good.

Their competition over the gaze comes to a point of culmination in *Harry Potter and the Deathly Hallows: Part 2*. As a silent voyeur, Harry witnesses Snape's execution and Voldemort's leaving him behind. Although Harry despises Snape and is convinced he murdered Dumbledore, when Harry enters the room, he rushes to the dying man. The following minutes are like a tragic echo of their very first encounter at the sorting hat ceremony and serve as a frame for their relationship. Again, the other events become less important and less perceivable—the presence of Ron and Hermione, the battle at Hogwarts. As in *Harry Potter and the Sorcerer's Stone*, the camera work shifts from full shots of the boathouse to intimate close-ups, which are edited in a shot-reverse-shot mode. The over-shoulder shot is used to build a strong connection between the characters and aims at creating a strong emotional involvement for the viewer. After giving his memories deliberately to Harry,

The boathouse scene from *Harry Potter and the Deathly Hallows: Part 2* (2011). "Look . . . at . . . me"; Snape's death wish marks the final point in a constant struggle over the mastery of the gaze.

Snape has a request for the protagonist, his dying wish: "Look . . . at . . . me."[42] This command is highly significant, since it demands a queer gaze. As Harry will learn later through Snape's memories, Snape was deeply in love with Harry's mother, Lily, and hated his father, James, just as passionately. Snape's emotions towards Harry have always been contradictory: Harry has been a substitute for Snape's unfulfilled love for Lily, as well as a placeholder for Snape's desire for revenge on Harry's father.

When Harry follows the call and looks at him with compassion, Snape adds promptly, "You have your mother's eyes" (something Harry has heard quite often in the past), as if to find an excuse for the queerness of the situation and his "desire" for Harry.[43] Surely, Snape's request implies his desire to see Lily in Harry, but it is nevertheless Harry who is looking at him, and not her, which hints again at the unstable gender identity of the protagonist. The eyes become Snape's fetish. In his exhibitionistic desire, Snape simultaneously has to accept the hero's predominance through giving in to the power of his gaze. With this voluntary act of submission, he acknowledges Harry's as well as James' superiority, because, apart from his eyes, Harry is an image of his father. As in *Harry Potter and the Sorcerer's Stone*, Snape finally interrupts their connection; his head sinks to one side, his eyes become gazeless, and he dies.

Conclusion

Of course, Severus Snape is not the only character that can be analyzed in terms of his status as a male object for Harry's and/or the audience's desires. There are more examples in the saga of male characters who become objectified: Ron Weasley, Gilderoy Lockhart, Cedric Diggory, Remus Lupin, and most of all Draco Malfoy. We remember Harry's constant obsessive stalking of Draco through the voyeuristic device that is the Marauder's Map. But sometimes even Harry himself loses his power over the gaze in the film adaptations—as exemplified by the Yule ball sequence in *Goblet of Fire* or the dueling club in *Chamber of Secrets*. On the other hand, Hermione shows how a female character can be empowered through the deliberate choice of temporary objectification. Further, Parvati's desire for her shows how the heteronormative gaze codes known from classical Hollywood cinema can be queered and an activated distinct female gaze can become recognizable. In the end, however, Snape has always been the object of Harry's gaze, revolting against this role in the Occlumency lesson, and finally giving in to Harry's dominance with his wish to be looked at as he takes his last breath.

In a similar way to Halberstam's argument that the successful reception of *Boys Don't Cry* beyond queer audiences "depends absolutely on its ability to hijack the male and female gazes, and replace them surreptitiously with transgender modes of looking and queer forms of visual pleasure," the diversity in possible gaze formations and modes of desire in the *Harry Potter* series offers a broad spectrum of visual pleasures to its audience.[44] It can be argued that the universal appeal of Harry Potter as an artifact of mainstream popular culture is a result of this polymorphism and openness. Therefore, the observations made here may also apply to other successful pop-cultural artifacts, such as superhero films.

In contrast to the novels, the film adaptations allow a certain freedom from Harry's restricted perspective. Although the camera directs the attention of the audience, it does not channel the audience's sympathies in the same way as the novel. The audience must evaluate the characters and actions on screen on the basis of their own judgments, because the process of reception is no longer solely moderated by the animosities and sympathies of the protagonist. This allows, for example, the possibility for a character like Severus Snape to become more complex, more attractive, and in the end more desirable for viewers of all genders. Therefore, the subliminal tensions between Snape and Harry may become—from book to film—more explicit and easier to decode. This transformative influence of the *Harry Potter* movies has not only influenced fan culture, but also Rowling's writing in the later volumes of the series that were published parallel to the film releases.[45]

Although gaze politics are a concept specific to film analysis, the growing prominence of gaze politics described in the novels gives us the opportunity to more fully perceive the cinematic quality of Rowling's writing.[46] In addition to the interlocking process of alternating releases and constant adaptation and transformation of both the novels and movies, the Harry Potter storyworld must be understood in terms of its transmediality. Not only officially produced content and paratexts but also fans and their creative output through fan art, fan fiction, and fan videos must be taken into account in terms of their own gender dynamics, distributions of power, and modes of desire. Fannish re-writings and re-orientations of the *Harry Potter* series are widely available and distributed on the Internet—and much of this creative output is so-called Slash fiction, homoerotic re-imaginings that extensively play with the erotic possibilities that the texts offer. In terms of their re-evaluation of gaze politics and in their exploration of queer possibilities, fan works can therefore not only be seen as a part of an underlying logic, which has already been established by the fluidity of gender and desire in the movies, but also as a consequence of the transmedia constitution of the Harry Potter storyworld.

Notes

1. Laura Mulvey, "Visual Pleasure and Narrative Cinema," *Screen* 16.3 (1975): 6–18.

2. Samantha A. Lyle, "(Mis)recognition and the Middle-Class/Bourgeois Gaze: A Case Study of Wife Swap," *Critical Discourse Studies* 5.4 (2008): 319–30.

3. bell hooks, "The Oppositional Gaze: Black Female Spectators," *Black Looks: Race and Representation* (Boston: South End Press, 1992), 115–31.

4. E. Ann. Kaplan, *Looking for the Other: Feminism, Film, and the Imperial Gaze* (New York/London: Routledge, 1997).

5. Martha Gever, Pratibha Parmar, and John Greyson, eds. *Queer Looks: Perspectives on Lesbian and Gay Film and Video* (New York/Abingdon: Routledge, 1993).

6. Steven Drukman, "The Gay Gaze, Or Why I Want My MTV," *A Queer Romance: Lesbians, Gay Men and Popular Culture*, ed. Paul Burston and Colin Richardson (London/New York: Routledge, 2005), 89–105.

7. J. Jack Halberstam, *In a Queer Time and Place: Transgender Bodies, Subcultural Lives* (New York/London: New York UP, 2005), 83.

8. Steve Neale, "Masculinity as Spectacle: Reflections on Men and Mainstream Cinema," *Screen* 24.6 (1983): 2–17.

9. Halberstam, 83.

10. David N. Rodowick, "The Difficulty of Difference," *Wide Angle* 5.1 (1982): 8.

11. Mulvey, "Visual Pleasure," 13–14.

12. John Ellis, *Visible Fictions: Cinema—Television—Video* (London: Routledge, 1982), 47.

13. Laura Mulvey, "Afterthoughts on 'Visual Pleasure and Narrative Cinema' Inspired by King Vidor's *Duel in the Sun* (1946)," in *Visual and Other Pleasures* (Basingstoke: Palgrave Macmillan, 1989), 29.

14. Mary Ann Doane, "Film and the Masquerade: Theorising the Female Spectator," in *Feminist Film Theory: A Reader*, ed. Sue Thornham (Edinburgh: Edinburgh UP, 1999), 143.

15. Rivière argues that females, in order to achieve power, may put on a mask of womanliness: "Womanliness therefore could be assumed and worn as a mask, both to hide the possession of masculinity and to avert the reprisals expected if she was found to possess it—much as a thief will turn out his pockets and ask to be searched to prove that he has not the stolen goods." "Womanliness as a Masquerade [1928]" in *Formations of Fantasy*, ed. V. Burgin, J. Donald, and C. Kaplan (New York: Routledge, 1986), 38. To fully understand this concept, it is useful to envision one of its most obvious impersonations: Dolores Umbridge in *Harry Potter and the Order of the Phoenix*.

16. Doane, "Film and the Masquerade," 132.

17. Ibid., 143.

18. Ibid., 138.

19. Neale, "Masculinity as Spectacle," 14.

20. Paul Willemen, "Anthony Mann: Looking at the Male," *Framework* 15–17 (1981): 16.

21. Neale, "Masculinity as Spectacle," 8.

22. Ibid., 15.

23. Halberstam, *In a Queer Time*, 83.

24. Approximately two-thirds of all Harry Potter characters are male, according to Elizabeth E. Heilman and Trevor Donaldson, "From Sexist to (sort-of) Feminist: Representations of Gender in the Harry Potter Series," in *Critical Perspectives on Harry Potter*, 2nd ed. (London: Routledge, 2009), 141.

25. It is important to note that Rowling has in fact been criticized for her marginalization and poor depiction of female characters in earlier installments of the series. See Christine Schoefer, "Harry Potter's Girl Trouble: The World of Everyone's Favorite Kid Wizard is a Place Where Boys Come First," *Salon*, 01-13-2000; and Elizabeth E. Heilman, "Blue Wizards and Pink Witches: Representations of Gender Identity and Power," in *Critical Perspectives on Harry Potter* (London: Routledge, 2003), 221–39. In *Harry Potter and the Order of the Phoenix*, significantly more female characters are included and further developed. See Heilman and Donaldson, 142–44; and Vera Cuntz-Leng, *Harry Potter que(e)r: Eine Filmsaga im Spannungsfeld von Queer Reading, Slash-Fandom und Fantasyfilmgenre* (Bielefeld: transcript, 2015), 290–91.

26. *Harry Potter and the Goblet of Fire*, directed by Mike Newell (2005; Burbank, CA: Warner Brothers 2007), DVD.

27. Teresa de Lauretis, *Alice Doesn't: Feminism, Semiotics, Cinema* (Bloomington: Indiana UP, 1984), 83.

28. Heilman, "Blue Wizards and Pink Witches," 229.

29. Eliza T. Dresang, "Hermione Granger and the Heritage of Gender," *The Ivory Tower and Harry Potter: Perspectives on a Literary Phenomenon*, ed. Lana A. Whited (Columbia: University of Missouri Press, 2002), 233.

30. J. K. Rowling, *Harry Potter and the Chamber of Secrets* (New York: Scholastic, 1999), 333.

31. Cuntz-Leng, *Harry Potter que(e)r*, 283.

32. Ximena Gallardo and C. Jason. Smith, "Cinderfella: J. K. Rowling's Wily Web of Gender," in *Reading Harry Potter: Critical Essays*, ed. Giselle Liza Anatol (Westport, CT: Praeger, 2003), 200.

33. Cuntz-Leng, *Harry Potter que(e)r*, 281.

34. *Harry Potter and the Goblet of Fire*, directed by Mike Newell (2005; Burbank, CA: Warner Brothers 2007), DVD.

35. Heilman and Donaldson, "From Sexist," 153.

36. Although Harry's biological gender is not female, many attributes of his character and his actions imply that he reconciles the fantasy's role of the male quester with the Gothic novel's heroine. See Gallardo and Smith; Travis Prinzi, "The Well-Ordered Mind: How Imagination Can Make Us More Human," in *Hog's Head Conversations: Essays on Harry Potter*, ed. Travis Prinzi (Allentown, PA: Zossima, 2009), 115–17; and Cuntz-Leng, *Harry Potter que(e)r*, 121–23. Ika Willis points out that in "his interactions with Harry, Snape's villainy is conveyed in a way that recalls the romanticized conventions of the Gothic novel: after almost every line of dialogue (delivered 'silkily' or 'sleekly') Snape's eyes glitter [as do Alan Rickman's], or his lips curl into a sinister smile or sneer, and Harry reacts with emotions—fear, anger, wounded pride—which romantic conventions readily sexualize." Ika Willis, "Keeping Promises to Queer Children: Making Space (for Mary Sue) at Hogwarts," in *Fan Fiction and Fan Communities in the Age of the Internet: New Essays*, ed. Kristina Busse and Karen Hellekson (Jefferson, NC: McFarland, 2006), 160. Interestingly, this sounds like a recapitulation of Neale's description of the repressed homosexuality in gaze politics regarding males on screen.

37. *Gone with the Wind*, directed by Victor Fleming (1939; Burbank, CA: Warner Home Video, 2000), DVD.

38. To a certain extent, this same logic also applies to Ron's appearance at the Yule ball.

39. Cuntz-Leng, *Harry Potter que(e)r*, 272.

40. Harry also has private lessons with Dumbledore in *Harry Potter and the Half-Blood Prince*, in which the two explore selected memories through the Pensieve. In terms of gaze politics in the Harry Potter series, it may be fruitful to further explore the inherent fetishistic/voyeuristic aspect of this device.

41. *Harry Potter and the Order of the Phoenix*, directed by David Yates (2007; Burbank, CA: Warner Brothers 2007), DVD.

42. *Harry Potter and the Deathly Hallows, Part 2*, directed by David Yates (2011; Burbank, CA: Warner Home Video 2016), DVD.

43. Ibid.

44. Halberstam, *In a Queer Time*, 83.

45. Peter Appelbaum, "The Great Snape Debate," in *Critical Perspectives on Harry Potter*, 2nd ed. (London: Routledge, 2009): 83–100; Cuntz-Leng, *Harry Potter que(e)r*, 239–41; Vera Cuntz-Leng, "Snape Written, Filmed, and Slashed: Harry Potter and the Autopoietic Feedback Loop," in *Playing Harry Potter:*

Essays and Interviews on Fandom and Performance, ed. Lisa S. Brenner (Jefferson, NC: McFarland, 2015).

46. Deborah Cartmell, "Adapting Children's Literature," in *The Cambridge Companion to Literature on Screen,* ed. Deborah Cartmell and Imelda Whelehan (Cambridge: Cambridge UP, 2007), 167–80.

Part Two

Transmedia Adaptations

4

Harry Potter, Henry Jenkins, and the Visionary J. K. Rowling

Maria Dicieanu

1. Introduction

In 1992, Henry Jenkins published his first book exploring fandoms and participatory culture, *Textual Poachers: Television Fans and Participatory Culture*, setting the base of what was to become twenty years later the new hype of audio-visual productions: transmedia storytelling. Jenkins viewed the multi-platform storytelling as a way of enhancing the spectators' experience and understanding of narratives. Observing the patterns of fandoms, the author suggested consumers are more likely to invest, both on an emotional and material level, in a limited number of franchises rather than to shallowly explore multiple ones. Even more, while cross platform explorations ultimately aim at increasing consumerism, they also provide a "more complex, more sophisticated, more rewarding mode of narrative."[1]

In 1995, J. K. Rowling published the first installment of what was going to become one of the bestselling series of all times—the story of the eleven-year-old orphan Harry, who discovers he is a very famous wizard. Nine more books[2], eight films, a theme park, an online platform, numerous games, countless merchandise, and twenty years later, the magical world of Harry Potter is still in everyone's minds—so much so that 2016 saw the film release of *Fantastic Beasts and Where to Find Them* (the first out of three prequels), together with the launch of a sequel theater play, *Harry Potter and the Cursed Child: Parts One and Two.*[3]

By creating a narrative powerful enough to encompass and engage with multiple mediums, Rowling ended up practicing what Jenkins was preaching. This chapter will provide a framework for seeing *Harry Potter* as a transmedia project and will aim to investigate the elements that facilitate the transfer of the *Harry Potter* narrative through so many media. Further, my work will also reflect on the implications for other transmedia projects that Rowling's achievement makes possible.

2. Harry Potter—A Transmedia Project?

Viewing film adaptations in general, and the *Harry Potter* franchise in particular, as transmedia narratives proves challenging even when considering one of the most easy to encounter and basic definitions of transmedia storytelling such as this *Wikipedia entry*: "Transmedia storytelling is the technique of telling a single story or story experience across multiple platforms and formats using current digital technologies, and is not to be confused with traditional cross-platform media franchises, sequels or adaptations."[4]

The definition clearly excludes franchises and adaptations from being considered transmedia projects. The main reason for this distinction becomes clear when considering the approach to multiple mediums for a particular work. In a transmedia project, the creator(s) are well aware of the nature of multi-platform storytelling, and they want the spectators to interact as much as possible with each platform. Ideally, as Jenkins puts it, each medium should do "what it does best so that a story might be introduced in a film, expanded through television, novels, and comics, and its world might be explored and experienced through the game-play."[5]

However, this is not the case for most adaptations, as writers often don't see their work as being part of a bigger media project while writing it. For instance, the creative opportunities offered by the online platform *Pottermore* didn't even exist when Rowling first started working on the series.[6] Although quite aware she was generating more content than could ever be included in the books, Rowling never thought there would be substantial interest in her notes, nor that new media developments could provide such an immersive and interesting way for the material to be presented to her readers.[7]

In turn, screenwriters such as Syd Field also treat their adaptation work as an original process disconnected from their literary sources, preferring to reinvent the stories they base their work on:

> When you adapt a novel or any source material into a screenplay, you must consider your work an original screenplay based on other material. You can't adapt a novel literally and have it work.
>
> The verb to adapt means "to transpose from one medium to another." Adaptation is defined as the ability "to make fit or suitable by changing or adjusting," modifying something to create a change in structure, function, and form. It only starts with the novel, book, play, article or song. That is the source material, the starting point—nothing more.[8]

According to Field, the *adaptation* would be a process of *transferring* a work belonging to one platform into another medium. *Adaptation* would thus imply *transformation*, while transmedia narratives deal with an *expansion* on different mediums, each of them acting simultaneously.

Jenkins also favors this distinction between adaptations and transmedia projects. He starts by defining transmedia storytelling as "a process where integral elements of a fiction get dispersed systematically across multiple delivery channels for the purpose of creating a unified and coordinated entertainment experience. Ideally, each medium makes its own unique contribution to the unfolding of the story."[9] This definition suggests that adaptations and transmedia projects cannot be viewed as similar, as the former does not satisfy the conditions of a "unified and coordinated entertainment experience." However, in my essay "Adaptations: Primitive Transmedia Narratives?" I explain why there are instances when we can consider adaptations to be transmedia projects.[10] These instances rely on the spectators' being exposed to both the source material and the film adaptation, which is something that stands true also for most of the people fascinated by the *Harry Potter* universe.

In addition, I will test if Henry Jenkins's four essential functions that transmedia content should comply with are also valid for the *Harry Potter* universe. According to Jenkins,

Most transmedia content serves one or more of the following functions:
1. Offers back-story
2. Maps the World
3. Offers us other character's perspective on the action
4. Deepens audience engagement.[11]

The information offered in the books easily ticks all boxes, as the medium allows Rowling to better describe more things than could be included in the films, such as the practicing of various spells, Harry's attending the Quidditch World Cup in *Harry Potter and the Goblet of Fire*, his extensive training with Dumbledore's Pensieve in *Harry Potter and the Half-Blood Prince*," etc.[12] But this franchise actually deepens the immersion even further. Publishing the *Quidditch Through the Ages* book allowed Rowling to better explain how this sport for wizards works, as well as to present a short fictional history of the game. The clear rules outlined in this companion book have made it possible for the fictive game to become a real sport, complete with an International Quidditch Association and a yearly World Cup, thus deepening fan engagement.[13]

The other companion books also comply with Jenkins's four functions. *Fantastic Beasts and Where to Find Them* has the format of a Hogwarts textbook with Harry and Ron's marginal markings and comments, giving readers more insight into their classroom experiences. *The Tales of Beedle the Bard* is filled with Dumbledore's notes, offering fans the opportunity to better understand this enigmatic character as well as to enjoy a set of wizard stories.

Rowling's website also helped enhance the experience, being the first platform to feature a genealogical tree of the main characters, thus revealing new information about what ends up happening to them.[14] Fans could, for instance, find out the name of Luna Lovegood's husband and child and that George Weasley marries fellow Quidditch teammate Angelina Johnson and has a boy named Fred and a girl named Roxanne.[15] All this information was previously unreleased in either books or movies, contributing to the backstory and the overall connection between the users and the franchise.

As far as Rowling is concerned, everything that she created aside from the books suggests that if transmedia narratives would have been more clearly defined when she started working on *Harry Potter*, she might have chosen this cross platform exploration instead, as she knew she was not going to be able to include everything she created for the *Harry Potter* universe in books.[16]

Aside from the above mentioned criteria, Jenkins also talks about having one person or creative unit maintaining control over the franchise.[17] This is yet another area where Rowling excelled as she successfully managed to remain the lead person responsible for all the major developments involving the expansion of the *Harry Potter* franchise. Whether dealing with the films, the online platform *Pottermore*, the more recent theater play *Harry Potter and the Cursed Child*, or the trilogy spin-off based on *Fantastic Beasts and Where to Find Them*, Rowling was consulted and involved in the creative process so that no resulting outcome would contradict her artistic vision.

There are thus limited reasons why this franchise should not be considered a transmedia project, mainly revolving around Rowling's initial intention of creating a simple yet engaging book series. Given her work process, however, and her handling of the development of this multi-platform project, together with the fact that multi-platform storytelling was not so clearly defined, and hence was not an option, when she started working on the narrative, we can safely consider the *Harry Potter* world a definite example of transmedia exploration. I will now consider the elements that made this series so incredibly suitable for a cross platform environment.

3. Spreading *Harry Potter* on Various Platforms

In the summer of 2011, it was announced that a new companion website for the *Harry Potter* series would be launched. Used to the regular marketing purposes for such websites, few people expected *Pottermore* to be any different or to bring additional layers to the story. However, with 8 million unique users, 5 million accounts, an average user session of 23 minutes, and 46 average page visits in just the first month, *Pottermore* quickly became a game-changer for transmedia practices.[18] This would not have been possible if the *Harry Potter* series had not been blurring the boundaries between cross-media and adaptations, ever since the first novel was created.

THE BOOKS
In 1997, Rowling published *Harry Potter and the Philosopher's Stone*, the story that introduced everybody to her magical world and followed the adventures of eleven-year-old orphan Harry, who finds out he is not a regular boy, but a wizard with very famous parents.[19] Although the series took ten years to be completed, the main plots, characters, and storylines were established from the very beginning. The character of Sirius Black (Harry's godfather) is, for instance, first casually mentioned in *Harry Potter and*

the Philosopher's Stone but only developed in the third book, *Harry Potter and the Prisoner of Azkaban*.[20] Thus a subliminal emotion of familiarity is constructed in the first installment but used only later in the series. This element is indicative of Rowling's working method—establishing a storyline and then arching it through an entire series—a similar principle to that of transmedia storytelling, which creates a narrative and then spreads it through multiple platforms.

In 2000, Rowling published two additional companion books to the series: *Fantastic Beasts and Where to Find Them* and *Quidditch Through the Ages*. Both titles had been previously mentioned in the *Harry Potter* novels, the former being one of Harry's textbooks, the latter one of his favorite books from the Hogwarts library. Both titles help fans immerse themselves further into the magical universe by getting a taste of Hogwarts and Harry's school time. The marginal annotations and comments written by Harry and Ron provide further insight regarding the two characters and make the overall reading of the series more enjoyable. Significantly, Rowling is not the author credited on the covers of the two books; both are attributed to characters belonging to the *Harry Potter* universe (Newt Scamander and Kennilworthy Whisp, respectively). The publication of these novels provided fans and readers an additional level of information, while also enhancing their immersion in the Potter world by bringing a real dimension to an otherwise fictional space.

In 2008, Rowling released another book which had previously been mentioned in the *Harry Potter* series and played a significant role in the last installment, *Harry Potter and the Deathly Hallows*: *The Tales of Beedle the Bard*.[21] Featuring comments from Professor Dumbledore, the book was actually more interesting for the insights it provided regarding the stories wizard parents read to their children. It was yet another way of getting a better taste of the magical world.

The collection of stories was initially published in only seven unique copies bound in brown Morocco leather, decorated with hand-crafted silver ornaments and semi-precious stones, with handmade illustrations by the author herself. Six of them were gifts given away by Rowling to people she thought had played a significant part in developing the *Harry Potter* universe, such as her first editor. The last of the custom-made books was sold in an auction for the record price of $4 million—the highest amount at auction for a modern literary manuscript.[22] Initially it was announced that Rowling would allow no other copies to be sold or auctioned, but following a wave of fan disappointment, the book was ultimately mass produced.

THE FILMS

In 1998, Warner Bros purchased the rights to adapt to screen the first two novels from the *Harry Potter* series. The deal was extremely advantageous for Rowling, allowing her to maintain control over the project. It was her decision to have a completely British cast, for instance. She was constantly consulted about the screenplay, and, in some instances, she gave directions to the actors. The extent of this influence is best reflected in a key moment occurring in the first film, *Harry Potter and the Sorcerer's Stone*, in which Harry meets Professor Snape, played by Alan Rickman. Throughout the series, Snape's loyalty is questioned, and for a good part of the first installment, he is considered the villain. Yet, a close-up of Snape seeing Harry for the first time reveals an unmistakable yet surprising reaction of pain. The justification for this reaction comes only in the seventh book—which at the time of shooting the scene, was not even written—when Snape's love for Harry's mother is revealed. Thanks to Rowling's direction, Rickman had known the true connection between the two characters all along, even at times when the scripts and books suggested otherwise. Later in an interview, the actor admitted Rowling had told him, and him alone, the outcome of the last volume, thus influencing his performances throughout the whole series.[23] This incident reflects the consistency of Rowling's transmedia thinking and the way she constantly connected the films to the books.

Though the movies clearly benefitted from Rowling's unitary vision and the mostly unchanging cast members, the films did experience different directors, and with them, various storytelling approaches. While Alfonso Cuarón (*Harry Potter and the Prisoner of Azkaban*) sacrificed large chunks of the action in order to focus on the atmosphere and emotions in the books, Chris Columbus (*Harry Potter and the Sorcerer's Stone* and *Harry Potter and the Chamber of Secrets*) and David Yates (*Harry Potter and the Order of Phoenix, Harry Potter and the Half-Blood Prince* and *Harry Potter and the Deathly Hallows*) tried to include as many details from the novels as possible, arguably to please the fans rather than building them up as necessary elements for the story. For instance, in the *Harry Potter and the Half-Blood Prince* film, the Pensieve—the memory-visualizing tool that allows Harry to gain insightful information about the behavior of his enemy Voldemort—is used more like an artifact for showcasing special effects, rather than playing the important dramaturgic role conveyed in the literary source. In the movies, we are never told how Harry gets the information necessary to defeat Voldemort, demonstrating that the films may be better suited as companions for the books rather than stand-alone projects, as Syd Field contends. Screenwriter Kloves also stated in an interview that he found it surprising to still encounter fans of the movie series who had not read the books.

THE EXHIBITION AND THEME PARK

In April 2009 "Harry Potter: The Exhibition" originally opened in Chicago, Illinois before touring in various cities around the world. Fans were given the option of immersing themselves even further in the magical universe as the exhibition displayed costumes and artefacts from all eight movies, showcased in elaborate settings inspired by Hogwarts locations such as the Great Hall, Gryffindor Common Room, and Hagrid's Hut.[24]

Only a year later in June 2010, the theme park "The Wizarding World of Harry Potter" was opened at Universal Orlando Resort, Florida, where visitors were given the opportunity of exploring both a full-sized Hogwarts with the adjacent shops of Hogsmeade, and some reenactments of exciting moments in the books, such as the Dragon Challenge, Flight of the Hippogriff, and the Forbidden Journey.[25]

In a similar way to Rowling's publication of the companion books, these experiences managed to make the fiction more tangible for the franchise's fans. People could walk around the park and feel like they were transported to the Potter world, while the rides attempted to recreate the excitement the characters experienced in the books. This sort of fan immersion thus occurs on two levels: on a *cognitive* level through the recognition of familiar magical elements from the *Harry Potter* universe, and then on an *emotional* level through the visceral experiences simulated by the rides. Visitors are not just enjoying a ride like they would in a regular theme park; they are invited to feel as the characters felt, and then go back to the texts and overlap their own emotions on the specific passages.

POTTERMORE

Immediately before the release of *Harry Potter and the Deathly Hollows: Part 2*, when fans were preparing to say goodbye to the series, rumors started that Rowling had something else prepared: the website platform *Pottermore*. It was initially thought that the website was set up only as an exclusive place for purchasing digital audio books and e-books, but Rowling explained that *Pottermore* was going to provide an "online reading experience unlike any other," with a few crucial additions, the most important being the involvement of the readers themselves.[26] Upon registration, users could join an official community of fans, explore never-yet-seen materials written by Rowling throughout the years, and share their own fan fiction art.

Pottermore even allowed a special category of fans to be involved in shaping the final adjustments for the online experience. One million "beta testers" got to explore the site beforehand, report bugs, and even submit feedback based on their experiences. Some creators might have been hesitant about granting public access to an unfinished product, but Rowling's decision proved very wise from several points of view. First, *Pottermore* was announced very close to the release of the last film of the series, thus maintaining the interest of the fans and giving everybody something new to anticipate. According to the original plan, *Pottermore* was supposed to be open to the public in October 2011, but this proved rather optimistic as the site was ultimately completed and launched only in April 2012.[27] If the website's creators had waited until the online platform was actually ready, they might have lost a significant part of the hype that the movie *Harry Potter and the Deathly Hollows: Part 2* generated, together with a considerable number of users.

Allowing fans to contribute to the shaping of *Pottermore* made them feel involved in the process. Rather than being disturbed by bugs found in testing the platform, users felt they were actively engaged in developing a unique and special experience. The fact that only a select few were able to access *Pottermore* at an early stage also made a difference. It helped keep people motivated and interested for the months needed to have the site ready, despite the rather limited content that could be explored in just a few hours.

Last, but not least, selecting beta testers gave creators the opportunity to organize a "7-day quest": *The Magic Quill Challenge*, launched exactly on Harry's and Rowling's birthday.[28] Again, this shows how Rowling always found ways to interlink the mediums, while also constantly connecting the real with the fictional world. The quest required users to find a magic quill while accessing *Pottermore*, which would redirect them to another website containing a question. The answer needed to be added in the URL on top of the page, at the end of *Pottermore*'s website address, granting the user access for creating an account. There were a limited number of quills offered every day, which were usually all found within two hours. In the first days, the time frames when people could expect to find quills on *Pottermore* were not made public, and the questions were also more difficult. Later on, however, the level of difficulty decreased, and time frames for the launching of quills could be found on fan websites. Producers made sure that people in different time zones around the world were provided a convenient time frame for finding the quill.

The hype of *The Magic Quill Challenge* was tremendous, with hard-core fans refusing to go to sleep, fearing they might miss the quills. Some lucky users managed to create multiple accounts, which they later tried to sell on eBay for as much as £100, despite the organizers' attempts to discourage such practices.[29] After the challenge ended, beta testers had to wait until their accounts were activated. As the website was still under development, access was granted gradually, the whole process stretched out over two months. This again could have been a turning point for the project. A series of sometimes angry, sometimes disappointed e-mails and tweets were sent to the platform's administrators, requesting more specific information with regard to when the website's exploration could begin. Some users even felt cheated, thinking that if they received access too close to the official launching date in October, all the struggle would have been for nothing. Under different circumstances, people could have ended up losing interest altogether. However, as *The Magic Quill Challenge* was so intense, leaving many fans without early access, the lucky ones selected eventually had their turn to explore the site.

Pottermore allowed the fans to get sorted into houses, find clues, and buy objects in Diagon Alley, which they would later use in the website's games sections to pick wands and pets. Once users started their courses at Hogwarts, they could also "brew potions" and duel other users in order to get points for the House Cup. The winning house team was awarded earlier access to other sections of the website that were dedicated to the second book. The process was repeated, and access to specific chapters was always granted earlier to the winners of the previous House Cup competition. This system of quest/reward was a very effective way of keeping users engaged in the activity of their Houses.

In September 2015, however, shortly after the last House Cup competition and the release of the final interactive chapters of the *Deathly Hallows*, *Pottermore* announced a series of changes.[30] The interactive exploration of chapters was dropped, together with most of the imagined artwork, the duels, the brewing of potions, and the online community. The House sorting and wand picking were initially disabled but in early 2016 were once again made available, while fans were also promised a section meant to determine their Patronus.

The new website better highlighted Rowling's specially written content as well as providing tie-ins to the *Fantastic Beasts* magical universe and

The House Cup scoring page, Diagon Alley, and the Gryffindor Common Room from the original *Pottermore* site. The site was radically redesigned in 2015 away from a primary focus on the books to accommodate a more transmedia understanding of *Harry Potter*.

details about the *Cursed Child*. By no longer being focused solely on the action in the initial *Harry Potter* books, *Pottermore* became more of a "meeting place" for everything related to Rowling's magical world. From the franchise's point of view, it provided more cohesion as it gathered together all the different ways of exploring this universe: the books, the films, and the theater play. The new *Pottermore* also brought a certain degree of unity in the representations. All characters were mostly referred to by means of their cinematic versions, with stills from the films.

The extra content made sure the fans would find reasons to return as well as ease the transition to the new dimension that the film *Fantastic Beasts and Where to Find Them* was going to provide. Users could read all about the history of the Ilvermorny Magical School (the American equivalent of Hogwarts), get sorted into Houses, and pick wands. Those holding an old *Pottermore* account could choose if they wanted to merge its details with the new one, or go through the sorting/choosing procedures again. Also, due to the new design, the website was prompted to be easier to use on smart-phones and tablets, devices considerably more integrated in our lives now, compared to when the platform was first launched.

FAN ENGAGEMENT

A group of online platforms dedicated to *Harry Potter* emerged shortly after the release of the first two books, the most notable being *The Leaky Cauldron*[31] and *MuggleNet*.[32] The websites allowed fans to get together, discuss their favorite parts of the books and films, speculate on what would happen in future books and who would be cast for various parts in the films, deliver the latest news related to anything connected to the *Harry Potter* universe, and submit their fan fiction and fan art. For the first time, the vastness of *Harry Potter* fandom could be grasped, and the engagement and immersion of the visitors ultimately inspired Rowling to create *Pottermore*. Moreover, important official announcements, exclusive interviews with Rowling, and information regarding *Pottermore's* launch were released through *Leaky Cauldron* and *MuggleNet*.

The dedication of the platforms did not go unnoticed and unrewarded, and for the first time, founders of a fan site were invited to a press preview on a film set: Warner Bros asked *Leaky Cauldron* creator Melissa Anelli to visit the *Harry Potter and the Prisoner of Azkaban* set.[33] Fans might not have had a voice with regard to the narrative of the series and the destiny of the characters, but Rowling did personally check feedback she received from readers through the online platforms.[34] In one notable way, fans did influence the *Harry Potter* narrative: via the Neville/Luna romance. This represented a massive fan request, and ended up being included in the films even though the books suggested no love interest between the two, and the additional information released by Rowling via her initial website paired Luna with a different wizard. Yet in the films, the two were a pair. This compromise was enough to reinforce to an ever-growing fan base that their opinions mattered.

Fans also took to engaging in the magical world that Rowling created at a very serious level. Inspired by the originality of Quidditch game, and fueled by the extensive information provided in *Quidditch Through the Ages*, in 2005, ten teams decided to compete in a real version of a Quidditch World Cup (riding on brooms included!). An International Quidditch Association was also launched on that occasion. By 2012, there were already 175 competing member teams from forty-five US States and five other countries, showing the growing popularity of the sport.[35]

WONDERBOOK: BOOK OF SPELLS AND COLLABORATION WITH PLAYSTATION

Throughout the years, several *Harry Potter* video games have been released, including a Lego version. However, none seem to have made a lasting impression in the fan community. In 2012, PlayStation launched *Wonderbook: Book of Spells*, a game shaped as a companion manual (similar to *Fantastic Beasts and Where to Find Them*), credited to Miranda Goshawk, a character from the *Harry Potter* universe. Using the PlayStation 3's augmented reality technology—resulting from the interaction of the PlayStationEye digital-camera with the SonyMove controller—the game/book allowed players to transform the world around them, to cast spells by gesturing with their arms or with a wand included with the game, and also to access original content provided by Rowling.[36] *Wonderbook* in itself lacked a cohesive narrative structure and end goal, failing to engage users unfamiliar with the *Harry Potter* universe. While it represented a wonderful extension for those willing to experience every aspect of the magical world, it failed to appeal to non-Potter fans, as had also happened with the other three published companion books.

At the beginning of April 2013, Sony also released a *Pottermore* version for their PlayStation Home platform. Although the game mirrored its web-based version environments and actions, through the fully-realized 3D environments and the possibilities of user interaction, the game provided quite a significantly immersive experience.[37]

It was, however, short-lived, as on March 31, 2015, the PS3 gave up on its virtual world PlayStation Home environment and, together with it, the *Pottermore* game for this platform.[38] This withdrawal was also followed in September 2015 by the massive revision of the web version of *Pottermore*. Even though the *Pottermore* creators seemed to base their decision on the realization that the target audience was more mature than anticipated, along with their wish to have a website more smart-phone-and-tablet-friendly, it is very likely Sony's exit also played an important role.[39]

The fans were desolate. Comments poured in on *MuggleNet* and similar websites, criticizing the updates. Users missed the games, the interactions, the fan art and, perhaps most importantly, what was left to the imagination in the representation of the characters. Even more, they complained that the magic was lost and *Pottermore* had become no different from a fan site, its creators more interested in selling merchandise than providing an experience. [40]

The updated website had indeed left out a series of things that had made *Pottermore* so special. It also featured a number of inconsistencies generated by the different outcomes some protagonists faced in the books as opposed to the movies. As long as the characters had various representations in the media, fans were willing to overlook these differences. With the new *Pottermore,* however, stills from the films were associated with the descriptions of certain characters, all representations being blended into one. The different outcomes no longer made sense.

Some users also had problems with the resorting into Houses. While the new version of the website offered the possibility of maintaining the house a person was initially assigned to on the old *Pottermore*, many chose to retake the test, unsurprisingly reaching different outcomes. For some people that had invested time in group competitions and getting their House to win, suddenly being placed in another one was devastating.

The fact remained, however, that the old platform was becoming not only increasingly difficult to manage and to browse in the current media landscape, but it also had little room to grow once all chapters had been covered. Users could continue brewing potions and dueling, but only until they ran out of resources. Even more, the bridge the new website established between *Harry Potter* books, films, theater play, and *Fantastic Beasts* would have been very difficult, if not impossible, to achieve through the old version.

In terms of user engagement, updating *Pottermore* seemed to be an example of "killing your darlings." Many fans were left disappointed by the new direction, and the project did lose parts of its originality, but undoubtedly it was the best move for the franchise and for the expansion towards an international wizarding world.

THE *FANTASTIC BEASTS* SPIN-OFF AND THE *HARRY POTTER* THEATER PLAY

In 2016, the *Harry Potter* franchise reached yet another set of important milestones. November saw the launch of the first out of three films based on the *Fantastic Beasts and Where to Find Them* companion *Harry Potter* book. The story is set in North America, seventy years prior to the events in the *Harry Potter* series, and features as protagonist Newt Scamander, the well-known author of the *Fantastic Beasts* Hogwarts textbook. The script for the first installment was written by Rowling, thus marking her debut as a screenwriter. It remains to be seen in the long term how fans will respond to the idea of a magical universe with a different setting and another protagonist, but if the trilogy proves successful, it will be an incredible accomplishment for the franchise suddenly confronted with the possibility of further expansion.

Taking the story line in a different direction, the *Harry Potter and the Cursed Child* theater plays deal with events that take place nineteen years after those described in the books. Though featuring the series' well-known characters, the story is centered around Harry and Ginny's son Albus, who finds himself struggling with a legacy he never wanted. Apart from expanding on one of the few mediums left unexplored by this franchise—the theater—this story also flirts with the idea of new protagonists in the same universe. While Rowling reinforced her assertion that this was the last we'd be hearing of Harry,[41] there's no saying we will not get more adventures from the new generation of Potters, Weasleys, and Malfoys. Several fan fiction writings have already explored the subject of the Potter kids having their own adventures; it would not be completely unlikely for Rowling to ultimately present her own vision on the subject.

The play also brings significant changes regarding the characters' identification. So far, the images of the *Harry Potter* characters were strongly connected to the faces of the actors that played them in the films. The various international stagings of the theater play, however, will make it possible for each country to have its own Harry Potter. It will be interesting to see how fans respond to this change and if it affects the franchise in any way. Up until this point, the fandom has been extremely favorable towards the release of the new material, embracing the launch of *The Cursed Child*'s print text with the same enthusiasm as for any of the previous books.

4. The Legacy of the *Harry Potter* Franchise

J. K. Rowling might have started as a writer back in the 90s, but by constantly innovating and unleashing her imagination, she has been able to take the *Harry Potter* universe into realms yet to be explored by any other book author. A genuine trendsetter, she has prompted other writers as well to both maintain control and be open to other media interpretations of their own works. If before Rowling it was quite common for the book author to have nothing to do with the screen adaptation of their works, the past years have witnessed a definite shift. Successful writers such as Veronica Roth, George R. R. Martin, and E. L. James have had important production roles in the adaptations of their novels, while others such as Gillian Flynn and Paula Hawkins even wrote the scripts of their corresponding screen adaptations.

In addition, for the time being, transmedia projects resulting from book adaptations have been considerably more successful than genuine transmedia projects. *The Truth About Marika*, a Swedish "participation drama" in which regular people were asked to solve the mystery of the disappearance of the young girl Marika, using clues provided via a television show, website, and Alternate Reality Game (ARG) activities, managed to reach an audience on the order of tens of thousands of people at best. Though very well received by critics and other cross-platform creators, having been awarded an International Emmy for Best Interactive TV service and considered one of the trailblazers of transmedia projects, *The Truth About Marika* remained quite unknown to average media consumers. In contrast, transmedia projects based on adaptations of books, such as *Harry Potter*, *Lord of the Rings*, and the *Twilight* series have reached audiences of hundreds of millions of people (the *Harry Potter* book series alone has sold over 450 million copies and 5 billion movie tickets). There is, thus, a considerable difference in exposure between the two types. *Harry Potter* was a pioneer, showing big studios how much money they can make with a good concept once they expand it beyond traditional media. As I also conclude in "Adaptations: Primitive Transmedia Narratives?" genuine transmedia storytellers can learn a lot about fan engagement and immersion by having a good look at projects similar to *Harry Potter*.

Although usually created for different reasons than genuine transmedia projects, such as the potential of an existing story or a character from text to migrate to the screen and engage a new audience, in some instances projects like *Harry Potter* end up giving fans the opportunity to prolong their immersion within a fictional space. *Pottermore* was also initially thought of as a "gift" for the fans, letting them share their Potter-inspired works while also accessing additional information Rowling had written about the Potter universe.[42] Although in these instances viewers are not usually influencing the story line but rather are engaging in the story world to generate their own unique experiences, it suggests that authors are creating content specifically with fans in mind. Franchises similar to *Harry Potter* emphasize the importance of fandoms and community formations specific to genuine transmedia narratives, recognizing fans' wishes to contribute to the fictional universe; to be more in control of the story line; and to simulate the experiences of protagonists, while being able to connect with other fans around the world. Ultimately, this sets a great example for all content creators.

Notes

Sections of the chapter have been published as part of the "Adaptations: Primitive Transmedia Narratives?" chapter in the *Words, Worlds and Narratives: Transmedia and Immersion* collection published by Inter-Disciplinary Press.

1. Henry Jenkins, "Transmedia Storytelling," *MIT Technology Review*, January 15, 2003, www.technologyreview.com/s/401760/transmedia-storytelling/.

2. Including *Fantastic Beasts and Where to Find Them* (New York: Scholastic Press, 2000), *Quidditch Through the Ages* (New York: Scholastic Press, 2000), and *The Tales of Beedle the Bard* (New York: Scholastic Press, 2008).

3. J. K. Rowling, John Tiffany, and Jack Thorne, *Harry Potter and the Cursed Child: Parts One and Two* (New York: Scholastic Press, 2016).

4. *Wikipedia, The Free Encyclopedia*, s.v. "Transmedia storytelling" (accessed December 17, 2012), http://en.wikipedia.org/wiki/Transmedia.

5. Jenkins, "Transmedia Storytelling."

6. Anita Singh, "JK Rowling Launches Pottermore Website," *The Telegraph*, June 16, 2011, www.telegraph.co.uk/culture/harry-potter/8579560/JK-Rowling-launches-Pottermore-website.html.

7. "Pottermore Launched: J. K. Rowling on New Harry Potter Material," *The Telegraph,* June 23, 2011, YouTube Video, www.youtube.com/watch?feature=player_embedded&v=_NS6fNQMpns.

8. Syd Field, *Screenplay: The Foundations of Screenwriting* (New York: Bantam Dell, 2005), 258–259.

9. "Transmedia 202: Further Reflections." *Confessions of an ACA—Fan, the Official Weblog of Henry Jenkins,* August 1, 2011, http://henryjenkins.org/2011/08/defining_transmedia_further_re.html.

10. In *Words, Worlds and Narratives: Transmedia and Immersion,* ed. Tawnya Ravy and Eric Forcier (Oxford: Inter-Disciplinary Press, 2014).

11. "Transmedia 202."

12. J. K. Rowling, *Harry Potter and the Goblet of Fire* (New York: Scholastic, 2000) and *Harry Potter and the Half-Blood Prince* (New York: Scholastic, 2005).

13. *International Quidditch Association,* September 15, 2016, http://iqaquidditch.org/.

14. *J. K. Rowling,* September 15, 2016, www.jkrowling.com. This information has since moved to *Pottermore,* September 15, 2016, www.pottermore.com.

15. *Harry Potter Wiki,* s.v. "George Weasley" (accessed September 15, 2016), http://harrypotter.wikia.com/wiki/George_Weasley.

16. Olivia Solon, "J. K. Rowling's Pottermore Reveal: Harry Potter E-books and More," *Arstechnica* June 23, 2011, http://arstechnica.com/gaming/2011/06/jk-rowlings-pottermore-reveal-harry-potter-e-books-and-more/.

17. "Transmedia Storytelling."

18. "Q_A with Pottermore CEO Charlie Redmayne," *Vimeo,* September 15, 2016, https://vimeo.com/145700816.

19. J. K. Rowling, *Harry Potter and the Philosopher's Stone* (London: Bloomsbury, 1997). Published in the United States as *Harry Potter and the Sorcerer's Stone* (New York: Scholastic, 1998).

20. J. K. Rowling, *Harry Potter and the Prisoner of Azkaban* (New York: Scholastic, 1999).

21. J. K. Rowling, *Harry Potter and the Deathly Hallows,* New York: Scholastic, 2000.

22. Bryan Patterson, "Enthusiastic Fans Await New Release," *Melbourne Herald Sun,* November 30, 2008, www.heraldsun.com.au/news/victoria/enthusiastic-fans-await-new-release/story-e6frf92f-1111118176695.

23. " 'Harry Potter': Alan Rickman Looks Back on Decade of Dark Magic," *Hero Complex,* December 30, 2011, http://herocomplex.latimes.com/movies/harry-potter-alan-rickman-looks-back-on-decade-of-dark-magic/#/0.

24. *Harry Potter: The Exhibition*, September 16, 2016, www.harrypotter exhibition.com.

25. "The Wizarding World of Harry Potter," May 9, 2013, www.universal orlando.com/harrypotter/.

26. Ward, Victoria, "JK Rowling Unveils Pottermore Website," *The Telegraph*, June 23, 2011, www.telegraph.co.uk/news/uknews/8593930/JK-Rowling-unveils-Pottermore-website.html.

27. Salvador Rodriguez, "Pottermore Launches Competition to Select Beta Users," *The LA Times*, August 1, 2011, http://latimesblogs.latimes.com/technology /2011/08/pottermore-launches-competition-to-select-beta-users-.html.

28. "J. K. Rowling's Pottermore Site Launches Magical Quill Challenge," *The Wall Street Journal*, July 31, 2011, http://blogs.wsj.com/speakeasy/2011/07/31/j-k-rowlings-pottermore-site-launches-magical-quill-challenge/.

29. Harriet Walker, "First Sight: Pottermore.com, the Internet," *The Independent*, August 16, 2011, www.independent.co.uk/arts-entertainment/books/ news/first-sight-pottermorecom-the-internet-2338170.html.

30. "Press Release—11 Sept 2015," *Pottermore*, August 30, 2016, www .pottermore.com/about/press-11-Sept-2015.

31. *The Leaky Cauldron*, May 9, 2013, www.the-leaky-cauldron.org/.

32. *MuggleNet*, May 9, 2013, www.mugglenet.com.

33. Gwynne Watkins, "Portrait of an Influential Fan: Melissa Anelli, Webmistress of Harry Potter's Leaky Cauldron," *Vulture*, October 17, 2012, www .vulture.com/2012/10/influential-fan-harry-potter-melissa-anelli-leaky-cauldron.html.

34. Anelli and Spartz.

35. "About," *International Quidditch Association*, September 19, 2016, www .iqaquidditch.org/about.php.

36. "Wizard Training for Muggles: Sony Creates New Book of Spells Game to Keep Harry Potter Fans Happy," *Daily Mail*, June 4, 2012, www.dailymail .co.uk/sciencetech/article-2154725/Calling-Harry-Potter-fans-Sony-creates-new-Book-Spells-game-Muggles-happy.html.

37. *Wonderbook: Book of Spells*, PlayStation.com, May 9, 2013, http:// us.playstation.com/games/wonderbook-book-of-spells-ps3.html.

38. Liam Martin and Matthew Reynolds, "PlayStation Home Closes Its Doors for Good: A Look Back at Its Best Moments," *Digital Spy*, April 1, 2015, www.digitalspy.com/gaming/feature/a638593/playstation-home-closes-its-doors-for-good-a-look-back-at-its-best-moments/.

39. "Pottermore Prepares for Relaunch to Showcase Wider Wizarding World," *MuggleNet*, July 12, 2016, www.mugglenet.com/2015/09/pottermore-prepares-for-relaunch-to-showcase-wider-wizarding-world/.

40. Ibid.

41. Andrew Liptak, "Harry Potter's Journey Has Come to an End with The Cursed Child," *The Verge*, July 31, 2016, www.theverge.com/2016/7/31/12333626/harry-potter-journey-end-the-cursed-child.

42. "Full Text from J. K. Rowling Pottermore Press Conference," *The Leaky Cauldron*, June 23, 2011, www.the-leaky-cauldron.org/2011/6/23/full-text-from-j-k-rowling-pottermore-press-conference.

5

Epoximise!

The Renegotiation of Film and Literature through *Harry Potter* GIF Sets

Katharine McCain

Back in 2015, Chilean artist Javier Jensen crafted a series of animated book covers that added movement and life to a number of classic tales: *The Hobbit* features clouds drifting over The Misty Mountains, planets spin beside Le Petit Prince, smoke curls up from Sherlock Holmes's pipe, and the fearsome whale surfaces briefly on the cover of *Moby Dick*. Jensen has commented that he wants his work to "reflect what you see when you look deeply" at books, and he suspects that he's only begun to demonstrate what GIFs are able to do for both art and literature.[1] Indeed, fans—specifically media fans who are active in producing transformative works and sharing them in online spaces—are proving that GIFs are capable of transforming, perhaps *transfiguring*, familiar works into something entirely new.[2]

Over the past two decades, *Harry Potter* scholarship has focused primarily on J. K. Rowling's books, her adaptive films by Warner Bros., or these two texts in comparison with one another, yet scholars have made little attempt to assess how *Harry Potter* is interpreted through intertextual mediums that combine the two, the screen and the text, mediums such as individual GIFs and GIF sets. Here I would like to examine GIFs as a type of fanfiction: a genre of fiction crafted by fans that relies on an intimate knowledge of a canonical source or sources, building on the original framework to create a new creative piece. In splicing and pairing GIFs, *Harry Potter* fans bridge perceived gaps and attempt to rediscover a sense of fidelity, even authenticity, between the novels and the films in the following ways: 1. Using GIFs as a means of fixing apparent mistakes in the films, 2. Recreating significant, canonical scenarios that didn't make it into the films, and 3. Creating new scenarios that help to continually expand the *Harry Potter* universe and keep the fandom alive. By transferring *Harry Potter* to a flexible medium, combining the core visual and textual elements of the series that has gone through not just two or three but numerous layers of remediation, fans continue to push the definition of fanfiction; explore what GIFs can bring to literature; and demonstrate how like-minded fans in the twenty-first century can craft non-traditional works that both creatively and critically show their devotion to one of the greatest stories ever told.

Confundo: Unraveling the GIF Set

GIFs (short for Graphic Interchange Format) are looping animations that are either presented as single pieces or with multiple, related GIFs collected in a grid form, often referred to as GIF sets. CompuServe introduced GIFs back in 1987 as an early way of getting moving images up online. However, they've only come into widespread use within the last fifteen years or so, and it has only been in the last decade that GIFs have caught on as an artistic medium.[3] "Artistic" is obviously a broad and loaded term, but here I use it to mean GIFs as Jason Eppink describes them, as having "an ethos, a utility, an evolving context, a set of aesthetics. . . . They are not simply viewed; they are created, used, posted, collected, copied, modified, performed."[4] GIFs are used by fans and non-fans alike as a way of reacting to the world, telling short stories, and highlighting imagery and information that warrants careful attention. They are not merely tools, but *aesthetic* tools. This is particularly evident given that GIFs are a visual medium, emphasizing fans' desire to spread material that is both informative *and* aesthetically entertaining. They also allow for faster, "dirtier" analyses, to say nothing of a more detailed knowledge of the canon. Gone are the days when fans lost time to rewinding VHS tapes or even, more recently, to scouring back through individual episodes, struggling to find specific moments across multiple seasons. With the rise of GIFs, information deemed collectively important by fandoms—such as defining character traits, plot twists, hair-raising moments from premiers and finales—is condensed into bite-sized, repetitive pieces, uploaded for the masses, and consumed just as quickly as it takes to glance at a screen. This allows fans to re-familiarize themselves with the text at a previously unheard of rate and draw conclusions about it just as fast. Nowadays online interaction is all about speed, to the extent that a TV show edited down into GIF form is considered more useful than a written summary, and the only thing limiting fans' communication with these new HD texts is the space available within the technology itself.[5] Tumblr, in particular, is notorious for its size restrictions and its mobile app that, in not loading GIFs, refuses to load the conversation.

It's no surprise then that with this newfound speed, crediting works has largely fallen by the wayside. Oftentimes the authorship of GIFs is either unknown or de-emphasized, and they pass from person to person in an anonymous string that allows them to seamlessly merge with the current culture, becoming a visual language for anyone to use.[6] Tumblr—a micro-blogging social media website that went up in 2007[7]—is one of the few online spaces that continually fights for GIFs to maintain a secure authorship, calling out anyone who dares to appropriate or "steal" GIFs for their own use without linking to or otherwise acknowledging the creator.[8]

This mindset, which works against the normal accessibility and speed by which GIFs are shared, has converted Tumblr into a unique space, wherein GIFs are *both* universally available tools and works attributed to single (or in rare cases, pairs of) authors. Fans on Tumblr expect to be able to appropriate and use GIFs in whatever manner they please—just like any other language—whereas GIF creators expect their work to remain "untarnished" or, at the very least, for others to acknowledge their ownership, thus limiting how much GIFs are able to merge with fan culture. In many ways, this tension between letting go of fanworks and maintaining control of them reflects similar questions regarding the ownership and accessibility of fanfiction.[9]

As mentioned previously, GIFs are used by fans for a variety of reasons, four of which I'd like to briefly outline here. One of the most common usages beyond mere entertainment is the spread of information considered relevant to other fans, such as other shows that weave *Harry Potter* into their own mythos. For example, a GIF set of David Tennant from *Doctor Who* has him lamenting to his companion, "Wait 'till you read Book 7. Oh, I cried."[10] Not only does this GIF set alert fans to other series that might interest them (surely if the Doctor likes *Harry Potter*, he must be worth watching), but it spreads *potential* information as well. That episode, "The Shakespeare Code," was released just four months before *Harry Potter and the Deathly Hallows*, playing off of the Doctor's status as a being who can travel through space and *time*. Fans enjoy the idea that the Doctor can

For a few years there, there were the Harry Potter films.

And there was a whole family of ginger people.

I thought at somehow, I might be a part of that.

Never happened.

Eddie Redmayne's interview on *The Graham Norton Show* (2015) paired with Warner Bros.' *Fantastic Beasts and Where to Find Them* (2016) announcement.

"spoil" them, and this is a safe choice of spoiler: no fan doubts that they will in fact cry after reading the final *Harry Potter* book.

More concrete, yet no less significant, is the passing of information such as the announcement that Oscar winner Eddie Redmayne would be playing Newt Scamander in *Fantastic Beasts and Where to Find Them*. Here, a grid of four GIFs cover Eddie's desire to be a part of the film franchise: "For a few years there, there were the *Harry Potter* films. And there was a whole family of ginger people. I thought somehow, I might be a part of that. Never happened."[11] These images and transcribed dialogue are paired with the Warner Brothers' official tweet announcing his role, providing *Harry Potter* fans not only with a crucial bit of Potter-information, but also a sense of closure (in that Eddie has finally achieved a decades-long dream) and satisfaction, as Eddie's words confirm that Warner Brothers has granted this opportunity to a fellow fan. That alone lends the film a certain level of authenticity in other fans' eyes.

Further information spread through GIFs includes trivia, with fans offering a visual element for viewers to associate with the presented fact. A popular GIF set, with 993,732 "notes" (likes and reblogs) as of May 2016, shows another two-by-four grid setup with Fred (or is it George?) Weasley doing homework in the great hall, a rather befuddled look on his face.[12] Text beneath it claims that, "The child actors in Harry Potter would do their actual schoolwork in the movie to make the school setting seem more real." This tidbit of trivia allows fans to draw a direct connection between the information offered and this particular (no longer purely fictional) scene. Now, an assumption is made on the part of the viewer that this image depicts not merely acting on the part of James or Oliver Phelps, as previously thought, but rather shows a real-life boy doing his actual schoolwork. Another fan added a bit of humor, suggesting what type of homework might elicit such confusion. The addition says simply, "Math."

Above all, though, fans use GIFs as a way of reflecting on their own status *as* fans: poking fun at themselves, engaging in "cracky" humor, and reliving *Harry Potter*'s emotional impact in a significantly shorter timespan than it takes to re-read the books or re-watch the films. GIFs illustrating the atmosphere of Hogwarts, catchy one-liners, significant battle moments, and Mrs. Weasley's defense of her daughter against Bellatrix Lestrange are all popular moments for fans to GIF, as they allow them to access what are collectively considered the "best" moments in the series, without the hassle of fast forwarding or skimming through hundreds of pages of text. These GIF'ed scenes not only provide fans with a way of re-experiencing the text, but also with a more practical way of analyzing it. The repetition inherent in GIFs allows fans to pick up on details they may have previously missed, and Tumblr's grid formatting enables GIFs from the different films to be placed side by side, making it easier for fans to spot potential parallels and connections.

Fans define "cracky" humor as a work that is ludicrous in its premise and yet highly addictive, playing off of the slang for crack cocaine.[13] The term may be applied to crack fics, crack vids, or crack pairings, and whether there is a negative or positive connotation depends on the individual using the term as well as the context. Here, crack scenarios emphasized or portrayed through GIFs allow fans to poke fun at themselves and maintain a certain level of humor in what can sometimes be a charged and heated community.[14] For example, one GIF of Harry showcases him at the end of *Prisoner of Azkaban*, zooming around on his broomstick, mouth open wide and heading straight for a floating cupcake, added via Photoshop. This is a scenario that is in no way constructed as canonical, that is in fact so preposterous as to be funny.[15] The creator of the GIF presumably "must be on drugs" to produce something so ridiculous, yet at the same time there's a certain level of sincerity, given that the joke derives from Daniel Radcliffe's exaggerated expression in the scene and the fact that the *Prisoner of Azkaban* producers chose to end the film on a freeze frame of said expression, with Harry's face comically contorted. Many fans found the ending absurd or just outright bad, and they comment on this by increasing the absurdity within their GIFs. At the same time, fans derive enjoyment both from the humor itself and from the satisfaction of parodying what might be considered "deeper" themes within the canon. In the case of Harry and his cupcake, GIFs move the narration away from Harry's sense of profound relief (learning that Sirius is safe at the end of *Prison of Azkaban*); freedom (rocketing through the sky on his broomstick); and joy (receiving a Firebolt, currently the fastest broom on the market and, more importantly, a gift from his godfather); and instead present the viewer with a mockery of these emotions—though it's a mockery done with love.

Finally, expanding on this kind mockery, GIFs are used by fans to self-referentially make fun of their community, pointing out what they know to be their own obsessions and flaws. One popular example of this kind of work is a GIF set that shows Hagrid from *Prisoner of Azkaban*, preparing to teach his Care of Magical Creatures class to a group of third-year Slytherins and Gryffindors. In the film, the class's focus is on hippogriffs, and Hagrid warns his students of the creatures' proud—and potentially deadly—nature. But rather than the expected lesson on hippogriffs, Hagrid in the GIF says, "You do not want to insult a fangirl's OTP. It may just be the last thing you ever do."[16] This is a case in which the image is lifted directly from the film, unedited, but added text is what changes the meaning. The second half of Hagrid's warning, "It may just be the last thing you ever do," is similar to his canonical warning about the dangers of insulting hippogriffs, but here the "danger" is in insulting an OTP—a fan's "one true pairing." The joke lies in the exaggeration of a fangirl's devotion to fictional characters (particularly their romances), and the respect is in the GIF creator's ability to tie the joke so closely to the film's original scene. The more these GIFs look and sound like canon, the funnier they're considered to be.

Similarly, a GIF set of Harry and Luna from *The Order of the Phoenix* keeps Luna's dialogue exactly as it was but changes the visuals, and by doing so manages to apply the words to fans as a whole. The duo observes a group of thestrals—skeleton-like horses that can only be seen once someone has witnessed death—but Luna challenges their bad reputation, saying, "People avoid them because they're a bit . . . different."[17] What was once a tender, educational moment in the film becomes humorous when the word "Tumblr" appears over the thestrals' heads, implying that members of Tumblr's community are the ones who are "different." Luna is thus no longer defending a truly misunderstood creature, but rather speaking plainly about a "creature" that needs no defense. Here, fans revel in their own "difference," making fun of it, yes, but also using GIFs to celebrate it.

Reparo: Cleaning Up the Film Franchise

Justifying GIFs as not merely forms of entertainment, humor, self-referential reflection, or news outlets, but as new forms of fanfiction, is a tad bit more complicated. Admittedly, the ways in which the two differ are numerous: GIFs are not textually based; they utilize actors, sets, costuming, and other visual aspects of film or television; they are produced using Photoshop or free online convertors; they're consumed by fans far faster than a fic—often resulting in the inaccurate assumption that not as much effort goes into their production. All that being said, though, the similarities between the transformative nature of GIFs and fanfiction—as well as the way in which they both engage in analysis of their canonical texts—provide a basis for reading GIFs with the same level of detail that has been afforded to fanfiction studies since the early 1990s.

I am far from the first to suggest that fringe fan creations might usefully fall under the broader term of "fic." Back in 2009, Paul Booth expanded on Levy's work (1997) to argue that wikis—websites created for the communal sharing of media content—allowed fans to "articulate a new conception of narrative constructions," what he terms "narractivity."[18] In short, Booth argues that wikis are a medium that, like fic, are at their core written works that allow fans to re-think and expand upon specific source materials. They are narrative creations that treat plot points, specifically spoilers, as "not just guesses as to what *might* happen, but rather indications of what *would* happen in a different possible narrative."[19] Notably, GIFs are re-contextual-izations like fic, crafting new meanings and re-imaginings. Both genres are digital forms of art existing in an affinity space.[20] They each circulate unof-ficially; encourage communal authorship; build on pre-established knowl-edge of the canon/fanon; emerge within a gift culture;[21] and exist as unstable rather than fixed texts, with endless additions, comments, and edits. Be-yond these similarities, Booth significantly examines how wikis move away from certain assumptions about fanfiction, in that they need not be linear, or limited to an authorship of no more than three authors, or even "go be-yond" the original text, principles laid out by scholars like Henry Jenkins. By arguing that wikis are both diverse from, yet remain a type of "interac-tive fan fiction," Booth's work opens the door for considering other types of narrative constructions by fans *as* fic, including the GIF set.

Like fic, much of the work GIFs do nowadays involves fixing perceived mistakes within the canon. In the realm of one-shots and chapters, this could be as simple as rewriting scenes to edit out behavior perceived to be OOC (Out of Character), or as large as erasing a protagonist's death. For *Harry Potter* GIFs, the "mistakes" are rarely attributed to Rowling's origi-nal text. Only within the last few years has Rowling fallen from her "per-fect" pedestal within the Tumblr community, as fans who grew up with the books are now old enough to recognize (or rather, articulate) the need for more diverse representation.[22] That being said, fans are still more likely to view the books as the "correct" version and any deviation in adaptation as "flaws," which speaks more to the status of *Harry Potter* as a beloved cul-tural phenomenon than to fans' loyalty to whatever text is created first. Paul Flesher, speaking specifically of film adaptations, says that those which "ad-here closely to their base text can draw authority and authenticity from the text onto the film itself."[23] Warner Brothers changed a great deal when they moved *Harry Potter* to the big screen, reimagining everything, from plot, to characterization, to splitting the final book into two films—and thus, ac-cording to Flesher, they lessened the authenticity of the films. On the other hand, working to fix these mistakes seems to *raise* the authenticity of GIFs, despite their non-canonical status.

Fans often quote Jenkins's belief that fic is "the culture repairing the damage done in a system where contemporary myths are owned by corpo-rations instead of the folk," and nothing quite speaks to the folk *as* fans so much as an attention to minor detail and a rejection of the larger picture—that is, what's more likely to earn a text money.[24] Financially speaking, the delivery of a single line by Michael Gambon (who replaced Richard Harris as Dumbledore in *Prisoner of Azkaban* through *The Deathly Hallows Part 2*) presumably had no impact on the billions of dollars the *Harry Potter* films have raked in over the years. Nevertheless, fans have become hyper-attuned to his reading of a particular line in *The Goblet of Fire,* and many consider it to be one of the films' largest mistakes, despite its briefness.

In the book scene, Harry has just learned that his name has appeared in the Goblet of Fire itself, naming him as the fourth contestant in the Triwizard Tournament, despite the fact that he is too young to compete and Hogwarts isn't allowed two champions (the "tri" in "Triwizard" is a strict guideline). Bombarded with accusations of cheating, Harry is finally approached by the headmaster himself:

> Professor Dumbledore was now looking down at Harry, who looked right back at him, trying to discern the expression of the eyes behind the half-moon spectacles.
>   "Did you put your name into the Goblet of Fire, Harry?" he asked calmly.
>   "No," said Harry.[25] (276).

The key word is "calmly." Deviating from the scene, Gambon—who was notorious for choosing not to read Rowling's books—plays out the scenario by rushing at Harry, grabbing him by the shoulders, and backing him roughly into a display case, while growling his line in anger and disbelief. Gambon's conflicting interpretation is duly noted by fans in their reviews, metas, and endless YouTube comments attached to the clip, with "Did you put your name in the Goblet of Fire?" quickly rising to the status of a meme within the *Harry Potter* community.

It may be hard to understand why such a minor change caused such discord, particularly since fans should expect (and understand) a need for modification in adaptations. However, fans (like scholars) have attuned themselves to details, both out of a passion for the text and in order to further their critical analysis of it, and this change, while seemingly small, has rather large consequences for the series, particularly for Dumbledore as a character. By changing the tone of the line, Gambon and director Mike Newell changed Dumbledore himself, altering the wise and tranquil persona for which he is loved and instead making him explosive, even violent. Rowling's description of Dumbledore's line is an indicator of his core personality: a man who remains calm under intense pressure, never judges, always listens, and above all believes his students when they claim they've done no wrong. Moral implications of "the greater good" aside, Dumbledore is a protector—the wise man archetype—but Gambon's portrayal of the character isn't doing much protecting here; rather, he goes so far as to manhandle Harry when he's already in a vulnerable position. For many fans this is an unforgivable lapse. Certainly, there is humor in the cry for such an obsessively accurate translation of the books, but there's also logic and justification too. Dumbledore's "calmly" encompasses too much of his character for fans to ignore.

With this in mind, it hardly comes as a surprise that the scene is a favorite for GIFing and ultimately "fixing" by fans. When discussing fanfiction, many scholars and outsiders focus on their subversion, a reworking of stories that deliberately veer away from the canon in an attempt to provide social commentary (or simply "originality"), in the form of potentially taboo subjects such as homoeroticism;[26] male pregnancy;[27] and the so-called Mary Sue (a derogatory term used to describe an idealized, too perfect protagonist who functions as the author's self-insert),[28] as well as on the ways in which they promote a gift-based culture through the creation and distribution of fic itself.[29] One fan, who goes by Executrix, classifies subversive fanfiction as "discordant" (as opposed to concordant), characterized by a desire to "seek to change some important aspect of the [text]."[30] To classify further, discordant fics come in two forms: those that seek to transform the very values within the text (such as those genres mentioned above) and those that work on a much smaller level to re-establish *logic* within the canon universe, such as fixing a moment of discrepancy, rather than what's perceived as a larger failing on the text's part, such as in plot or characterization.[31] It is this second category that GIFs from *The Goblet of Fire* fall into.

There are more versions of GIFs fixing the Goblet of Fire scene than can possibly be discussed here, but one of the most popular creations is by a fan who identifies as "Sabrina, 27 . . . Biiiig fan of harry potter's books."[32] Back in 2014 Sabrina created a simple GIF of Richard Harris from *Harry Potter and the Sorcerer's Stone*, his expression notably calm, with overlapping text asking, "Harry, did you put your name in the Goblet of Fire?" The scene Sabrina GIFed is from the very end of *Sorcerer's Stone*, wherein Dumbledore explains to Harry what occurred during his fight with Professor Quirrell and tries out a Bertie Bott's Every Flavor Bean at the end of the conversation. This is significant because the scene is a humorous one—Dumbledore is hoping for a toffee-flavored bean but gets earwax instead—and readily recognizable by fans. Bypassing other scenes with Gambon, Sabrina chose a moment where Harris's expression is not simply calm but jolly, teasing, fully embodying the role of a kind yet quirky mentor. Sabrina provides a "fix-it" GIF that does not merely repair the perceived damage but actually manages to transcend it, focusing in on what fans prize about the book scene in the first place: Dumbledore's compassion. Indeed, the 188,000 notes attest to this, compounded by the comments, which include things like, "I feel much better now," "This is so satisfying," and "It's like a Michael Gambon sized weight has been lifted from my chest."[33] Fans can spend thousands of words of fanfic fixing the mistakes of the canon, but GIFs can do just as much in a far more concise format.

Accio: Summoning Up New Scenes

Similar to correcting perceived mistakes that stem from changes in the text, fans also use GIFs as a way of correcting the "mistake" of withholding whole book scenes from the film adaptations. Screenwriters take numerous concerns into account when choosing what scenes to adapt—time constraints, budget, what translates well to the screen, etc.—but there are some moments that fans see as crucial to the heart of *Harry Potter,* and their exclusions are taken as a smack in the face. The existence of the corrective GIFs implies a desire for a completely "authentic" film franchise, one that translates *all* of *Harry Potter* and allows fans to see the entirety of the series up on the big screen.

Lufttsu, also known as Ksenia, whose Tumblr bio begins, "I love Harry Potter," completed a challenge back in 2015 to adapt fifty *Harry Potter* book quotes into GIF sets. The sheer number of quotes, as well as the fact that Ksenia is just one of many fans engaging in this activity, speaks to the amount of book material that fans want to have visually represented. Ksenia is particularly adept at bridging the gaps between *Harry Potter's* narrative and visuals that weren't crafted for that context, choosing scenes where the actors' expressions and gestures match up exceptionally well with the dialogue. The quote used in number forty-seven out of fifty is one such GIF set, wherein Ginny announces that she told Romilda Vane (another Hogwarts student with a crush on Harry) that Harry has a Hungarian Horntail tattoo and that Ron has a far less impressive Pygmy Puff, "but I didn't say where."[34] This set is actually composed of visuals from two film scenes, split between the left and right panels, but the fact that they both take place in Gryffindor Tower allows fans to easily imagine that the characters are actually speaking to one another, a very willful suspension of disbelief. Ginny plays with a book in her hands, helping to support the casualness of the dialogue, and each expression matches the mood perfectly: Harry looks puzzled as he asks what tattoo Ron got, Ginny smiles as she drops the joke, Ron loses his own smile at the punch line. All in all, this GIF set does a remarkable job of persuading the viewer that this scene was actually adapted, and the only thing stopping fans from believing it's real is their own intimate knowledge of the films.

Other GIFs of Ksenia's use a separation between two moments (two individual GIFs) to emphasize the overall message that the book quote is trying to convey. Ksenia could have simply taken the GIF of Harry and Ron chatting, overlaid it with the quotation, "What about those Monster Books, eh? The assistant nearly cried when we said we wanted two," and left it at that, trusting in fans to understand the scene's meaning.[35] Instead, Ksenia included a GIF directly above of Harry fighting with his own Monster Book in *Prisoner of Azkaban*, allowing the visuals of the film to succinctly convey why the store assistant "nearly cried" at the boys' request. Here the dialogue is once again well matched with the visuals, but Ksenia equally uses the films' strength to enhance the impact of Rowling's dialogue. Still other sets in her collection add subtle new layers to Rowling's scenes, simply as a result of their acting as visual accompaniments. Unlike the before-mentioned tattoo scene, GIF set number forty-five conveys expressions that don't quite match with the dialogue, yet can still be read as viable interpretations. Ron smiles when he asks Hermione, "What are you doing with all these books, anyway?" and then responds, "Oh, of course. I forgot we'll be hunting down Voldemort in a mobile library."[36] The dialogue is neutral, with the visuals coding this exchange as gentle teasing, yet Hermione's expression in the last GIF is one of dejection, suggesting that Ron has, perhaps unintentionally, hurt her feelings. By overlaying book quotations with film visuals, artists like Ksenia manage to provide a more complex interpretation of the scenes than is possible in either the books or the films alone.

Alohomora: Pushing the Boundaries of the Canon

Finally, Harry Potter fans utilize GIFs as a tool not only to reconcile the books with the films, but also—as Ksenia's work begins to show—to extend the series farther than either medium can accomplish on its own. Like written fanfiction, GIFs are capable of dropping Harry and his friends into entirely new scenarios, most prominently by crafting AUs (alternate universes), presenting crossovers with other fandoms, or using these fictional displays as a way of commenting critically on the canon itself.[37] All of this can and is done through traditional fanfiction, but, as with vidding, the merging of the books *and* films adds a layer of perceived authenticity that isn't always present in textual-based fic.

Alternate universes alter at least one element of the canon and can encompass anything as small as changing one character's choice of words in a conversation, to a change as large as reimagining the state of the universe itself—such as developing a steampunk AU, a zombie AU, etc.[38] Changes in perspective can also fall under the category of AU, such as one fan's summary explanation of the series through Fred and George Weasley's eyes.[39] Though the plot is unchanged, by focusing on events through the point of view of someone other than Harry, the author is able to point out potentially overlooked connections and emotional resonances, such as the fact that *The Chamber of Secrets* took place during the year the twins "almost lost our sister," and the pride the twins must have felt in *Prisoner of Azkaban* when they "passed on James's legacy" by gifting Harry the Marauders' map. Each of these headers—many of them touching on death or destruction—is accompanied by a GIF of the twins laughing or playing, except for the final image, a looping picture of Ron and George sobbing over Fred's corpse: "The year 'we' became 'I.'" By leading up with so many happy images, the author of this set is able to deliver the emotional punch of Fred's death as well as to emphasize the development of the series' minor characters, in a more resonant, encapsulated way than mere words would allow.

More "traditional" AU's include larger changes, such as one set where James and Lily survive Voldemort's attack, getting the chance to raise Harry in peace. Imagining Karen Gillan as Lily and Aaron Johnson as James, this set pulls from both of their film histories in order to craft scenes that simply don't exist within the canon, such as James playing guitar for his family and Lily baking in the kitchen.[40] Though obviously fans can and do write out these kinds of scenes, crafting these fics through visuals provides a much clearer idea of what the author is imagining and yet, paradoxically, also forces fans to work harder to buy into the fantasy. Anyone who knows Gillan's work needs to actively fight against seeing her as Amy from *Doctor Who* (the show that provides at least three of her images in this set), and when fans see Harry receiving the snitch in the fifth GIF, they know it is Oliver Wood handing it to him in the film, yet they must suspend their disbelief when the GIF suddenly cuts to Johnson giving the snitch to his

AU (Alternate Universe): James and Lily Live.

"son." This sort of work, while difficult, nevertheless makes the imagining of scenes all the more worth it.

Still other GIFs, like the vast majority of fanfiction out there, includes slash, with the Draco/Harry pairing being one of the most prominent within the fandom. Tumblr user Isa demonstrates the difference a single detail can make when they edited a scene so that Harry is now wearing a Slytherin green and silver tie, while Draco is dressed in Gryffindor red and gold. Overlaid text has Ron and Hermione asking Harry, ". . . are you wearing a Slytherin tie?" with Harry confusedly responding, "Er . . . no?"[41] Of course, Draco's entrance in the next GIF proves that they *have* accidentally switched clothing and Isa summarizes her visual fic with, "In which Draco and Harry dress a little too quickly after a meeting." Every drarry fan out there knows exactly what kind of "meeting" this was and the GIF set is received well because it concisely pulls together all the best aspects of fanfiction: a popular pairing, originality, ties to the canon, and the "nudge, nudge, wink, wink" aspects in vocabulary like "meeting." Yet if fans are craving something longer and more traditional, Isa notes that there are "Three fics related to this gif set discussed here" and helpfully provides a link. Just because fans now embrace GIF sets as a new kind of fanfiction doesn't mean the fanfiction of old has lost any of its popularity.

Indeed, with the emergence of new technology fans are now using not just GIFs, but tweets, vines, roleplaying, playlists, and text posts to tell their stories—to name just a few. "Fanfiction" has long moved past the zines of the 1940s–60s, though it no longer simply means text-based works attached to archives either. Given the immensity of *Harry Potter* as a cultural phenomenon, it's no surprise that this fandom is one of the most prominent in pushing the boundaries of what "fanfiction" is and, much more broadly, questioning how we tell stories and what it is we're looking for when we tell them, what it means to reconcile different versions of a text and which of those versions are granted authenticity. The choice to fix, expand, and go beyond Warner Brothers' franchise—as well as Rowling's canon—speaks both to a need to have more *and* have it all: every variation of *Harry Potter* imaginable, and a version for every medium; not just the books and the films, but now, something in-between. In *Deathly Hallows Part 2*, Dumbledore famously tells Harry that, "Words are, in my not-so-humble opinion, our most inexhaustible source of magic, capable of both inflicting injury and remedying it." Fans are steadily proving that GIFs also have a magic all their own.

Notes

1. Claire Fallon, "These Living Book Covers Are as Magical as Anything in Harry Potter," *The Huffington Post*, September 16, 2015, www.huffingtonpost.com/entry/book-cover-gifs_us_55f88e62e4b0b48f6701102d.

2. Henry Jenkins, *Textual Poachers: Television Fans and Participatory Culture* (New York: Routledge, 1992).

3. David Pogue, "The Strange Magic of Micro Movies," *Scientific American*, May 2013: 34.

4. Jason Eppink, "A Brief History of the GIF (So Far)," *Journal of Visual Culture* 13.3 (2014): 298.

5. Tumblr, known for its interconnected format where "no blog is an island," is notorious for its size restrictions and its mobile app that, in not loading GIFs, refuses to load the conversation.

6. Kevin Maney, "GIFs Are Replacing Words . . . Even Thoughts," *Newsweek*, March 29, 2016, www.newsweek.com/2016/04/08/gifs-are-replacing-words-thoughts-441499.html.

7. Amanda Kooser, "Understanding Tumblr," *Restaurant Business*, August 27, 2013, www.restaurantbusinessonline.com/ideas/social-media/understanding-tumblr.

8. "Reblog Not Repost! A Masterpost," *Reposting Is Stealing*, October 8, 2013, http://repostingisstealing.tumblr.com/post/63482164012/anothermind palace-hello-so-recently-i-found.

9. See Robin Hobb, "The Fan Fiction Rant," *Internet Archiv,* June 30, 2005, http://web.archive.org/web/20050630015105/, www.robinhobb.com/rant.html, and Viktor Mayer-Schonberger and Lena Wong, "Fan or Foe: Fan Fiction, Authorship, and the Fight for Control," *IDEA: The Intellectual Property Law Review* 54.1 (2013): 1–22.

10. *Mad Potter Until the Very End*, September 30, 2016, http://madpotter headuntiltheveryend.tumblr.com/post/15446991956.

11. "Mischief Managed," June 2, 2015, http://papertownsy.tumblr.com/post/120485486096.

12. *Mad Potter Until the Very End*, September 30, 2016, http://madpotterhead untiltheveryend.tumblr.com/post/66661035852/songbard5683-fiestyhysteria-the-child-actors.

13. "Crack," *Fanlore Wiki*, August 21 2015, http://fanlore.org/wiki/Crack.

14. Melissa M Brough and Sangita Shresthova, "Fandom Meets Activism: Rethinking Civic and Political Participation," *Transformative Works and Cultures* 10 (2012), http://journal.transformativeworks.org/index.php/twc/article/view/303/265.

15. *Mad Potter Until the Very End*, May 8, 2012, http://madpotterheaduntil-theveryend.tumblr.com/post/22658555971.

16. "Welcome to the Shire," September 30, 2016, http://hobbitsunite.tumblr .com/post/63253859752/life-lessons-with-hagrid.

17. *Mad Potter Until the Very End*, September 30, 2016, http://madpotter headuntiltheveryend.tumblr.com/post/41604897064.

18. Paul Booth, "Narractivity and the Narrative Database: Media-based Wikis as Interactive Fan Fiction," *Narrative Inquiry* 19.2 (2009): 372.

19. Ibid., 389.

20. Jayne Lammers, "Fangirls as Teachers: Examining Pedagogic Discourse in an Online Fan Site," *Learning, Media and Technology* 38(2013): 368–386.

21. Abigail De Kosnik, "Should Fan Fiction Be Free?" *Cinema Journal* 48.4 (Summer 2009): 118–24.

22. Henry Jenkins, "Fandom Studies as I See It," *Journal of Fandom Studies* 2.2 (2014): 89–109.

23. Paul Flesher, "Being True to the Text: From Genesis to Harry Potter," *Journal of Religion and Film* 12 (2008), http://digitalcommons.unomaha.edu/jrf/vol12/iss2/1/.

24. Amy Harmon, "In TV's Dull Summer Days, Plots Take Wing on the Net," *The New York Times*, August 18, 1997, www.nytimes.com/1997/08/18/business/in-tv-s-dull-summer-days-plots-take-wing-on-the-net.html?pagewanted=all&src=pm

25. J. K. Rowling, *Harry Potter and the Goblet of Fire* (New York: Scholastic, 2000), 276.

26. Hongwei Bao and Ling Yang, "Queerly Intimate: Friends, Fans and Affective Communication in a Super Girl Fan Fiction Community," *Cultural Studies* 26.6 (2012): 842–71.

27. Berit Åström, " 'Let's Get Those Winchesters Pregnant': Male Pregnancy in *Supernatural* Fan Fiction," *Transformative Works and Cultures* 4 (2010), http://journal.transformativeworks.org/index.php/twc/article/view/135/141.

28. Anupam Chander and Madhavi Sunder, "Everyone's a Superhero: A Cultural Theory of 'Mary Sue' Fan Fiction as Fair Use," *California Law Review* 95.2 (2007): 597–626

29. John Fiske, "The Cultural Economy of Fandom," *The Adoring Audience: Fan Culture and Popular Media*, ed. Lisa A. Lewis (New York: Routledge, 1992), 30–49.

30. Sheenagh Pugh, *The Democratic Genre: Fan Fiction in a Literary Context* (Bridgend, Wales: Seren, 2005), 199.

31. Ibid., 55.

32. "I'm the Two Sides of the Coin!" February 27 2015, http://i-m-a-good-viper.tumblr.com/post/112273494285/dontsayclazy-ms-meryl-imjustthe mechanic (site discontinued).

33. Ibid.

34. Lufttsu, "Quotes from the Harry Potter Books [47/50]," August 3, 2015, http://lufttsu.tumblr.com/post/57164469479/quotes-from-the-harry-potter-books-4750.

35. Lufttsu, "Quotes from the Harry Potter Books [2/50]," October 5, 2015, http://lufttsu.tumblr.com/post/33635476895/quotes-from-the-harry-potter-books-250.

36. Lufttsu, "Quotes from the Harry Potter Books [45/50]," April 30, 2015, http://lufttsu.tumblr.com/post/49251728815/quotes-from-the-harry-potter-books-4550.

37. Jenkins, *Textual Poachers*.

38. "Alternate Universe," *Fanlore Wiki*, August 21, 2015, http://fanlore.org/wiki/Alternate_Universe.

39. *Mad Potter Until the Very End*, September 30, 2016, http://madpotterheaduntiltheveryend.tumblr.com/post/50811811645/iou-a-call-sherlock-just-for-the-reblogs.

40. *Mad Potter Until the Very End,* September 30, 2016, http://madpotterheaduntiltheveryend.tumblr.com/post/60626331255/au-james-and-lily-live.

41. "Obsessive Thoughts," February 12, 2015, http://snowgall.tumblr.com/post/110854647855/scaredpotter-in-which-draco-and-harry-dress-a.

6

Harry Potter and the Surprising Venue of Literary Critique

Michelle Markey Butler

Internet memes—used here in the sense of captioned images—are usually discussed as if they are the Twinkies of web culture. Alluring, evoking pleasant memories of childhood, but ultimately unsatisfying, possessing no depth, no redeeming value, by definition unsuitable as a venue for sustained, engaging, and rewarding thought. Indeed, in this mindset, the only thing memes are really good for is wasting time. Such an assumption underlies a rather meta version of the Dos Equis / Most Interesting Man in the World Meme.[1] The familiar Dos Equis man leans on one elbow, his usual stance. "I don't always waste time at work," proclaims the upper caption. "But when I do, I do it with memes," adds the lower. Despite (or perhaps because of?) the widely accepted notion that memes have no purpose beyond facilitating work-related time-wasting, memes have nonetheless started to receive scholarly attention. However, such attention nearly always focuses on the characteristics of a successful meme (for instance, Michelle Coscia's "Competition and Success in the Meme Pool: A Case Study on Quickmeme.com")[2] or on the ways in which memes participate in political or pop culture discussions (e.g. Limor Shifman's 2013 *Memes in Digital Culture*).[3] While I don't dispute the importance of understanding why some memes succeed and others do not or the usefulness of studying how memes participate in political discourse, I intend to make the case that an overlooked role of memes is as a venue for literary critique.[4] While meme-based critique is made by fans and everyday readers/viewers rather than professional literary scholars, the types of questions asked and the observations made draw upon the same literary analytical tools and techniques that the pros employ. In this chapter, I show that memes about Harry Potter demonstrate literary analysis of plot, character, worldbuilding, evaluative critique, comparative analysis of the books and their movie counterparts, and comparative analysis with other works of fantasy like *Lord of the Rings, Twilight,* and *Game of Thrones.*

Plot

More than a few Harry Potter memes consider questions of plot. A significant category of such memes are those that question whether a particular element constitutes a plot hole, and one of the most common potential plot holes weighed by memes is the Marauder's Map from *Harry Potter and the Prisoner of Azkaban*.[5] If Fred and George Weasley have been in possession of the map for years, and Peter Pettigrew has been hiding as a pet rat with first Percy, then Ron, shouldn't they have noticed him on the map?

One such meme, for instance, uses the Philosopher Raptor[6] image with the upper caption: "If the Weasley twins owned the Marauder's Map" and the lower caption: "Why didn't they notice that Ron slept with Peter Pettigrew every night?"[7] This meme's phrasing poses it as a straightforward question: shouldn't Fred and George have noticed? The implication of a deeper question is clear: shouldn't Peter have been discovered earlier? Is the Marauder's Map a gaping plot hole? Other memes ask the question more covertly. One shows an image of Fred and George, in which both are laughing, with the captions "Sees brother sleeping with a man named Peter every night on Marauder's Map" (upper) and "Doesn't say a damn thing" (lower).[8] The implication is that Fred and George would be highly unlikely to pass up a golden opportunity to harass their brother. Hence they did not in fact learn this information from the Marauder's map, and hence there is a plot hole. Similarly, another meme shows an unsmiling image of Fred and George with the captions "Sees brother in Marauder Map [*sic*] sleeping with man named Peter every night" (upper) and "Doesn't bring him up or judge him" (lower).[9] Like the previous example, this meme uses the tongue-in-cheek method of ascribing uncharacteristic behaviors to Fred and George to suggest that, in fact, they did not learn about Peter Pettigrew from the map (because they would never have reacted as the meme pretends they would have), and thus this is a potential plot hole.

While there are many memes arguing that the existence of the Marauder's Map in Fred and George's hands for so long while Peter Pettigrew remains undiscovered reflects a flaw in the plot, another set of memes takes the same approach with Harry himself, implying Harry's failure to notice Peter when the map was in his possession is also a plot hole. One, for instance, uses the Scumbag Hat meme[10] (a snowclone[11] of Scumbag Steve,[12] which involves moving the hat to another image to indicate the figure's scumbag status, in this case Harry) with the captions "Sees Peter Pettigrew sleeping next to Ron's bed every night for months" (upper) and "Doesn't care" (lower).[13] Yet another meme—this discussion will be representative but in no way exhaustive as there are hundreds of examples—imagines a conversation between Harry, George, and Fred. Harry: "According to this map, Ron is in bed with some dude named Peter Pettigrew." Fred: "Yeah, we noticed that a while ago. We think it's just a typo."[14] Here again, we see the strategy of ascribing ludicrous attributes to Fred and George in order to highlight the unlikeliness of their noticing the situation but taking no action.

Of course, memes are not the *only* venue for such discussion. Even setting aside professional literary scholars' handling of the topic, other web-based fan discussion sites take up the question. Hundreds of discussion boards,[15] question-and-answer websites,[16] articles in the popular online press,[17] and Tumblr posts[18] address the issue.

However, the widespread discussion in web-based fan culture of the potential plot hole of the Marauder's Map reinforces rather than undercuts the claim that memes can and do tackle serious, literary critique-type considerations. Indeed, it is worth noticing the conciseness, efficiency, and cleverness with which memes do so. Online pop media articles are assuredly shorter than scholarly articles (200–500 words compared to 4000–8000, so roughly a factor of ten smaller). The same is true of memes. Memes typically have two dozen words at most. Elaborate, multi-image memes might run as high as 100–300 words. The ability of memes to raise and analyze the same question with many fewer words, in juxtaposition with an image or images, is impressive.

There are other potential plot holes and plot considerations raised by memes, as well as by the wider online fan community (Hagrid's assertion that Hogwarts is the safest place to be after Gringotts, for instance), but the

Marauder's Map is perhaps the most widely discussed and is certainly sufficient to illustrate the point.

Character

Character analysis is another literary critique-type consideration that we see in Harry Potter memes. Several memes, for instance, consider what Harry does with his invisibility cloak and what he might have done instead. Two of them are particularly interesting because while they use the same text (Upper caption: "Gets invisibility cloak," lower caption: "Doesn't go into the girls' showers"), they employ different images. One shows a serious-looking, young Harry, from a *Harry Potter and the Sorcerer's Stone* movie still.[19] This image juxtaposed with the captions suggests Harry not only did not go into the girls' showers using his invisibility cloak, he was not tempted to do so. The situation is less clear with the second meme, which uses an older, smiling Harry, from a *Harry Potter and the Goblet of Fire* movie still.[20] This meme's juxtaposition of image and text implies that while Harry would never actually use the invisibility cloak this way, he might have been tempted to do so, but doesn't because of the inherent goodness of his character. Other memes likewise argue for Harry's honorable nature by emphasizing what he does with the invisibility cloak, in implicit comparison with what he might have done. This one, for instance, points out that Harry "gets invisibility cloak" (upper caption) but rather than the many nefarious things a person could do with such an item, he "goes to the library" (lower caption).[21] According to these representative examples, memes evaluate Harry as not necessarily well-behaved at all times, and perhaps tempted towards naughtiness, but ultimately as someone who does the right thing.

Dumbledore is another character frequently assessed in memes. One, for instance, critiques Dumbledore for having Filch clean Hogwarts manually rather than assisting him with magic: "Can use magic to clean up any mess instantly" (upper caption) and "Makes Mr Filch clean Hogwarts with physical labor."[22] Another meme takes the same observation, however, and argues that a different conclusion should be drawn: "Could clean up Hogwarts using magic" (upper caption) and "Doesn't so that Mr Filch is guaranteed a job."[23] Both memes use similar movie stills of Dumbledore (as played by Michael Gambon), but make very different arguments about his character. The first asserts that Dumbledore is questionable because he makes Filch do

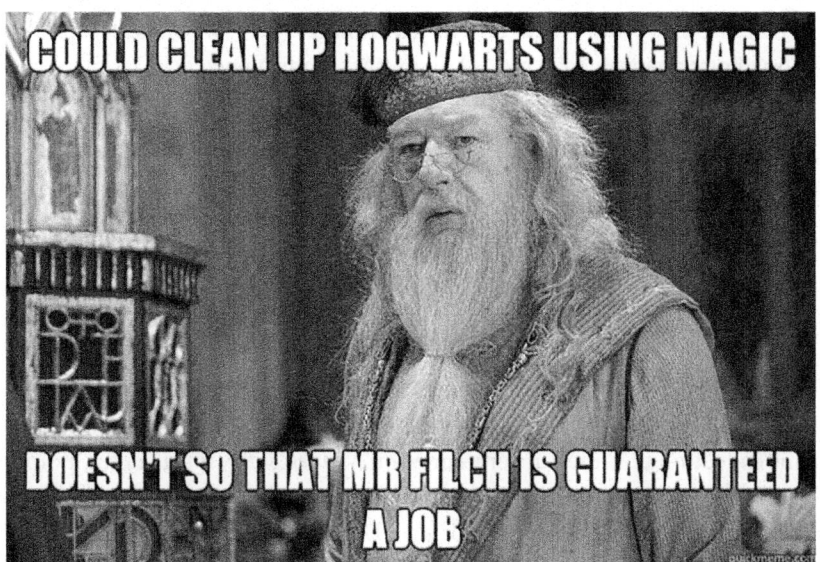

Benevolent Dumbledore Meme.

unnecessary work. The second argues that for this precise reason, Dumbledore is a good guy; he provides Filch work that could easily be done with magic, thus allowing him to stay within magical society despite being a squib.

This pair is illustrative of how many memes handle Dumbledore, and it is interesting that memes, like "professional" literary criticism, point to the potential ambiguity of Dumbledore's character. Christopher Bell's "Heroes and Horcruxes: Dumbledore's Army as Metonym" argues that Dumbledore's defining characteristic is, problematically, pride: "Whether one views Dumbledore's pride as rightfully-earned confidence or dangerous arrogance, it is the defining feature of Dumbledore."[24] Memes that consider Harry may make tongue-in-cheek arguments about what Harry might have done with the invisibility cloak, but they continue to suggest that Harry is the good guy, with good intentions if not always good judgment. Dumbledore is a different matter. At the beginning of the series, for Harry and for the reader, Dumbledore is a wise, inerrant father figure. We write off statements of self-congratulation such as in *Harry Potter and the Sorcerer's Stone* ("It was one of my more brilliant ideas, and between you and me, that's saying something") as jokes, but they are less amusing and harder to brush off as the series moves forward.[25] Dumbledore's pride skirts close to arrogance, as Bell discusses, and we realize his flaws along with Harry. The creators of Harry Potter memes have picked up on that ambivalence.

Worldbuilding

Harry Potter memes also engage with and comment upon elements of worldbuilding. As with plot and character, worldbuilding memes cover a lot of ground, but some paths end up better trodden than others. One worldbuilding topic that receives significant attention in memes is the Time-turner from *Prisoner of Azkaban*. Memes tend to argue that the Time-turner is a serious breakdown of worldbuilding in the Wizarding World. This collection of Time-turner memes on *MemeCenter*, for instance, points out that Hermione uses the Time-turner to take extra classes, but not to go back in time and kill Voldemort or save Dobby.[26] The fact that the Ministry of Magic's stock of Time-Turners has been destroyed (in *Order of the Phoenix*) by the time Dobby dies in *Deathly Hallows* does not negate the overall question: does the possibility of time travel held out by the existence of the Time-turner cause problems with the credibility of the worldbuilding?

The handling of the Time-turner in memes suggests that, for many fans, it is a source of concern, if not an outright problem. One shows a movie still of Dumbledore with the upper caption, "I'm sorry about your parents, but no spell can awaken the dead, Harry. I trust you know that," and the lower caption, "Except for the Time-turner. We'll use that to save Buckbeak."[27] Another also shows a still of Dumbledore with the upper caption, "Lets Hermione use Time-turner to take more classes," and the lower, "Never lets you use it in life or death situations."[28] Yet another shows Hermione and Harry with the upper caption "Has Time-turner," and lower "Doesn't go back in time to kill Voldemort."[29] This meme makes its opinion of that choice abundantly clear by photoshopping the Scumbag Hat onto Hermione. A final example is not content to merely raise questions about the Time-turner by giving one example of where it might have been used to great effect. Instead, over an image of a Time-turner, it gives a list:[30]

Time-turner
Situations it could have been used:
Preventing the Potters' murder
Witnessing Peter Pettigrew's Muggle slaughter

I'M SORRY ABOUT YOUR PARENTS, BUT NO SPELL CAN REAWAKEN THE DEAD, HARRY. I TRUST YOU KNOW THAT.

EXCEPT FOR THE TIME TURNER. WE'LL USE THAT TO SAVE BUCKBEAK.

Snarky Critique of Time-Turner Use Meme.

Preventing escapes from Azkaban
Diminishing Auror casualties
Killing/arresting the young Tom Riddle

Below this, the meme provides a second list:
Situations it has been used:
Taking an extra class

The conclusion intended by the juxtaposition is clear: if the Time-turner exists in the Wizarding World, it has not been used to its full potential. The suggestion about witnessing Pettigrew's (or, as was assumed, Sirius Black's) mass murder of Muggles is particularly evocative. Why *aren't* Time-Turners a regular part of Ministry of Magic investigations, visiting the past not to change anything but to establish the facts of an event?[31] Once pointed out, that seems like an obvious investigative strategy. With the Time-Turner in particular but also with other topics, memes provide a venue for concise but thoughtful, logical, and often surprisingly developed critique of aspects of Harry Potter worldbuilding.

Evaluative Critique

Some memes engage the *Harry Potter* series as a whole, considering the wider implication, meanings, or values the books convey. Such memes tend to be more complicated, involving a series of images with captions rather than one or two pictures with an upper and lower caption. This meme, for instance, lays out what its creator views as the message learned from a character or group of characters.[32] The meme gives a series of sixteen movie stills, each with an accompanying caption:

[Weasleys' vacation in Egypt]: They taught me that family is important
[adult James Potter]: He taught me that a bully can become a great man
[adult Lily Potter]: She taught me that no one loves you more than your mom does
[adult Sirius Black]: He taught me that your family does not define who you are
[adult Remus Lupin, superimposed with a howling wolf's head]: He taught me to judge people by who they are, not what they are
[Fred and George]: They taught me to smile when the world becomes dark
[Luna]: She taught me to see the world with an open mind
[Neville]: He taught me that hard working and determination will lead to success
[Ginny]: She taught me that size is no guarantee of power
[Snape, shielding Harry, Ron, and Hermione from wolf-Lupin]: He taught me that love is the most powerful magic
[Dumbledore]: He taught me to look past prejudices
[Hermione]: She taught me to fight for equality
[Ron]: He taught me to overcome fear

[Harry]: He taught me to do what is right instead of what is easy
And finally . . .
[Harry, Ron, and Hermione]: They taught me to cherish friendship
['True Story' meme line drawing][33]: Thank you, Ms. Rowling

This meme provides a developed evaluation of the series as a whole, focusing upon the major characters and what the creator/reader learned from them during the overall story arc of the books. Of course, with sixteen images and accompanying captions, the meme is capable of more detailed analysis than is possible in memes like those cited previously, which consist of one or two images with brief captions, totaling perhaps two dozen words. Even so, this seeming abundance is relative. There are fewer than two hundred words in this meme, or roughly half a page of text in most standard fonts. Half a page is not much space in which to make as complex and varied a set of assertions as this meme does. The argument for each claim is largely implicit, which is unsurprising given the literary critique in a haiku-like format that is a fundamental characteristic of memes. The observation about Fred and George, for instance, relies upon the viewer knowing their role as jokesters in the series. But memes in general are aimed at a knowing audience; even memes that are merely entertaining, without providing thoughtful critique of the work, rely upon the viewer's preexisting knowledge. Similarly, the claim that Ron taught this meme's creator to overcome fear relies upon the viewer remembering the number of times Ron had to overcome fear, from childlike incarnations such as in *Chamber of Secrets*—in which Ron has to push past his fear of spiders— to the decidedly adult fears that the Horcrux whispers to him in *Deathly Hallows* (his mother loves him least, Hermione prefers Harry).

While necessarily relying upon the viewer to bring existing knowledge of the books to bear in support of its assertions, the meme makes a surprisingly sophisticated argument about the main characters and their effect on readers. It is not difficult to imagine a full-scale academic article or book chapter following the outline provided by the meme, with more complete citation of evidence from the books to bolster the claims. Any one of the sixteen images and captions would be an interesting literary meme, but together they provide a comprehensive consideration of the main characters, their development over the course of the books, and their effects upon readers that is astonishing in its concision. This meme, and others like it, demonstrate beyond a doubt that memes engage in literary criticism, comparable to, let's say, professional literary critics publishing their thoughts on Twitter. That is, memes are limited in how many words they may employ, so of course their points are made more concisely than an academic article would. Nonetheless, the observation holds. Analysis of character development over the series and the lessons the text offers are clearly concepts within the purview of literary criticism.

Comparative Analysis of *Harry Potter* Books and Movies

Evaluative analysis of the *Harry Potter* series is a more complex type of literary analysis than those discussed previously: critiques of plot, character, and worldbuilding. Thus, our next example of literary-type analysis in memes is another step along the complexity continuum. This set of memes considers the movie adaptations in comparison to their source books.

Probably the best known is the "Did You Put Your Name in the Goblet of Fire" meme. This meme shows up in a wide range of styles, images, and wording, but all of them point out the marked contrast between how this moment in described in the book *Harry Potter and the Goblet of Fire* and how it occurs in the movie.[34] In *Goblet of Fire*, after the other champions for the Tri-Wizard tournament have been selected, one from each wizarding school, the Goblet shoots out another name: Harry's. A short time later, the four champions and a small group of adults, consisting of each school's headmaster or headmistress; Ludo Bagman and Barty Crouch representing the Ministry of Magic; and Professors Snape, McGonagall, and "Moody" (really Barty Crouch Junior in disguise), gather to discuss what to do in the wake of this unexpected development. There is a great deal of hostility in the room. The heads of Durmstrang and Beauxbatons react angrily, claiming it is unfair for Hogwarts to have two champions. Professor Snape adds the opinion that the problem is Harry's fault, with his history of rule-breaking. In the midst of this crackling, tense scene, Dumbledore speaks: "'Did you put your name into the Goblet of Fire, Harry?' he asked calmly."[35]

The rendering of this scene in the film has been a topic of discussion—that is, displeasure—in the fandom since the movie was released.[36] Just today (July 25, 2016), a post appeared on the Facebook fandom page, "Doctor Who and the T. A. R. D. I. S.," about this topic.[37] It contained a screenshot of a Tumblr discussion thread[38] from November 2014, based on a meme originally found on a gamer fan site:[39]

*Whirls Snape out of the way
Did you

*Shoves Minerva in a wall
Put your name
*Shoves over a table aggressively
In the Goblet
*Grabs Harry and slams him into the wall
Of Fire!?!?!?1111?!?11132113591130583FERGEKLJRKGJGRLGJWRLKGV
   JLKJ G" Dumbledore asked calmly.

Another user commented below this (still part of the November 2014 post): "we're never gonna get over this, are we?"[40]

Another rendering of fan displeasure with this scene in the film of *Goblet of Fire* is a GIF of movie-Dumbledore striding over to Harry.[41] The GIF is headed with the quotation from the book: " 'Did you put your name into the Goblet of Fire, Harry?' he asked calmly." Over the GIF itself is the caption, "Harry! Did yah put yah name in da Goblet of Fiyah?!" The phonetic spelling of this line is clearly meant to critique its delivery as not calm at all. In the same vein, another meme includes an image of the page from the book with the word "calmly" circled in red.[42] The comments for this post include a link to a cartoon meme, "Book Dumbledore vs Movie Dumbledore," which demonstrates in its visual presentation a "calm" Book Dumbledore followed by an agitated Movie Dumbledore.[43] Yet another[44] accompanies the above-discussed GIF with the above-cited line from the book and the Rage Guy meme, followed by increasingly large versions of the word "calmly" to make clear the creator considers the movie's interpretation of this scene to be blatantly at odds with the book.[45] Another one "fixes" the problem by putting the question ("Harry, did you put your name in the Goblet of Fire?") over a movie still of Richard Harris as Dumbledore, so calm his eyes are nearly closed.[46]

Memes critiquing the movie's presentation of the "Did you put your name in the Goblet of Fire, Harry?" scene are clearly engaging in literary analysis. For one thing, we see the same subject addressed in other venues and formats. For another, the memes are not simply objecting that the scene is different from the book. Rather, they assert the change to the scene has important consequences for our perception of Dumbledore and his role in the scene, as well as Harry's reaction to and relationship with Dumbledore. Instead of being the lone calm presence in the midst of upset adults, as he is shown in the book, Dumbledore *becomes* one of the upset adults, undercutting both his character and our belief in his ability to remain an objective judge in this situation. While questioning Dumbledore does indeed become, in the later books, an important element of Harry's, and the reader's, development, in *Goblet*, Harry still trusts Dumbledore completely and unquestioningly. This hot-headed presentation of Dumbledore in the movie suggests Harry is foolish to continue to do so. The memes' critique highlights the central problem with the movie's portrayal of this scene.

Comparative Analysis of *Harry Potter* and Other Works

Some memes compare the *Harry Potter* series with other works, most commonly other works of fantasy. Some make detailed comparisons with a single, specific other work, such as a meme that presents a point-by-point analysis of four major aspects of *Harry Potter* and *Lord of the Rings* ("Mentor," "Best Friend," "Villain," and "Third Person"), with four sub-categories for each, providing a brief description of that element.[47] The meme then assigns a winner, loser, or tie in each sub-category and overall category. The supposed purpose of the meme is to determine whether *Harry Potter* or *Lord of the Rings* is better, but the meme assigns six wins, six losses, and four draws, ending with "Shit. That didn't settle anything, did it?" I suspect this result is precisely what the meme's creator meant it to be, concluding that both series are excellent and it is impossible to choose between them. The meme is a fine example of the detailed literary analysis that, by this point, we should not be surprised to find within this supposedly good-only-for-wasting-time internet genre. Many memes comparatively analyze *Harry Potter* and *Lord of the Rings*, and [48] there are likewise memes considering *Harry Potter* alongside *Star Wars*.[49]

Perhaps even more intriguing are those memes that cross-compare *Harry Potter* and multiple other works. In one, for instance, Harry and two other heroes (the manga ninja hero Naruto and Obi-wan Kenobi from *Star Wars*) are marshalled for comparison to Edward Cullen from the *Twilight* series, who appears decidedly out-classed:[50]

> [image of Naruto]: I kill rogue ninjas.
> [image of Obi-wan]: I kill Sith lords.
> [image of Harry Potter]: I kill dark wizards.
> [image of Edward Cullen]: I sparkle.

This pattern repeats in a number of cross-comparative memes: *Twilight* is nearly always referenced as a negative example and/or lesser work. This one, for instance, compares Edward to other heroes of fantasy, among them Harry:[51]

> [image of Gandalf]: Here are your missions, boys . . .
> [image of Frodo]: Frodo, destroy the Ring.
> [image of Harry]: Harry, destroy the Horcruxes.
> [image of Luke Skywalker]: Luke, bring balance to the Force.
> [image of Edward]: and Edward . . .
> [different image of Gandalf, looking weary]: just stop sparkling, my son.

From those two memes, it would seem Edward's sparkling is the chief criticism leveled at Twilight, but his use of his immortality is also critiqued, among other things.[52] Indeed, critique of *Twilight* in memes is widespread, as the "Still a Better Love Story than Twilight" meme[53] and the "Real Vampires Don't Sparkle" meme, among others, demonstrate.[54]

Perhaps the most fascinating cross-comparative memes, though, are those focusing upon female characters. Such memes almost universally present *Twilight* negatively. Indeed, when we look at critiques of Edward and Bella side by side, we might conclude that Edward gets off easy. He is criticized for being an inadequate vampire (the repeated criticism of his "sparkling") and for his unimaginative and somewhat creepy wasting of immortality by using it to repeat high school and date teenagers. Bella, on the other hand, is regularly criticized for being an utterly passive figure compared to other heroines of fantasy. One meme depicts the problem this way:[55]

> [image of Eowyn]: I will fight in this war . . .
> [image of Hermione]: I will save the Wizarding World . . .
> [image of Bella]: I'll just lay here and let my sparkling boyfriend do all
>   the work . . .

There are quite a few memes of this sort, comparing Bella to other women in fantasy (Hermione nearly always among them), which fall into two overall groups. The meme described above is representative of the first group, in which Bella's actions, or lack thereof, are critiqued. It is a basic example, with three images and an adequate but not expansively developed argument: Eowyn chooses to fight; Hermione chooses to fight; Bella chooses to let Edward fight.

Other examples build a more detailed case. This meme begins with a title, "Female Role Models in Y/A Fiction," signaling an organized, coherent argument will follow, and it does, by way of four examples:[56]

> [image of Hermione]: Hermione Granger.[57] It's cool to be smart. In a fight, brains are just as important as brawn.
> [image of Katniss]: Katniss Everdeen. You are not insignificant. By taking a stand against tyranny, you can create a spark that ignites a revolution and changes the world.
> [image of Annabeth]: Annabeth Chase. Winning requires strategy, not luck. Thinking, reasoning and careful planning will lead you to victory.
> [image of Bella]: lol i boinked a blood sucking demon but its cool cuz we got married n stuff.

It's worth noticing the strategies the meme uses to make its argument. Evidence-based argumentation is predominant, in the description of the first three characters and their actions, as if spoken by the character herself. However, when we get to Bella, the phrasing, capitalization, and spelling assigned to her imply a judgment. Not only does she not choose to act bravely, as the others do, but she might not actually be smart enough to do so. A similar judgment is reflected in the images chosen. For the first three examples, the images are positive and attractive; the movie still for Bella shows her with her eyes half-closed and her eyebrows furrowed. This meme, then, takes full advantage of the range of strategies available to the form in support of its argument. The argument is made by the visual as well as the text, and the text is varied in support of the argument. While professional literary critics would shy away from loading the dice quite so blatantly, evidence is nonetheless provided here for a recognizably literary argument, and we can certainly acknowledge the meme's marshalling of all available strategies while recognizing not all of them would be acceptable in professional literary critique.

Many more such memes exist, but these two illustrate the category.[58] The second group of memes that compare the female characters of *Harry Potter* to Bella Swan, along with those of other fantasy franchises, focus specifically on the female characters' reactions to losing their romantic male leads. As with the first category, there are dozens if not hundreds of examples, so we will look at an illustrative but not exhaustive set.

This meme compares Annabeth, Hermione, Katniss, and Bella, and how each of them react to losing their love:[59]

[drawn image of Annabeth]: Annabeth Chase: When this demigod thought for sure that she would lose her friend and true love to Rachel Dare, she still stuck through it all and fought to defeat the Titan of Time. This girl didn't let being hung up on a boy control her life.

[drawn image of Hermione, as portrayed in movies]: Hermione Granger: When this witch was abandoned by Ron Weasley in the Deathly Hallows, she was heartbroken. But she still stuck through it and never stopped trying to defeat the most evil wizard in the world. This girl didn't let being hung up on a boy control her life.

[drawn image of Katniss]: When in the Third Quarter Quell, Peeta was the only one she knew she could trust. When he was captured by the Capitol, she was devastated. But she still led the rebellion as the Mockingjay and never stopped fighting. This girl didn't let being hung up on a boy control her life.

[movie still image of Bella]: When Edward left Bella, she curled up into a little ball, spent her days away from him depressed (well, that wasn't really a difference), then jumped off a cliff. This girl let being hung up on a boy control her life.

I think something is wrong here.

This meme is approaching a mini five-paragraph essay. There's not a stated thesis at the beginning, but there are essentially four paragraphs, each of which have a clearly stated topic and provide evidence for that topic, and a fifth section that serves as the conclusion. Again, the meme's argument is not as detailed as it would be if it were delivered in a professional literary format, but there is clearly literary critique present. In this case, the argument that Bella's reaction to losing Edward, compared to Annabeth, Hermione, and Katniss's behavior in a similar situation, suggests her relationship to him is unhealthily dependent.

Similarly, this meme compares Ginny and Bella:[60]

[image of Ginny]: When Harry broke up with me for my safety, I tried to steal the sword of Gryffindor, I restarted DA with Neville and Luna to defy Snape's regime, and later fought during the Battle of Hogwarts.

[image of Harry]: That's my girl!

[image of Bella]: When Edward broke up with me for my safety, I become near comatose for months, and I purposely put myself in danger just to hear Edward's voice.

[image of Edward grimacing]

This one is interesting because it not only compares the female characters, with the assertion that Ginny's behavior is more admirable, but makes an argument about the possible, or perhaps desirable, reaction of the male characters. Harry, the meme argues, approves of Ginny's actions, as of course we see him do in the book. The last panel posits that Edward is revolted by Bella's co-dependent passivity, which is not necessarily supported by the text. Rather, this panel seems another component of the meme's argument: Bella's behavior is so extreme and unhealthy that Edward *should* have been revolted by it.

A set of related memes address this issue as well. Intriguingly, while some characters used to highlight Bella's shortcomings in the wake of Edward's departure change, Hermione remains a constant. One meme compares Bella to Hermione and Daenerys Targaryen, arguing that when the love of each woman's life left her, Hermione and Daenerys continued their fights, while Bella lay unmoving for months.[61] Another meme[62] is identical to the previous one, except it substitutes Rose Tyler for Daenerys, while yet another one uses Leia in the third panel.[63] However, the meme I want to look at in detail from this subset incorporates the Leia version of the meme and adds an additional panel:[64]

[image of Hermione]: When the love of Hermione's life left her, she continued to search for the keys to destroying the world's most powerful dark wizard.

[image of Bella]: When the love of Bella's life left her, she curled up in the fetal position, went numb for months, and then jumped off a cliff.

[image of Leia]: Bitches, please.[65] When the love of Leia's life was encased in carbonite by Boba Fett and Darth Vader and taken to Jabba the Hut, she disguised herself as a bounty hunter and rescued him.

[image of Captain Janeway]: Saved the ship. Pwned the Borg. Saved Earth, fuck it, saved the Alpha Quadrant. Didn't need to be motivated by 'the love of her life.' Someone get this woman some goddamn coffee.

This is an example of a one-upmanship meme, in which a meme is picked up by another reader/creator and added to; the others in this set are as well, each adding to a meme that originally consisted of the two panels of Hermione and Bella. Such interacting memes, sparking one another in new directions, are a fairly common occurrence, accomplishing the same sort of critique using different comparisons: Hermione, Daenerys, Leia, and Rose react to the loss of their beloved actively, whereas Bella reacts passively. The final meme, however, puts a different twist on the discussion, introducing Captain Janeway as a comparison and arguing she has impressive and worthwhile accomplishments without being inspired by the loss of love. Setting aside whether we entirely accept the assertion,[66] it is an interesting and at least partially true argument that deepens the feminist approach of the original, positing that while Ginny and the others are certainly more admirable than Bella, a more admirable figure still might be Janeway, who stands as her own person.[67] The meme engages in literary critique, and in conversation with peers, quite similar to the operation of professional literary criticism.

Conclusion

I have argued throughout this chapter that many memes, not just a few isolated examples, demonstrate thoughtful literary critique. Memes consider elements such as character, plot, and worldbuilding. They engage in evaluative critique. They compare movies with their sources in books, and make arguments about why those changes affect how we perceive characters. Memes engage in comparative analysis of works. I have shown how memes demonstrate these types of literary critique with *Harry Potter*, but the same is true for other works.

Meme-based literary criticism, as I have worked to illustrate, handles the same types of concerns, takes the same sort of approaches, and often comes to the same conclusions as that of professional critics. I have stressed this point because it feels necessary to do so, to help us in the academic world take meme-based and other online types of critique seriously, not because the creators of such memes use professional literary work as a yardstick to know if they're "getting it right" or because they are trying to beat us at our own game. There's no evidence that meme creators consider academic literary criticism at all, either positively or negatively. Meme creators produce literary criticism voluntarily, as part of their entertainment life, not because they are in graduate school or need tenure, but because they are interested in and have engaged thoughtfully with a work or works.

This voluntary participation in the world of the mind in general and with literature in particular is worth pausing to consider. Not only are people doing plot analysis and looking for logical inconsistencies in world-building in their free time, they do so not as isolated individuals but as part of a community. On most meme sites, anyone can create and submit memes, but not all memes are featured by the websites. Most have a voting system that factors into determining which memes become featured (often called "making the front page"). Memegenerator, for instance, has ranked categories of memes, depending upon how they were received by the community ("God Tier," "Demigod Tier," "Legendary Tier," "Top Tier," "Fascinating Tier," "Meh Tier," "Lame Tier," and "Fail Tier"). Memes are—dare we say it?—peer-reviewed. We see community input in the interactive development of memes as well. Memes often respond to one another, such as the last set of memes discussed above, comparing various female characters in SFF fandoms and weighing their relative merits as strong characters. The longer the conversation goes on, the more we see interpretative consensus: the Time-Turner is a plothole, Bella Swan does not hold a candle to other women in SFF, and Michael Gambon is a lesser Dumbledore. You can, of course, find dissenting voices, but their rarity underscores that fan opinion has coalesced.

It is time to acknowledge the existence of a sophisticated web-based community of literary critique, largely disconnected from the academic literary world. There is a growing body of scholarship about what is called "citizen science." According to Andrea Wiggins and Kevin Crowston's 2011 article, "From Conservation to Crowdsourcing: A Typology of Citizen Science," citizen science is "a form of research collaboration involving members of the public in scientific research projects to address real-world problems."[68] Memes (and other forms of online critique) function as crowdsourced literary criticism. Anyone can submit a meme, successful memes are those chosen by the community, memes are often created as part of an ongoing conversation about the work(s), and consensus emerges as that conversation continues. Memes and other online forms of critique are "citizen humanities."

Recognizing the emergence and existence of citizen humanities should come as something of a reassurance. It is often argued that the internet is making us stupid. Nicholas Carr's *The Shallows: What the Internet is Doing to our Brains* suggests our use of the web is decreasing our attention span and destroying our ability to engage in projects that require long-term thought. In everyday conversation, and perhaps ironically through internet-enabled communication such as Facebook and Twitter, such assertions are repeated as if they are established fact. I hear colleagues state categorically that students nowadays refuse—nay, cannot—read long books because their attention spans have been wiped out by television and movies, fast cuts, short BuzzFeed style listicles, and yes, memes. We should be skeptical in general about such assertions. Older generations have an observable history of panicking about the next generation's technology; perhaps the most infamous example in (relatively) recent years is the 1954 Senate sub-committee hearings about whether comic books cause juvenile delinquency.[69] The same technology that makes listicles possible also enables fanfiction running into the hundreds of thousands of words (the best known example in the area of Harry Potter being *My Immortal*), which should at least give us pause before too readily accepting assertions about the loss of our attention span.[70]

Which is not to say that the web is the utopia we were once promised it would be. Two decades ago, as the internet emerged, technological utopians argued that web-based interaction would be free of gender, racial, social class, and ageist biases, that the internet would provide a place for people to converse freely without the influence of advertising and other lenses of capitalism, and without the need for intermediaries, moderators, or gatekeepers.[71] The assumption was, of course, that we would converse in good faith and good behavior, wanting to hear and learn from one another. We've learned otherwise. People remain people, even online, and they bring their biases with them. Trolling, harassment, bullying, and threats are enormous problems.[72] But the same web that facilitates swatting and doxing, issues death threats against female critics of game culture, and mercilessly torments Leslie Jones also makes possible the emergence and development of widespread, voluntary participation in literary culture and critique. The internet is probably not making us stupider. It might be making us more likely to participate in movements, good and bad, by making such participation easier. While we come to terms with the reality that the web is not the venue of earnest and open interaction that its early adherents hoped for, and we struggle with undesirable outcomes like Twitter harassment and death threats, it is worth acknowledging that while the web is not a utopia, it's not a dystopia either. For literary scholars in particular, the use of memes to engage a wide readership in a literary conversation is deeply encouraging. We've been told the humanities are dying. They are not. There is pressure on the humanities within academia, but on the web, literary criticism—citizen humanities—is thriving.

Notes

1. To avoid any potential copyright issues, I have not included images of the memes here but rather described them. "The Most Interesting Man in the World," *Meme Generator*, September 1, 2016, https://memegenerator.net/instance/66698802.

2. *Proceedings of the Seventh International AAAI Conference on Weblogs and Social Media* (2013), 100–109.

3. Cambridge: MIT Press, 2013.

4. See my chapter "The Wisdom of the Crowd: Internet Memes and *The Hobbit: An Unexpected Journey*" in *The Hobbit and Tolkien's Mythology: Essays on Revisions and Influences*, ed. Bradford Lee Eden (Jefferson, NC: McFarland, 2014), which relatedly argues that memes about *The Hobbit: An Unexpected Journey* provide critical analysis of the movie's plot and characters.

5. J. K. Rowling (New York: Scholastic, 1999).

6. *Know Your Meme*, September 1, 2016, http://knowyourmeme.com/memes/philosoraptor.

7. *Quick Meme*, September 1, 2016, www.quickmeme.com/meme/359fsp.

8. *Quick Meme*, September 1, 2016, www.quickmeme.com/meme/3qwgv8.

9. *Quick Meme*, September 1, 2016, www.quickmeme.com/meme/3ogpjv.

10. *Know Your Meme*, September 1, 2016, http://knowyourmeme.com/memes/scumbag-hat.

11. *Know Your Meme*, September 1, 2016, http://knowyourmeme.com/memes/snowclone.

12. *Know Your Meme*, September 1, 2016, http://knowyourmeme.com/memes/scumbag-steve.

13. *Quick Meme*, September 1, 2016, www.quickmeme.com/meme/3q36rt.

14. *Flickr*, September 23, 2012, www.flickr.com/photos/47804730@N03/8017138531.

15. "Talk: Marauder's Map," *Harry Potter Wiki*, September 1, 2016, http://harrypotter.wikia.com/wiki/Talk:Marauder's_Map; "Why couldn't Harry or anybody else see Peter Pettigrew," *Science Fiction and Fantasy Stack Exchange*, September1,2016,http://scifi.stackexchange.com/questions/11447/why-couldnt-harry-or-anybody-else-see-peter-pettigrew-aka-scabbers-on-the-marau; "I found a plothole," *Reddit*, September 1, 2016, www.reddit.com/r/harrypotter/comments/1698oh/i_found_a_plothole_didnt_fred_george_see_peter/;

"Harry Potter Discussion," *Goodreads,* September 1, 2016, www.goodreads.com/topic/show/1259051-plot-hole.

16. "When examining the Marauder's Map," *Quora,* September 1, 2016, www.quora.com/When-examining-the-Marauder%E2%80%99s-Map-how-did-Fred-and-George-fail-to-notice-that-their-brother-Ron-had-another-man-Peter-Pettigrew-in-bed-with-him-every-night-or-that-Voldemort-was-always-beside-Quirrel-in-the-first-book.

17. Bill Bradley, " 'Harry Potter' Has One Huge Plot Hole You Might've Missed," *The Huffington Post,* May 28, 2015, www.huffingtonpost.com/2015/05/28/harry-potter-plot-hole_n_7447500.html; http://hellogiggles.com/harry-potter-plot-hole/.

18. "Why Fred and George Didn't See Voldemort and Pettigrew On The Marauder's Map?" *Potter Plotholes,* September 1, 2016, http://potter-plotholes.tumblr.com/post/112134776057/fred-george-weasley-marauders-map-voldemort-pettigrew.

19. "Gets Invisibility Cloak," *Humoar,* September 2, 2016, www.humoar.com/gets-invisibility-cloak-doesnt-go-into-girls-showers/.

20. "Gets Invisibility Cloak, Doesn't Go Into Girls Shower," *Quick Meme,* September 16, 2016, www.quickmeme.com/meme/3qz40v.

21. "Gets Invisibility Cloak, Goes to the Library," *Meme Generator,* September 2, 2016, https://memegenerator.net/instance/53202987.

22. "Can Use Magic to Clean Up Any Mess Instantly," *Pinterest,* September 2, 2016, www.pinterest.com/pin/157977899399801841/.

23. "Could clean up Hogwarts using magic," *Quick Meme,* September 6, 2016, www.quickmeme.com/meme/3qbezg.

24. *Wizards vs. Muggles: Essays on Identity in the Harry Potter Universe,* ed. Christopher Bell (Jefferson, NC: McFarland, 2016), 78.

25. J. K. Rowling, *Harry Potter and the Sorcerer's Stone* (New York: Scholastic, 1998), 100.

26. "The Time Turner," *MemeCenter,* September 6, 2016, www.memecenter.com/fun/1555081/time-turner.

27. "I'm sorry about your parents," *Quick Meme,* September 6, 2016, www.quickmeme.com/meme/35rfd2.

28. "Lets Hermione use time turner," *Quick Meme,* September 6, 2016, www.quickmeme.com/meme/35fw92.

29. "I Don't Get Harry Potter," *Tumblr,* September 6, 2016, http://idontgethp.tumblr.com/page/2.

30. "Time Turner Situations I Could Have Been Used For," *WeKnowMemes,* February 1, 2012, http://weknowmemes.com/2012/02/time-turner-situations-i-could-have-been-used-for/.

31. *Harry Potter and the Cursed Child*, released during the writing of this chapter, provides more information about the working of Time-Turners, most of which seems intended to deflect or refute critiques that the Time-Turners are a plot hole. It is worth mentioning that some of the suggestions (going back and killing Voldemort, for instance) are addressed by this additional information, but some (such as the Minister using them for investigative purposes) are not. In any case, it is fascinating that the new work contains elements that inevitably seem aimed at addressing this criticism. J. K. Rowling, Jack Thorne, and John Tiffany, *Harry Potter and the Cursed Child, Parts 1 & 2* (New York: Arthur A. Levine, 2016).

32. "Harry Potter Morals," *MemeCenter*, September 6, 2016, www.meme center.com/fun/897027/harry-potter-morals.

33. "True Story," *KnowYourMeme*, September 6, 2016, http://knowyour meme.com/memes/true-story.

34. J. K. Rowling, *Harry Potter and the Goblet of Fire* (New York: Scholastic, 2000).

35. Rowling, *Goblet of Fire*, 276.

36. For instance, this topic is first in the *BuzzFeed* listicle, "17 Things that Harry Potter Fans Still Aren't Over." September 10, 2015, www.buzzfeed.com /stephanierhesa/17-things-that-harry-potter-fans-still-arent-over-1tkri.

37. "Dr. Who and the T.A.R.D.I.S," *Facebook*, July 25, 2016, www.facebook .com/Doctor-Who-and-the-TARDIS-276710412383657/?pnref=story.

38. Discussion threads are not, strictly speaking, memes, according to the definition of memes as captioned images. However, screenshots of discussion threads often circulate on meme sites and tend to serve the same functions as captioned image memes.

39. "Whirls Snape Out of the Way," *Smash 4 Link Player*, September 7, 2016, http://mycastiel.co.vu/post/99930594303/whirls-snape-out-of-the-way-did-you-shoves.

40. Indeed, an image of this same Tumblr discussion thread is included in the BuzzFeed listicle mentioned above.

41. "Harry! Did yah put yah name in da Goblet of Fiyah?!" *Lindsay Favreau*, June 30, 2014, http://lindseyfavreau.tumblr.com/post/90378699861.

42. "Well, Harry?" *Imgur*, April 21, 2013, http://imgur.com/gallery/e7UT02F.

43. "Book Dumbledore vs Movie Dumbledore," *Imgur*, September 7, 2016, http://i.imgur.com/OFGFoA6.jpg.

44. "Did you put your name into the Goblet of Fire, Harry?" *Tumblr*, September 7, 2016, http://29.media.tumblr.com/tumblr_m1z5csFMUqlrsfiixol_400.gif.

45. "Rage Guy," *Know Your Meme*, September 7, 2016, http://knowyourmeme .com/memes/rage-guy-fffffuuuuuuuuu.

46. "leela-summers," *Tumblr*, September 7, 2016, http://66.media.tumblr. com/35128c1147c5fc7e4a03b9c2c03be088/tumblr_ndydqnqYxS1qcvd0oo4_ 540.png.

47. "Lotr Vs Harry Potter," *MemeCenter*, September 7, 2016, www.me-mecenter.com/fun/191137/lotr-vs-harry-potter.

48. "Lotr and Harry Potter Similarities," *MemeCenter*, September 7, 2016, www.memecenter.com/fun/942326/lotr-and-harry-potter-similarities. Another version of this one adds an image of Rowling writing, with the caption, "I'm sure no one will notice." Clearly the creator of that meme believes that HP is a knock-off of LOTR; "LOTR vs. Harry Potter," *9Gag.Com*, September 7, 2016, http://9gag.com/gag/4278294.

49. *Harry Potter vs Star Wars*, September 7, 2016, https://mir-s3-cdn-cf .behance.net/project_modules/disp/9fc1fb21127611.562fbf0be5d39.jpg; "The Uncle," *Tumblr*, September 7, 2016, http://66.media.tumblr.com/tumblr_ln-vqc4zKuH1qk2jwqo3_1280.jpg; "VS," *Tumblr*, September 7, 2016, http://media. tumblr.com/tumblr_loyenoCpmf1qh5nc9.jpg.

50. *I kill rogue ninjas*, September 7, 2016, http://img0.joyreactor.com/pics /post/Harry-Potter-Star-Wars-Naruto-edward-cullen-199656.jpeg.

51. https://s-media-cache-ak0.pinimg.com/564x/ab/1c/73/ab1c732cc8dc 14094f8640c1c800e764.jpg

52. For instance: https://s-media-cache-ak0.pinimg.com/236x/9c/f3/e3/9cf 3e323dd4a5b88950e8d6625c4f27f.jpg

53. http://knowyourmeme.com/memes/still-a-better-love-story-than-twilight

54. http://knowyourmeme.com/memes/real-vampires-don-t-sparkle

55. www.memecenter.com/fun/95780/LOTR-Harry-Potter-twilight-0

56. http://cheezburger.com/7352670464; The logo for each franchise is also included, between the character image and its caption.

57. The characters' names are given in a larger font than the descriptive text.

58. For example: https://s-media-cache-ak0.pinimg.com/236x/68/33/90/68 3390554127ab1d00bd43b8d42f146e.jpg; www.pinterest.com/pin/44543421937082 0238/; https://s-media-cache-ak0.pinimg.com/736x/5a/74/3d/5a743d33d83348 b221cb3eaffd357565.jpg; http://kmeaghan.deviantart.com/art/Real-Heroines-16958 2866

59. https://s-media-cache-ak0.pinimg.com/236x/c7/93/bf/c793bf230ac8ef 26b7905609a6391bd6.jpg

60. www.memecenter.com/fun/180507/wright-girl-for-harry

61. https://s-media-cache-ak0.pinimg.com/236x/99/10/71/991071bb7cae57f6701578dc0dd53fcb.jpg

62. https://s-media-cache-ak0.pinimg.com/236x/58/74/c6/5874c632ba366097b4bc98da900f7559.jpg

63. https://pics.onsizzle.com/Facebook-Submitted-by-Michael-Lake-464c43.png

64. www.memes.com/img/370730

65. As Know Your Meme explains, "Bitch, Please," is itself a meme, "used when someone claims to be superior at something, but well deserves to be countered by someone else who is way superior," September 12, 2016, http://knowyourmeme.com/memes/bitch-please.

66. I don't, at least in Hermione's case. It seems to me that she isn't so much inspired by Ron's abandonment as that she is determined to stick to the plan she developed with Harry, despite Ron's desertion.

67. I would accept the claim for Leia and Rose, and possibly Ginny.

68. Andrea Wiggins and Kevin Crowston, "From Conservation to Crowd-sourcing: A Typology of Citizen Science," HICSS 2011, Proceedings of the 2011, 44th Hawaii International Conference on Social Sciences, 1–10.

69. https://archive.org/stream/juveniledelinque54unit/juveniledelinque54unit_djvu.txt

70. http://myimmortalrehost.webs.com/

71. https://www.prospectmagazine.co.uk/magazine/morozov-web-no-utopia-twenty-years-short-history-internet

72. See, for instance, Whitney Phillips's *This is Why We Can't Have Nice Things: Mapping the Relationship Between Online Trolling and Mainstream Culture* (Cambridge, MA: MIT Press, 2015).

7

Taking Tea at Elephant House

How Potterheads Researched *Harry Potter* During a Fandom-Focused Study Abroad

Liza Potts, Kelly Turner, and Emily Dallaire

Introduction

Across physical and digital spaces, people participate in memory-making activities to enact their fandoms and engage with others as a form of adaption, shaping and extending their experiences with their fan communities. This merging of collective memory and participatory culture, herein referred to as *participatory memory*, can often lead to spaces where such interaction is contested or even prohibited. In others, this participation is welcomed, celebrated, or even commodified. For fans of *Harry Potter*, examples of these spaces of memory in the United Kingdom include Elephant House in the city of Edinburgh, the "Making of *Harry Potter*" Warner Brothers Studio Tour near London, and Platform 9¾ in King's Cross Station in London. Participation in these spaces exemplifies how participatory fan culture represents an important new form of adaption in the digital age.

When we examine participatory spaces, we can ask several questions to explore the social, political, and economic implications of participatory memory. How do fans respond in physical spaces that are sacred to their fandoms? Where can fans participate and where can they simply consume their fandom? How are these physical spaces different from the digital ones, with regards to participation, empowerment, and interpretation by the fans? And, one of the key questions for this book chapter:

Much like fans of Quidditch, fans of *Harry Potter* are eager to adapt and adopt their fandom's icons and show pride in their community.

What happens to adaptation when memory-making is in play for the fans of *Harry Potter*?

For the students and the faculty leader of a 2014 study abroad to the United Kingdom, these questions were paramount as they studied how fans interacted in digital and physical spaces. Their challenge was to consider these interactions, as well as how producers allowed for or prohibited certain kinds of participation. In this chapter, we discuss the framing of this fandom-focused study abroad, the experiences of these students, and how these interactive fan experiences were used as pedagogical tools for understanding participatory culture.

An important part of this study abroad experience involves showing students how fandoms operate like miniature or micro-cultures; similar activities that create shared experiences, stories, and histories help develop cultures more broadly. Exploring spaces of memory for these micro-cultures helped students to see influences across the digital and built environment. These links are important to help students extend their understanding of culture more generally, while connecting with the topic of *Harry Potter* specifically. Such moves help to contextualize their studies and let them make broader connections to the world.

As they reflect on this experience as a whole, Emily and Kelly find that their deep dive into *Harry Potter* fandom helped them reach a better understanding of cultures and communities. Heading into the study abroad program as fans, they were focused on *Harry Potter* online fandom. By researching and analyzing how knowledge-sharing contributes to and encourages fandom growth during the study abroad trip, Emily and Kelly were able to understand broader implications of how communities are sustained through this kind of curation work. By focusing on a variety of spaces that fans visit and participate in, they were able to examine how crowdsourced knowledge evolves over time. Through their analysis of these spaces, they were able to pinpoint the convergence of media and fan connections across platforms, countries, and perspectives.

In this chapter, we examine issues of memory and adaptation for fans of *Harry Potter* by presenting a reflection on the research study abroad experiences of Emily Dallaire and Kelly Turner, along with their study abroad leader, Liza Potts. We begin with a discussion about the construction of this research-focused study abroad program, move into an overview of memory studies, and then open up a dialogue among the three authors. This dialogue includes questions from Liza that help frame the discussion, with answers supplied by Emily and Kelly. We end with a short reflection and consideration of how the 2014 study abroad trip influenced the 2016 trip. By presenting this information in this way, we illustrate how study abroad trips to examine micro-cultures can help students better understand how adaptation works in built environments. And, in the case of *Harry Potter*, how fans can influence and alter these experiences—and thus create their own adaptations of the canon. The work of participatory fan culture as adaptation is a reason to approach this topic through the discursive exploration of student fan experience.

Framing the Fandom-Focused Study Abroad Program

In considering how to create a study abroad program, the faculty leader wanted to find a way to engage her students, talk about a new concept called *experience architecture,* and follow her own research interests in participatory memory. Experience architecture refers to the ways in which we research, design, and develop user experiences in the built and digital environments from the perspective of the humanities. Think of this term as similar to the ways in which computer scientists deploy human-computer interaction, and art programs use design thinking to talk about how we build people-focused technologies. The leader, Liza Potts, launched the study abroad in 2014 with the idea that she would give the students a full buffet of choices, from examining historically significant monuments to engaging with fan-produced spaces. She quickly recognized that the majority of her students gravitated towards spaces produced for or by fans of television, literature, and film. This moment helped her shift gears to focus more on her students' fandoms, and it helped her recognize how valuable these fandoms were for her students' ability to create a sense of community abroad. The experiences on the 2014 study abroad trip helped Liza develop a second version of this trip in 2016, solely focused on popular culture fandoms.

In selecting a location for the study abroad, the United Kingdom emerged as a prime location choice, given the recent popularity of several books, television shows, and films set there. In addition, historical monuments and memory-spaces dedicated to royalty and world wars made it an appealing spot as well. Given the students' interests, the (somewhat) familiarity of the language, and the (somewhat) recognizable culture, the U.K. was an easy choice. Liza set out to ensure major locations of interest to fans were visited, such as filming sites, museums, and fan-directed spaces of memory. In addition to these visits, several students arranged their own pilgrimages to specific sites, such as the "*Doctor Who* Experience" in Cardiff Bay, the Warner Brothers Studio Tour for the "Making of *Harry Potter*" outside of London, and Shakespeare's birthplace in Stratford-upon-Avon.

In shaping the summer student experience, Liza turned to the literature on pedagogy and study abroad. Michigan State University (MSU) has one of the largest study abroad programs in the country, so there were many resources available to her in the form of workshops, manuals, and support personnel. There are also key research projects on study abroad maintained at MSU. In particular, the History of Education Abroad project provides a wealth of material for understanding study abroad innovations at the institution.[1]

There are a multitude of topics and choices that professors can make when building a study abroad program. Thankfully, a body of work exists about building and running these programs. This research includes well-cited work by Anderson et al. on cultural sensitivity,[2] Dwyer's research into the duration of programs,[3] and Williams's work on intercultural communication skills.[4] Liza specifically wanted to do something around the topic of participatory memory, looking at memory-making activities by mourners, celebrants, and fans at various spaces of memory throughout Europe. She consulted the "Overseas Study at Indiana University Bloomington" guide from 2009, which contains sections on participation, student gains, and academic outcomes. That research points to data stating that the majority of study abroad students are women, which helped in her program planning, as her study abroad program indeed had a majority of women participants.[5] Realizing that she needed to center the program in a handful of cities, she consulted research on locations and space for study abroad programs. Specifically, the 2010 work of Eric Freedman helped her recognize how facilitating such a study abroad experience "requires a significant commitment of time, creativity, and energy" while providing her "opportunities for professional development, research, and curriculum enrichment."[6]

Brian D. Ballentine's 2015 work on creativity and study abroad points to the work of scholars who are making study abroad a key part of their curriculum to help their students think creatively and learn about the world around them, such as Michael Salvo and Tammy Conard-Salvo at Purdue, and Rich Rice at Texas Tech.[7] Rather than asking students to assimilate into a culture, Ballentine points to the need for biculturalism—a deliberate attempt to identify with the home and host cultures—as "the desired acculturation strategy, and integrative complexity and its associated creativity are among the desired learning outcomes."[8] This kind of thought leadership is permeating many of our study abroad programs today.

Focusing on collective memory, we read from different scholars researching memory studies. Barbie Zelizer's 1995 work on collective memory studies is a foundational work for those of us studying rhetoric, narrative, and memory.[9] Her work on Holocaust studies and collective memory formed the baseline for us to examine spaces of memory. Students also read from the classic *On Collective Memory*, by Maurice Halbwachs, to think about cognition, memory, and imagery.[10] Finally, *The Collective Memory Reader* provided readings on the concepts of canon and archives by Jan Assmann, museums as memory-making spaces by Theodor W. Adorno, and film and popular memory by Michel Foucault.[11] Taken together, these readings gave students a better understanding of what memory studies is about, and how they might extend these ideas into their own study abroad projects.

Finally, we examined the work of scholars in participatory culture and fan studies to learn about these concepts and recent research practices. Henry Jenkins's twentieth anniversary edition of his foundational work originally published in 1992, *Textual Poachers*, provides an outline for understanding the basis of fan culture.[12] As our students have discovered, at the core of a fan community is a basic need for fans to express themselves. Fans establish groups and relate to each other through pooling knowledge, resources, and creativity, encouraging engagement in meaningful conversations around a particular subject. Leaning on the work of Matt Hills[13] and Ross Garner,[14] who explore concepts such as cult geographies and paratextual framing strategies respectively, we can better perceive the inspiration to be found in spaces such as Cardiff Bay (for *Doctor Who*), London (*Sherlock Holmes*), and Edinburgh (*Harry Potter*). Studying the work of Suzanne Scott, we can understand how "as convergence culture increasingly affects media production and consumption, fan-producers are contending with both intricate new storytelling matrices and the persistent cycles of consumption these narratives encourage."[15] Fandom ecosystems and cultures, formed through tight-knit communities and nurtured online, encourage creativity and fan-made work through knowledge sharing and discussion within these fan circles. Fan communities that trace themselves through the convergence cultures of literature, film, television, comics, and games not only provide spaces for fans to commemorate and remember their experiences about their favorite stories, but also create a space to stimulate intellectual discussions between fans and producers.

In the following sections, the authors present a research-based reflection and discussion of the 2014 study abroad program. Focusing primarily on participatory memory and *Harry Potter* fandom, the authors discuss the work of the study abroad, their own work as fans, and the insights they gained from learning, participating, and engaging with these memory-making spaces in the United Kingdom.

Preparing for the Study Abroad Journey

In preparing for the study abroad, students were asked to select a fandom and pick from a set of readings on fandom, memory, and semiotics. Next, they were asked to take a deep dive into the digital spaces where fans discuss, debate, and celebrate their fandoms. They were asked to pay particular attention to spaces where fans catalog, describe, and map public physical spaces of memory in the areas we were going to be visiting. For most students, this meant learning more about their fandoms as they were embodied in spaces in London. For other students, this meant planning side trips outside of the city.

In deciding on side trips, Kelly and Emily considered Jenkins's view that "there are questions we can only answer by examining our own emotional experiences with forms of culture that matter to us."[16] They felt they could only begin to understand their own stance and experiences in the fandom by reflecting on their interactions within the fan community itself and deeply immersing themselves in the culture. They hoped to do this work at two sites of memory: Elephant House in Edinburgh, the tea room where J. K. Rowling wrote some of *Harry Potter*, and the Warner Brothers Studio Tour for the "Making of *Harry Potter*" outside of London. The following sections include excerpts from interviews with Emily and Kelly reflecting on their study abroad experiences with their instructor, Liza.

Question: What were your understandings of the Harry Potter *fandom before leaving for the study abroad trip?*

We both grew up reading the books but didn't get into the digital side of the *Harry Potter* fandom, such as digital forums and social media communities, until our late teens and early twenties. As our interest grew, the exposure through digital forums and online communities expanded our views and opinions of the *Harry Potter* world and connected us with other fans around the world. The *Harry Potter* fandom grew with digital media and allowed us to share our love of *Harry Potter* across the globe; we came to the realization later on that we had become members of and contributors to the global fandom. Kelly's first realization of this was when the last movie, *Harry Potter and the Deathly Hallows: Part 2,* premiered in London. She remembers watching the live stream from her house, the swarms of people chattering with excitement, the entire cast arriving on the red carpet—and then J. K. Rowling herself. She vividly remembers Rowling's speech, and crying her eyes out in front of her computer screen. That moment was so special for Kelly as a fan because even though she couldn't be there, she was able to experience the last formal gathering of the actors that brought the story to life as well as hear from the author that started it all.

Question: Did you figure out where you would visit before you left? What references did you use to track these places down? Why these references?

We were interested in the distinction between spaces that were strictly connected to the books versus the films. First, we looked into physical places such as Platform 9¾, King's Cross, Millennium Bridge, Warner Brothers Studio Tour for the "Making of *Harry Potter*," Elephant House, and *Harry Potter* walking tours around London. We decided not to do the walking tours because we wanted to be in control of how and when we experienced the spaces. Essentially, we could do the walking tours for free—we had the domain knowledge and we knew enough from fans online.

Diving into the digital world, we looked at Tumblr tags, fan accounts, and reviews of these spaces to see what people were happy, upset, or pleased about while they visited them. For example, perusing the TripAdvisor reviews for the Warner Brothers Studio Tour led to a fascinating spectrum of fans and critics. These accounts were more geared towards the traveler and the tourist, whereas digging through the Tumblr tags for the Studio Tour gave more of a fan's viewpoint of their visit. Both sites gave us valuable insights into what people were most engaged with in these spaces. Through these accounts, we learned which places were touristy, preparing us for the crowds we would find there. We also learned how film fans were drawn to the heavy presence of props and sets from the films at the Warner Brothers Studio Tour.

Before we left, we outlined the spaces we wanted to visit, but we didn't schedule anything. We didn't really estimate the volume of *Harry Potter* spaces in the city or how much we had to see. We planned to go to Elephant House, Platform 9¾, and the Studio Tour together, but we were also going to tackle spaces that were movie-exclusive on a self-guided tour, such as the space used as the Leaky Cauldron, Millennium Bridge, and Westminster Station. For some spaces, we actually planned additional visits, since we knew there would be heavy traffic and/or it was an important site, such as Platform 9¾. We planned on visiting at least four times: once for ourselves as fans; once with a tour for the experience; once for observation as a researcher; and once more, an after hours visit, when the public spaces were closed but still available for viewing.

Experiencing *Harry Potter* in the United Kingdom

In the interest of being thorough, Emily and Kelly invested time in researching their fandom and fans before leaving for the study abroad trip. While they possessed a fair amount of knowledge about the subject itself, they were not as knowledgeable about other people's experiences with the series. They wanted to use this study abroad to reflect on their own fan journeys online through Tumblr blogs and in person at conventions, and then trace journeys taken by other fans to compare their experiences. During the UK visit, the students rapidly noticed that physical spaces impacted them more than they'd thought, leading them to want to explore more information posted online by other fans to see which spaces were the most visited and interesting to focus on. Turning to digital fan communities such as

MuggleNet, Leaky Cauldron, fan blogs, and Pinterest, the students delved into fan and media perceptions of the series. They wanted to refresh their memories about the finer details of the book series and the films in order to fully perceive the differences in translation from page to screen to physical space.

Through their readings of Henry Jenkins, they were able to gain a more nuanced understanding of media convergence. By stepping back and putting their research goggles on before their fan goggles, they were able to look at fandom in a critical, productive, thought-provoking way while still maintaining the significance of their experiences as fans. They were able to see what Jenkins meant when he asserted that "media convergence is more than simply a technological shift. Convergence alters the relationship between existing technologies, industries, markets, genres and audiences."[17]

Question: How did you examine the Harry Potter *fandom as researchers and fans? How do you handle this dichotomy?*

Approaching this project as fans, we understood that opinions and views about the series differ from person to person, and so we expected fan experiences would most likely differ from space to space. In regards to the project, we made sure we were mindful of other's experiences as we became careful observers in each space and not just focused on our own experiences. We had to take off our fan goggles and try to experience these spaces without the fan filter. However, we knew it was important not to remove our perspectives as fans altogether—we needed that emotional investment in order to dig deeper and reflect more genuinely. This experience forced us to look at each space in two different ways, as a researcher and as a fan. We ended up visiting spaces multiple times in an effort to not restrict the space to one memory or experience either.

Question: What was your experience like during your study abroad? What spaces of memory worked and why? What was it like when the spaces didn't work? What patterns did you notice, as researchers, fans, and students?

Our whole experience of study abroad revolved around duality: fan and research experiences, physical and digital spaces, and even the dual existence of the books and films. Perhaps the most important has been the duality of our experiences before our research started and after. Our research has impacted the way we view the *Harry Potter* fandom, but the spaces that created the biggest impression on us allowed fans to participate and create personalized memories.

The spaces that "worked" allowed fans to not only participate but also create a personalized, uninhibited experience for themselves. While the Warner Brothers Studio Tour of the "Making of *Harry Potter*" includes a guided portion at the beginning to control crowd numbers, in the rest of the space, fans are free to roam and experience on their own. Due to scheduling issues, we visited the "Making of *Harry Potter*" Studio Tour separately, which allowed us to compare our individual experiences. Kelly went alone, while Emily went with a group. Throughout her time at the studio tour, Emily was able to form friendships and swap stories with people who loved the movies and books, as well as to share the space and weigh the significance of certain artifacts, sets, and props with others. While Kelly explored the space alone, she was able to take her time perusing the grounds and deeply reflect on her experience as an individual. Because she was on her own, Kelly was more aware of how others interacted with the sets presented on the tour. For example, she observed a woman who sat in the corner of an exhibit room and knitted what looked like a scarf. When Kelly looked at her, she simply beamed, as if this was the best way to spend her day. She was content just to be in this space with other fans.

For us, the ability to create an impression and make a mark on the space held the most value in terms of participation as both fans and researchers. At Elephant House, we were able to visit a place that has become a memory space for many *Harry Potter* fans. Since Rowling wrote a lot of *Harry Potter* in this café, Elephant House is considered the birthplace of the series—a sacred space offering an unparalleled connection with the author herself. In particular, the single-toilet bathroom has become a central site of fandom. We had the opportunity to add our names to the other thousands on the bathroom wall. Many of the scrawls covering the walls include thank-you notes to Rowling. The visit to the space was crucial to us not only as fans but also as researchers—we were able to literally see the history of participation in *Harry Potter* fandom over the years. It was magical.

Places that were not considered active "fan spaces" did not allow for a good opportunity for fans to participate. We found that the Millennium Bridge, where an infamous scene in the sixth film was shot, and the building that stood in for the Leaky Cauldron in the first film were not popular visiting spots. These sites didn't provide an environment for fan engagement and reflection on their experiences with *Harry Potter*. The walking tours posed problems with authenticity. Platform 9¾ presented a re-creation of the site where Hogwarts students would race through the barrier between Platform 9 and 10, complete with a trolley carrying a suitcase and an owl's cage, buried halfway in the wall. For a considerable amount of money, you can have your photograph taken by staff. The heavy presence of consumerism here conflicted with our desire to interact with the space. The conflict between fan experience and fan consumerism was very apparent; visitors (customers?) had to stand in line for lengthy amounts of time, were pushed into participating in the same activity as the person in line before them, and weren't able to hang around the space once their picture was taken. They were allowed to enter an official Warner Brothers gift shop, selling the same merchandise that was available at other *Harry Potter* commercial spaces. We were able to share stories with our friends when we visited the space with them, but we weren't able to actually experience the trolley in the wall as we wanted to.

The space felt "fan-pushed," rather than "fan-led." As fans who mostly enjoy fan-led experiences, we felt we needed to visit Platform 9¾ on our own, after the official visiting hours, in order to fully experience it. We visited with a group of *Harry Potter* fans around 10pm, when only the prop trolley and the sign that said "Platform 9¾" were up. Our group was able to linger, personalize our own pictures, and reminisce about our own attachments to this sacred space. This after-hours experience felt much more personal because we were able to create our own memories and attach our own narrative to the space rather than having a commercialized experience.

Question: What technologies did you use to during the trip? How did you use them? Why?

We took many of our notes via our smartphones. Mostly these consisted of very specific observations on behaviors of people and fan reactions, and notes about stuff we wanted to tweet or post about later in the spaces we were studying. We wanted to take pictures to match up with notes if we were talking about a specific artifact. We took quick photos with our phones, and Kelly had brought a professional camera to take pictures of the spaces, fan notes, drawings, and fan interactions. It was important to take notes about each space itself, including how it was set up, how fans interacted with it, how we personally felt and experienced the space, and how it connected with the books or movies.

The next note-taking media we took advantage of was Twitter. We created our own hashtag, #HPWHO, so we could use Twitter as a quick and easy journal. This platform forced us to condense and think about our thoughts in more specific ways and to easily reference past thoughts. Because we were analyzing our data through Storify, a digital storytelling tool, Twitter made it easy to add our tweets on Storify and match up with our writings and images. We used Twitter mostly post-visit, so we had set aside reflection time to tweet and share our experiences for reference.

Question: What digital spaces did you use to do research during the trip? Why these spaces?

Searching the Internet helped in figuring out what spaces were worth visiting as fans and researchers. We looked to Twitter and Tumblr hashtags, blogs, and conversation threads, which directed us towards many *Harry Potter* blogs and fan pages where these spaces are given proper review and reactions from other fans. Searching for places to go via Google helped us find authentic fan spaces. We searched for fan reactions and previous visits to gauge how authentic the experience was before and after we went to these spaces. Exploring fan-curated spaces helped us analyze and compare experiences as well as track other fans' experiences before and after we visited these landmarks.

Question: As fans, did you see yourself wanting to visit spaces with the class or on your own? Did you visit spaces before we went as a class? Tell us why.

We knew that we were going to have a *Harry Potter*-themed day as a class, but we did want to experience most of the spaces that were dear to us (e.g., Elephant House, Platform 9¾, "Making of *Harry Potter*" Studio Tour) on our own first. We made these early visits so we could spend as much time as we needed, answer the questions we were looking to answer, and fully experience the landmark. Since these spaces are so iconic, it was important to us as fans to personalize the moment and create a connection within the physical manifestation of the series. In this way, we tied ourselves to the space and become part of the living narrative. When we visited with the group, we were relieved to have gone by ourselves for the first round, just because a lot of time with the class was spent attempting to teach students not as familiar with *Harry Potter* about our fandom, such as the importance of a brick wall in a train station.

By the time we had gone with the class to see Platform 9¾, we had already gone there three or four times and, through trial and error, participated how we wanted to participate with it. By visiting separately, we were able to provide insight for the other students about how they could improve their experience with the space by visiting it after hours. These repeated visits provided a multi-faceted look at the space, complete with fresh perspectives from outside the fandom to more experienced viewpoints from people who have visited these spaces previously.

Reflecting on Fan Experience as a Tool for Understanding Participatory Culture

In reflecting on what they learned during their study abroad experience, the students noted how Laurie Cubbison's research rang true to their experience.[18] She argues that "fans are the most active segment of the media audience, one that refuses to simply accept what they are given, but rather insists on the right to become full participants."[19] Across these spaces, the students discovered the ways in which fans were making them their own, often through participation that was not always sanctioned or expected by the owners of these spaces. Through this participation, the students gained a stronger understanding of the connections between the digital and physical communities for their fandoms.

Question: Did your experiences studying participatory memory change your views of or relationship to the Harry Potter *fandom? If so, how?*

Studying abroad in the UK allowed us access to some of the most sacred *Harry Potter* fandom spaces in relation to both the books and films. The study abroad experience guided our visits and research in these places by helping us focus our perspectives as both fans and researchers. We were able to participate as fans with the excitement and the understanding of the significance of the spaces, but we were also able to critically analyze and reflect on how we and other fans interacted with the spaces and with each other.

Our understanding of *Harry Potter* started with the knowledge that it was a huge phenomenon, still growing, and quickly spreading from books to physical spaces. We had a growing interest around *Harry Potter*, both of us visiting many conventions and events to meet like-minded people, but we were wanting to step back and take a look at just how ingrained *Harry Potter* is in our lives. As fans since our childhoods, we had experienced *Harry Potter* like many others—first the books, then digital communities, but by tracking *Harry Potter* from space to space, we were able to revive our love of the books and movies in new ways. We were able to not only gain a more in-depth understanding of fandom in general and how it works and grows, but also to grow and continue our love for *Harry Potter*. The participatory memory study abroad experience allowed us to take something we were passionate about and tailor a project around spaces we were looking forward to seeing. Tracking the differences between experiencing the story in the books and translating it in physical form was something we were looking forward to doing. We were able to trace that impact on ourselves, how it opened our eyes to the communities surrounding *Harry Potter*, and the power and influence of fan participation in a memory space.

Being in the UK for weeks, we had time to dive into the place and experience things more than once to fully understand the spaces we had loved for so long. We were able to recreate our experiences in different media, and making this trip to Britain allowed us to gain more credibility as *Harry Potter* fans. We were able to visit, share, brag, and learn from the spaces so ingrained into British and even American culture. Being able to fully experience places that have such a high importance to the fandom was a very important experience to us as fans.

Question: What digital spaces did you use to do your analysis and present findings?

During our travels, we knew we needed to document and analyze our data in various ways to contextualize it. We first started collecting our data digitally using Storify, a platform recommended to us by Liza. It is a storytelling tool that curates content from various social and digital media platforms to articulate our thoughts, feelings, and reflections. Storify allowed us to collect information on digital spaces related to *Harry Potter*, such as blogs, hashtags, websites, and tweets, into an archive of our experience. This platform helped us support our claims and gave a digital richness to our experience, and it also made us feel more connected to others' experiences. We wanted to map our research visually, so we set out to create a physical representation of the spaces that could be searched and experienced digitally. Pinterest allowed us to put the physical world of *Harry Potter* into the perspective of our world. Their mapping feature took the physical spaces out of the book and put them on our own map, adding a sense of realism to our own experiences.

Question: Why is this idea of visiting these places from the series important/ relevant/interesting in the HP fandom?

When we first started our research, we were in the period in which the *Harry Potter* fandom was seeing an end to the series—the ending of the textual source of the *Harry Potter* world: the book series and the movie series. Despite what many might see as the end of Harry's magical world, the fandom is still going strong; their online and physical presence is thriving and the fandom is continuing to grow. This culture of *Harry Potter* promotes cyclical consumption, which encourages fans to get involved in the fandom, share their thoughts, and re-experience the fandom in different ways. The original experience (i.e., the book/canon), even though it has officially "ended," has multiple iterations for fans diving in for the first time, or even for fans experiencing it for a second, third, or fourth time. Continuing material includes in-production spinoffs set in the *Harry Potter* world, such as *Fantastic Beasts and Where to Find Them* and *Harry Potter and the Cursed Child*. In addition is Rowling's constant presence on Twitter, through which she drops tidbits from the *Harry Potter* world into her fans' waiting hands via digital media such as *Pottermore*. There are also the Wizarding World of *Harry Potter* theme parks in Orlando and Hollywood, which continue to draw huge crowds and are building new experiences for fans through immersive, interactive rides and shops. The spaces are rich in detail and provide bountiful cinematic parallels to the films.

We also were very interested in how temporary and physical spaces allowed fans to keep their interest alive in *Harry Potter* even though the series had ended and the subsequent media coverage was dwindling. *Harry Potter* is so ingrained into society that sometimes people don't look back and think of how influential it is. There are spaces built around *Harry Potter* artifacts; people travel all over the world to experience the original set, themed rides, and conventions; families bond over reading the books; and lifelong friendships have begun and been maintained through the love of this series. People build businesses around *Harry Potter*, fans are still visiting these spaces, and memories are still being made. We not only wanted to see how these spaces translated the original text and survived in the post-series world but also how the participation of passionate people can impact a whole culture.

Conclusion

Throughout this study abroad experience, both the students and the instructor learned more about how fans can participate in physical and digital spaces across time and space. In their research on platforms such as Twitter and Tumblr as well as through first-hand accounts from friends, the students noticed the power of fans being able to visit the physical spaces that represent *Harry Potter*. These experiences had previously only existed for them in the books and movies. Because they wanted to witness the significance of the physical manifestation of the series and assess the accuracy of the translation from the books and films, they visited places such as Platform 9¾, the Leaky Cauldron, and the "Making of *Harry Potter*" Warner Brothers Studio Tour. They also wanted to visit spaces of memory for the fandom itself, such as Elephant House. To get the most out of this experience, it was essential to take note of how fans participated in these spaces and to reflect on their own interactions with each space.

This study abroad program helped these students learn about their fandom, participatory memory, and fan experiences. By visiting these spaces, they felt their own fan credibility increase, helping them understand why other fans would also visit these spaces. Combining experiences in physical spaces with their own research into these sites of memory in digital communities helped them realize a fan dream of theirs. It also helped them understand how the experiences we create for fans can include their participation through maps, notes, and conversations, both offline and online. They recognized that this connection would inform their future work as content writers and user experience researchers, positions they now hold in industry.

Media convergence, the relationships across technologies, companies, markets, and people, has changed the way we experience, consume, and relate to media and each other. Not only do we have easier access, but we also have an overwhelming number of media channels. There are so many different ways to participate in the conversation, consume the latest news, and share content with various audiences. Physical spaces allow for fans to meet and crowdsource this knowledge in person, networking within the community and learning about the significance and meaning of these fan experiences. Examining this activity online and in these physical spaces helped the participants enrich their study abroad and their worldview of how fans interact and how to create better experiences for them.

As Liza went on to develop her study abroad program in 2016, she took into consideration the experiences in spaces of memory mentioned in this chapter. Scholars, fans, and students grapple with the dichotomy of the fan scholar and the scholar fan, and perhaps, in the end, the line here is very porous and fuzzy. Taking into consideration the experiences of students such as Kelly and Emily, Liza refactored the study abroad program to focus completely on fan studies. She found the focus of this study abroad to be welcomed by the students, who engaged with the material and their fandoms as they learned about new cultures, witnessed and respected differences across the United Kingdom and Ireland, and embarked on their own research projects. Exploring the spaces and places of Irish culture early on in the 2016 study abroad program helped students to start to understand the heritage of these people. As they moved from Ireland over to England, looking specifically at *Harry Potter* and other fandoms, they could begin to understand how macro and micro cultures can be sustained and grow over space and time. Such connections are important to help students broaden their experiences oversees, and they help us contextualize and situate fan studies in the larger context of a humanities-based education.

Notes

1. "History of Education Abroad," Michigan State University, September 29, 2016, http://studyabroad.isp.msu.edu/history/.

2. Philip H. Anderson, Lawton Leigh, Richard J. Rexeisen, and Ann C. Hubbard, "Short-Term Study Abroad and Intercultural Sensitivity: A Pilot Study," *International Journal of Intercultural Relations* 30.4 (2005): 457–469.

3. Mary M. Dwyer, "More is Better: The Impact of Study Abroad Program Duration," *Frontiers: The Interdisciplinary Journal of Study Abroad* 10 (2004): 151–163.

4. Tracy Rundstrom Williams, "Exploring the Impact of Study Abroad on Students' Intercultural Communication Skills: Adaptability and Sensitivity," Journal of Studies in International Education 9.4 (2005): 356–371.

5. "Plans, Participation, and Outcomes: Overseas Study at Indiana University Bloomington Indiana University Bloomington," (May, 2009): 10, http://overseas.iu.edu/docs/UIRR_Overseas_Study.pdf.

6. Eric Freedman, "Media, Tourism, Environment, and Cultural Issues in Australia: A Case Study of a Study Abroad Program," *Applied Environmental Education & Communication* 9.2 (2010): 95.

7. Brian D. Ballentine, "Creativity Counts: Why Study Abroad Matters to Technical and Professional Communication," *Technical Communication Quarterly* 24 (2015): 291–305.

8. Ibid., 295.

9. Barbie Zelizer, "Reading the Past Against the Grain: The Shape of Memory Studies," *Critical Studies in Mass Communication* 12.2 (1995): 214–39.

10. Maurice Halbwachs, *On Collective Memory*, trans. Lewis A. Coser (Chicago: University of Chicago Press, 1992).

11. Jeffrey K. Olick, Vered Vinitzky-Seroussi, and Daniel Levy, eds., *The Collective Memory Reader* (Oxford: Oxford University Press, 2011).

12. Henry Jenkins, *Textual Poachers: Television Fans and Participatory Culture*, twentieth edition (New York: Routledge, 2013).

13. Matt Hills, *Fan Cultures* (New York: Routledge, 2003).

14. Ross Garner, "Symbolic and Cued Immersion: Paratextual Framing Strategies on the Doctor Who Experience Walking Tour," *Popular Communication: The International Journal of Media and Culture* 14.2 (2016): 86–98.

15. Suzanne Scott, "Authorized Resistance? Is Fan Production Frakked?" In *Cylons in America: Critical Studies in Battlestar Galactica,* edited by C.W. Marshall and Tiffany Potter (New York: Continuum, 2008): 210.

16. Jenkins, *Textual Poachers*, xii.

17. Henry Jenkins, "The Cultural Logic of Media Convergence," *International Journal of Cultural Studies* 7.1 (2004): 34.

18. Laurie Cubbison, "Russ T Davies, 'Nine Hysterical Women,' and the Death of Ianto Jones," in *New Media Literacies and Participatory Popular Culture Across Borders,* edited by Bronwyn Williams and Amy A. Zenger (New York: Routledge, 2012).

19. Ibid., 136.

Bibliography

"17 Things that Harry Potter Fans Still Aren't Over." *BuzzFeed.* September 10, 2015. www.buzzfeed.com/stephanierhesa/17-things-that-harry-potter-fans-still-arent-over-1tkri.

"About." *International Quidditch Association.* September 19, 2016. www.iqa-quidditch.org/about.php.

"All Time Box Office." *Box Office Mojo.* September 28, 2016. www.boxoffice-mojo.com/alltime/world/.

"Alternate Universe." *Fanlore Wiki.* August 21, 2015. http://fanlore.org/wiki/Alternate_Universe.

Anderson, Philip H., Lawton Leigh, Richard J. Rexeisen, and Ann C. Hubbard. "Short-Term Study Abroad and Intercultural Sensitivity: A Pilot Study." *International Journal of Intercultural Relations* 30.4 (2005): 457–469.

Anelli, Melissa, John Noe, and Sue Upton. "PotterCast Interviews J. K. Rowling, Part Two." *PotterCast #131* podcast, December 24, 2007.

Anelli, Melissa and Emerson Spartz. "MuggleNet and The Leaky Cauldron interview Joanne Kathleen Rowling." *The Leaky Cauldron.* September 10, 2007. www.the-leaky-cauldron.org/2007/09/10/jkr1/.

Anatol, Giselle Liza, ed. *Reading Harry Potter: Critical Essays.* Santa Barbara: Praeger, 2003.

Appelbaum, Peter. "The Great Snape Debate." *In Critical Perspectives on Harry Potter: Second Edition.*, ed. Elizabeth E. Heilman, 83–100. London: Routledge, 2009.

Asher-Perrin, Emily. "Albus Dumbledore Didn't Come Out at the Right Time (According to Everyone)." *Tor.* September 26, 2013. www.tor.com/2013/09/26/banned-books-week-harry-potter-jk-rowling-dumbledore-gay-icon/.

———. "Rewatching the *Harry Potter and the Deathly Hallows: Part 1* Film." *Tor.com.* June 2, 2016. www.tor.com/2016/06/02/rewatching-the-harry-potter-and-the-deathly-hallows-part-1-film/.

———. "Rewatching the *Harry Potter and the Deathly Hallows: Part 2* Film." *Tor.com.* June 9, 2016. www.tor.com/2016/06/09/rewatching-the-harry-potter-and-the-deathly-hallows-part-2-film/.

———. "The Anxiety of Power and the Love of Wise Men." *Tor.com.* June 30, 2011. www.tor.com/2011/06/30/the-anxiety-of-power-and-the-love-of-wise-men-harry-potter-and-the-half-blood-prince/.

———. "The Harry Potter Reread: *The Deathly Hallows,* Chapters 33 and 34." *Tor.com.* May 12, 2016. www.tor.com/2016/05/12/the-harry-potter-reread-the-deathly-hallows-chapters-33-and-34/.

———. "The Harry Potter Reread: *The Deathly Hallows,* Chapters 35 and 36." *Tor.com.* May 20, 2016. www.tor.com/2016/05/20/the-harry-potter-reread-the-deathly-hallows-chapters-35-and-36/.

Åström, Berit. " 'Let's Get Those Winchesters Pregnant': Male Pregnancy in Supernatural Fan Fiction." *Transformative Works and Cultures* 4 (2010). http://journal.transformativeworks.org/index.php/twc/article/view/135/141.

Baggett, David and Shawn Klein, eds. *Harry Potter and Philosophy: If Aristotle Ran Hogwarts.* Chicago: Open Court, 2004.

Ballentine, Brian D. "Creativity Counts: Why Study Abroad Matters to Technical and Professional Communication." *Technical Communication Quarterly* 24 (2015): 291–305.

Bao, Hongwei, and Ling Yang. "Queerly Intimate: Friends, Fans and Affective Communication in a Super Girl Fan Fiction Community." *Cultural Studies* 26.6 (2012): 842–71.

Barratt, Bethany. *The Politics of Harry Potter.* New York: Palgrave MacMillan, 2012.

Begley, Sarah. "The Magic is Gone but Harry Potter Will Never Die." *Time.* August 12 2016. http://time.com/4445149/harry-potter-cursed-child-jk-rowling/.

Bell, Christopher. "Heroes and Horcruxes: Dumbledore's Army as Metonym" In *Wizards vs. Muggles: Essays on Identity in the Harry Potter Universe,* ed. Christopher Bell, 72–88. Jefferson, NC: McFarland, 2016.

Benjamin, Walter. "The Task of the Translator." In *Illuminations: Essays and Reflections.* New York: Schocken Books, 1985.

Biondi, Carrie-Ann, ed. *Imagining Better: Philosophical Issues in* Harry Potter. *Reason Papers* 34.1. June 2102.

Black, Rebecca W. *Adolescents and Online Fan Fiction.* New York: Peter Lang International Academic, 2008.

Blay, Zeba. "Emma Watson Gives Smart Answer When Asked if She's A 'White Feminist.' " *The Huffington Post.* October 12, 2015. www.huffingtonpost.com/entry/emma-watson-gives-smart-answer-when-asked-if-shes-a-white-feminist_us_561bea68e4b0dbb8000f4ea9.

"Book Dumbledore vs Movie Dumbledore." *Imgur.* September 7, 2016. http://i.imgur.com/OFGFoA6.jpg.

Booth, Paul. "Narractivity and the Narrative Database: Media-based Wikis as Interactive Fan Fiction." *Narrative Inquiry* 19.2 (2009): 372–93.

Bortolotti, Gary R, and Linda Hutcheon. "On the Origin of Adaptations: Rethinking Fidelity Discourse and 'Success'—Biologically." *New Literary History* 38.3 (2007): 443–458.

Bourke, Liz. "They Are Coming: Harry Potter and the Deathly Hallows." *Tor.com.* July 5, 2011. www.tor.com/2011/07/05/harry-potter-and-the-deathly-hallows.

Bradley, Bill. "'Harry Potter' Has One Huge Plot Hole You Might've Missed." *The Huffington Post.* May 28, 2015. www.huffingtonpost.com/2015/05/28/harry-potter-plot-hole_n_7447500.html; http://hellogiggles.com/harry-potter-plot-hole/.

Brough, Melissa M., and Sangita Shresthova. "Fandom Meets Activism: Rethinking Civic and Political Participation." *Transformative Works and Cultures* 10 (2012). http://journal.transformativeworks.org/index.php/twc/article/view/303/265.

Bury, Liz. "Cuckoo's Calling by JK Rowling: Did you Know?" *The Guardian.* July 15, 2013. www.theguardian.com/books/2013/jul/15/cuckoos-calling-jk-rowling-did-you-know.

Butler, Michelle Markey. "The Wisdom of the Crowd: Internet Memes and *The Hobbit: An Unexpected Journey.*" In *The Hobbit and Tolkien's Mythology: Essays on Revisions and Influences*, ed. Bradford Lee Eden, 222–232. Jefferson, NC: McFarland, 2014.

"Can Use Magic to Clean Up Any Mess Instantly." *Pinterest.* September 2, 2016. www.pinterest.com/pin/157977899399801841/.

Cartmell, Deborah. "Adapting Children's Literature." In *The Cambridge Companion to Literature on Screen*, ed. Deborah Cartmell and Imelda Whelehan, 167–80. Cambridge: Cambridge UP, 2007.

Chander, Anupam, and Madhavi Sunder. "Everyone's a Superhero: A Cultural Theory of 'Mary Sue' Fan Fiction as Fair Use." *California Law Review* 95.2 (2007): 597–626.

Cleland, Gary. "Amazon Admits to Record Harry Potter Bid." *The Telegraph.* December 7, 2014. www.telegraph.co.uk/news/uknews/3669918/Amazon-admits-to-record-Harry-Potter-bid.html.

Coscia, Michelle. "Competition and Success in the Meme Pool: A Case Study on Quickmeme.com." *Proceedings of the Seventh International AAAI Conference on Weblogs and Social Media* (2013): 100–109.

"Could clean up Hogwarts using magic." *Quick Meme.* September 6, 2016. www.quickmeme.com/meme/3qbezg.

"Crack." *Fanlore Wiki.* August 21 2015. http://fanlore.org/wiki/Crack.

Cubbison, Laurie. "Russ T Davies, 'Nine Hysterical Women,' and the Death of Ianto Jones." In *New Media Literacies and Participatory Popular Culture Across Borders,* ed. Bronwyn Williams and Amy A. Zenger, 135–150. New York: Routledge, 2012.

Cuntz-Leng, Vera. "Harry Potter que(e)r: Eine Filmsaga im Spannungsfeld von Queer Reading, Slash-Fandom und Fantasyfilmgenre." Bielefeld: transcript, 2015.

Cuntz-Leng, Vera. "Snape Written, Filmed, and Slashed: Harry Potter and the Autopoietic Feedback Loop." In *Playing Harry Potter: Essays and Interviews on Fandom and Performance,* ed. Lisa S. Brenner, 55–74. Jefferson: McFarland, 2015.

Dawkins, Richard. "Why Everyone Should Read Harry Potter." *Richard Dawkins Foundation for Reason & Science* September 9, 2014. https://richard-dawkins.net/2014/09/why-everyone-should-read-harry-potter/.

De Kosnik, Abigail. "Should Fan Fiction Be Free?" *Cinema Journal* 48.4 (Summer 2009): 118–24.

Dicieanu, Maria. "Adaptations: Primitive Transmedia Narratives?" In *Words, Worlds and Narratives: Transmedia and Immersion,* ed. Tawnya Ravy and Eric Forcier. Oxford: Inter-Disciplinary Press, 2014.

"Did you put your name into the Goblet of Fire, Harry?" *Tumblr.* September 7, 2016. http://29.media.tumblr.com/tumblr_m1z5csFMUq1rsfiixo1_400 .gif.

"Dr. Who and the T.A.R.D.I.S." *Facebook.* July 25, 2016. www.facebook.com/ Doctor-Who-and-the-TARDIS-276710412383657/?pnref=story.

Doane, Mary Ann. "Film and the Masquerade: Theorising the Female Spectator." In *Feminist Film Theory: A Reader,* ed. Sue Thornham, 131–45. Edinburgh: Edinburgh UP, 1999.

Dresang, Eliza T. "Hermione Granger and the Heritage of Gender." In *The Ivory Tower and Harry Potter: Perspectives on a Literary Phenomenon,* ed. Lana A. Whited, 211–42. Columbia: University of Missouri Press, 2002.

Drukman, Steven. "The Gay Gaze, Or Why I Want My MTV." In *A Queer Romance: Lesbians, Gay Men and Popular Culture,* ed. Paul Burston and Colin Richardson, 89–105. London/New York: Routledge, 2005.

Dwyer, Mary M. "More is Better: The Impact of Study Abroad Program Duration." *Frontiers: The Interdisciplinary Journal of Study Abroad* 10 (2004): 151–163.

EdwardTLC. "J. K. Rowling at Carnegie Hall Reveals Dumbledore is Gay."

The Leaky-Cauldron.org. October 20, 2007. www.the-leaky-cauldron. org/2007/10/20/j-k-rowling-at-carnegie-hall-reveals-dumbledore-is-gay-neville-marries-hannah-abbott-and-scores-more/.

"Elder Wand." *Harry Potter Wiki*. September 27, 2016. http://harrypotter. wikia.com/wiki/Elder_Wand.

Eligon, John. "Rowling Wins Lawsuit Against Potter Lexicon." *New York Times*. September 8, 2008, www.nytimes.com/2008/09/09/nyregion/09pot-ter.html.

Eppink, Jason. "A Brief History of the GIF (So Far)." *Journal of Visual Culture* 13.3 (2014): 298–306.

Ellis, John. *Visible Fictions: Cinema—Television—Video*. London: Routledge, 1982.

Fallon, Claire. "These Living Book Covers Are as Magical as Anything in Harry Potter." *The Huffington Post*. September 16, 2015. www.huffingtonpost. com/entry/book-cover-gifs_us_55f88e62e4b0b48f6701102d.

Fantastic Beast and Where to Find Them. Directed by David Yates. Warner Bros, 2016.

Field, Syd. *Screenplay: The Foundations of Screenwriting*. New York: Bantam Dell, 2005.

Fiske, John. "The Cultural Economy of Fandom." In *The Adoring Audience: Fan Culture and Popular Media*, ed. Lisa A. Lewis, 30–49. New York: Routledge, 1992.

Flesher, Paul. "Being True to the Text: From Genesis to Harry Potter." *Journal of Religion and Film* 12 (2008). http://digitalcommons.unomaha.edu/jrf/vol12/iss2/1/.

Fraser, Lindsey. *Conversations with J. K. Rowling*. New York: Scholastic Press, 2001.

Freedman, Eric. "Media, Tourism, Environment, and Cultural Issues in Australia: A Case Study of a Study Abroad Program." *Applied Environmental Education & Communication* 9.2 (2010): 87–95.

"Full Text from J. K. Rowling Pottermore Press Conference." *The Leaky Cauldron*. June 23, 2011. www.the-leaky-cauldron.org/2011/6/23/full-text-from-j-k-rowling-pottermore-press-conference.

Gallardo, Ximena/Smith, C. Jason. "Cinderfella: J. K. Rowling's Wily Web of Gender." In *Reading Harry Potter: Critical Essays, ed.* Giselle Liza Anatol, 191–205. Westport: Praeger, 2003.

Gannon, Louise. "I Find Being Sexy Embarrassing, Reveals Emma Watson." *MailOnline*. February 6, 2009. www.dailymail.co.uk/home/moslive/article-1127838/I-sexy-embarrassing-reveals-Emma-Watson.html.

Garner, Dwight. "Ten Years Later, Harry Potter Vanishes from the Best-Sell-

er List." *The New York Times.* May 1, 2008. http://artsbeat.blogs.nytimes.
com/2008/05/01/ten-years-later-harry-potter-vanishes-from-the-best-sell-
er-list/?_r=1.

Garner, Ross. "Symbolic and Cued Immersion: Paratextual Framing Strategies
on the Doctor Who Experience Walking Tour." *Popular Communication:
The International Journal of Media and Culture* 14.2 (2016): 86–98.

"Gets Invisibility Cloak, Goes to the Library." *Meme Generator.* September 2,
2016. https://memegenerator.net/instance/53202987.

"Gets Invisibility Cloak. Doesn't Go Into Girls Shower." *Quick Meme.* September 16, 2016. www.quickmeme.com/meme/3qz40v.

"Gets Invisibility Cloak." *Humoar.* September 2, 2016. www.humoar.com/
gets-invisibility-cloak-doesnt-go-into-girls-showers/.

Gever, Martha, Pratibha Parmar, and John Greyson, eds. *Queer Looks: Perspectives
on Lesbian and Gay Film and Video.* New York/Abingdon: Routledge, 1993.

Gone with the Wind. Directed by Victor Fleming. MGM, 1939.

Gonzalez, Sandra. "J. K. Rowling Says There Will Be Five 'Fantastic Beasts'
Movies." *CNN.* October 20, 2016. www.cnn.com/2016/10/13/entertain-
ment/fantastic-beasts-five-movies/.

Granger, John. *Harry Potter's Bookshelf: The Great Books Behind the Hogwarts
Adventures.* New York: Berkley Books, 2009.

Halbwachs, Maurice. *On Collective Memory.* Translated by Lewis A. Coser.
Chicago: University of Chicago Press, 1992.

Halberstam, J. Jack. *In a Queer Time and Place: Transgender Bodies, Subcultural Lives.* New York: New York UP, 2005.

Harmon, Amy. "In TV's Dull Summer Days, Plots Take Wing on the Net." *The
New York Times.* August 18, 1997. www.nytimes.com/1997/08/18/business/
in-tv-s-dull-summer-days-plots-take-wing-on-the-net.html?pagewant-
ed=all&src=pm.

Harris, Mark. "Dumbledore's Outing: Why it Matters." *Entertainment Weekly*
October 30, 2007. www.ew.com/article/2007/10/30/dumbledores-out-
ing-why-it-matters.

"'Harry Potter': Alan Rickman Looks Back on Decade of Dark Magic." *Hero
Complex.* December 30, 2011. http://herocomplex.latimes.com/movies/
harry-potter-alan-rickman-looks-back-on-decade-of-dark-magic/#/0.

"Harry Potter Discussion." *Goodreads.* September 1, 2016. www.goodreads.
com/topic/show/1259051-plot-hole.

"Harry Potter Morals." *MemeCenter.* September 6, 2016. www.memecenter.
com/fun/897027/harry-potter-morals.

"Harry! Did yah put yah name in da Goblet of Fiyah?!" *Lindsay Favreau.* June
30, 2014. http://lindseyfavreau.tumblr.com/post/90378699861.

Harry Potter and the Chamber of Secrets. Directed by Chris Columbus. Warner Bros, 2002.

Harry Potter and the Deathly Hallows Part 1. Directed by David Yates. Warner Bros, 2010.

Harry Potter and the Deathly Hallows Part 2. Directed by David Yates. Warner Bros, 2011.

Harry Potter and the Goblet of Fire. Directed by Mike Newell. 2005. Warner Brothers, 2006.

Harry Potter and the Half-Blood Prince. Directed by David Yates. Warner Bros, 2009.

Harry Potter and the Order of the Phoenix. Directed by David Yates. Warner Bros, 2007.

Harry Potter and the Prisoner of Azkaban. Directed by Alfonso Cuarón. Warner Bros, 2004.

Harry Potter and the Sorcerer's Stone. Directed by Chris Columbus. Warner Bros, 2001.

Harry Potter vs Star Wars. September 7, 2016. https://mir-s3-cdn-cf.behance. net/project_modules/disp/9fc1fb21127611.562fbf0be5d39.jpg.

Harry Potter: The Exhibition. September 16, 2016. www.harrypotterexhibition. com.

The Harry Potter Lexicon. https://www.hp-lexicon.org.

Hayles, N. Katherine. *How We Became Posthuman: Virtual Bodies in Cybernetics, Literature, and Informatics.* Chicago: University of Chicago Press, 1999.

Heilman, Elizabeth E. "Blue Wizards and Pink Witches: Representations of Gender Identity and Power." In *Critical Perspectives on Harry Potter,* ed. Elizabeth E. Heilman, 221–39. London: Routledge, 2003.

———., ed., *Critical Perspectives on Harry Potter.* London: Routledge, 2003.

Heilman, Elizabeth E. and Trevor Donaldson. "From Sexist to (sort-of) Feminist: Representations of Gender in the Harry Potter Series." In *Critical Perspectives on Harry Potter.* Second Ed., ed. Elizabeth E. Heilman, 139–61. London: Routledge, 2009.

Heritage, Stuart. "Harry Potter Enters the Twilight Zone." *The Guardian* December 8, 2009. www.theguardian.com/film/filmblog/2009/dec/08/harry-potter-twilight.

Hills, Matt. *Fan Cultures.* New York: Routledge, 2003.

"History of Education Abroad." Michigan State University. September 29, 2016. http://studyabroad.isp.msu.edu/history/.

Hobb, Robin. "The Fan Fiction Rant." *Internet Archive.* June 30, 2005. http://web.archive.org/web/20050630015105/http://www.robinhobb.com/rant.html.

hooks, bell. "The Oppositional Gaze: Black Female Spectators." *Black Looks: Race and Representation*, 115–31. Boston: South End Press, 1992.

Hutcheon, Linda. *A Theory of Adaptation*. New York: Routledge, 2006.

"I Don't Get Harry Potter." *Tumblr*. September 6, 2016. http://idontgethp. tumblr.com/page/2.

"I found a plothole." *Reddit*. September 1, 2016. www.reddit.com/r/harrypotter/comments/1698oh/i_found_a_plothole_didnt_fred_george_see_peter/.

I kill rogue ninjas. September 7, 2016. http://img0.joyreactor.com/pics/post/Harry-Potter-Star-Wars-Naruto-edward-cullen-199656.jpeg.

"I'm sorry about your parents." *Quick Meme*. September 6, 2016. www.quickmeme.com/meme/35rfd2.

"I'm the Two Sides of the Coin!" February 27 2015. http://i-m-a-good-viper. tumblr.com/post/112273494285/dontsayclazy-ms-meryl-imjustthemechanic (site discontinued).

"If the Weasley twins owned the Marauder's Map." *Quick Meme*. September 1, 2016. www.quickmeme.com/meme/359fsp.

International Quidditch Association. September 15, 2016. http://iqaquidditch.org/.

"Internet-memes-marauders-map." *Flickr*. September 23, 2012. www.flickr. com/photos/47804730@N03/8017138531.

"Internet-memes-marauders-map." *Flickr*. September 23, 2012. www.flickr. com/photos/47804730@N03/8017138531.

Jenkins, Henry. "The Cultural Logic of Media Convergence." *International Journal of Cultural Studies* 7.1 (2004): 33–43.

———. "Fandom Studies as I See It." *Journal of Fandom Studies* 2.2 (2014): 89–109.

———. *Textual Poachers: Television Fans and Participatory Culture*. New York: Routledge, 1992.

———. "Transmedia 202: Further Reflections." *Confessions of an ACA—Fan, the Official Weblog of Henry Jenkins*. August 1, 2011. http://henryjenkins. org/2011/08/defining_transmedia_further_re.html.

———. "Transmedia Storytelling." *MIT Technology Review*. January 15, 2003. www.technologyreview.com/s/401760/transmedia-storytelling/.

J. K. Rowling. www.jkrowling.com.

"J. K. Rowling Gives Clues to Harry Potter's Future." *Beyond Hogwarts*. May 16, 2005. http://www.beyondhogwarts.com/story.200505163.html.

"J. K. Rowling's Pottermore Site Launches Magical Quill Challenge." *The Wall Street Journal.*, July 31, 2011. http://blogs.wsj.com/speakeasy/2011/07/31 /j-k-rowlings-pottermore-site-launches-magical-quill-challenge/.

"JK Rowling Law Firm Pays Damages Over Pseudonym Leak." *BBC News*. July 31, 2013. www.bbc.com/news/entertainment-arts-23515054.

"JK Rowling Under Fire from US Bible Belt After Outing Dumbledore as Gay." *Daily Mail* October 28, 2007. www.dailymail.co.uk/news/article-490261/ JK-Rowling-US-Bible-belt-outing-Dumbledore-gay.html.

Kaplan, E. Ann. *Looking for the Other: Feminism, Film, and the Imperial Gaze.* New York: Routledge, 1997.

Kermode, Mark. "5 Live Review: *Harry Potter and the Deathly Hallows—Part 1.*" *BBC.* November 23, 2010. www.bbc.co.uk/blogs/markkermode/2010/11/5_live_review_2.html.

Kill Your Darlings. Directed by John Krokidas. Sony Pictures, 2013.

Knight, Laura Bryan. "Pack Your Bags: Edinburgh's Elephant House." *Aspiring Kennedy.* May30, 2013. www.aspiringkennedy.com/blog-working/piring kennedy.com/2013/05/pack-your-bags-edinburghs-elephant-house.html.

Kulie, Casper Ter. "What Can Harry Potter Teach Us About Evil in Our World Today." *On Being.* January 31, 2015. www.onbeing.org/blog/what-can-harry-potter-teach-us-about-evil-in-our-world-today/7244.

Lammers, Jayne. "Fangirls as Teachers: Examining Pedagogic Discourse in an Online Fan Site." *Learning, Media and Technology* 38(2013): 368–386.

Lauretis, Teresa de. *Alice Doesn't: Feminism, Semiotics, Cinema.* Bloomington: Indiana UP, 1984.

The Leaky Cauldron. www.the-leaky-cauldron.org.

"leela-summers." *Tumblr,* September 7, 2016. http://66.media.tumblr.com/35128 c1147c5fc7e4a03b9c2c03be088/tumblr_ndydqnqYxS1qcvd0oo4_540.png.

Leitch, Thomas. "Twelve Fallacies in Contemporary Adaptation Theory." *Criticism* 45.2 (2003): 149–171.

Leonard, Laura. "The Trouble with *Twilight.*" *Christianity Today* February 19, 2010. www.christianitytoday.com/ct/2010/februaryweb-only/17.51.0.html.

"Lets Hermione use time turner." *Quick Meme.* September 6, 2016. www.quickmeme.com/meme/35fw92.

Liptak, Andrew. "Harry Potter's Journey Has Come to an End with The Cursed Child." *The Verge.* July 31, 2016. www.theverge.com/2016/7/31/12333626/harry-potter-journey-end-the-cursed-child.

"Lotr and Harry Potter Similarities." *MemeCenter.* September 7, 2016. www.memecenter.com/fun/942326/lotr-and-harry-potter-similarities.

"Lotr vs Harry Potter." *MemeCenter.* September 7, 2016. www.memecenter.com/fun/191137/lotr-vs-harry-potter.

"LOTR vs. Harry Potter." *9Gag.Com.* September 7, 2016. http://9gag.com/gag/4278294.

Lufttsu. "Quotes from the Harry Potter Books [45/50]." April 30, 2015. http://lufttsu.tumblr.com/post/49251728815/quotes-from-the-harry-potter-books-4550.

———. "Quotes from the Harry Potter Books [47/50]" August 3, 2015. http://lufttsu.tumblr.com/post/57164469479/quotes-from-the-harry-potter-books-4750.

———. "Quotes from the Harry Potter Books [2/50]." October 5, 2015. http://lufttsu.tumblr.com/post/33635476895/quotes-from-the-harry-potter-books-250.

Lyle, Samantha A. "(Mis)recognition and the Middle-Class/Bourgeois Gaze: A Case Study of Wife Swap." *Critical Discourse Studies* 5.4 (2008): 319–30.

Mabe, Chauncey. "Don't Ask, Don't Spell." *Sun Sentinel* October 23, 2007. www.sun-sentinel.com/sfl-mtblog-2007–10-dont_ask_dont_spell_1-story.html.

Mad Potter Until the Very End. May 8, 2012. http://madpotterheaduntilthevery end.tumblr.com/post/22658555971.

———. September 30, 2016. http://madpotterheaduntiltheveryend.tumblr .com/post/41604897064.

———. September 30, 2016. http://madpotterheaduntiltheveryend.tumblr .com/post/66661035852/songbard5683-fiestyhysteria-the-child-actors.

———. September 30, 2016. http://madpotterheaduntiltheveryend.tumblr .com/post/50811811645/iou-a-call-sherlock-just-for-the-reblogs.

———. September 30, 2016. http://madpotterheaduntiltheveryend.tumblr .com/post/60626331255/au-james-and-lily-live.

———. September 30, 2016. http://madpotterheaduntiltheveryend.tumblr .com/post/15446991956.

Maney, Kevin. "GIFs Are Replacing Words . . . Even Thoughts." *Newsweek.* March 29, 2016. www.newsweek.com/2016/04/08/gifs-are-replacing-words-thoughts-441499.html.

Marinovich, Milosh. "Harry Potter Goes Nude!" *CBS News.* July 28, 2006. www.cbsnews.com/news/harry-potter-goes-nude/.

Martin, Charlotte. "Nudes that make you go ewww." *The Irish Sun.* December 8, 2009. www.thesun.ie/irishsol/homepage/woman/2761965/The-worst-celebrity-nude-scenesWorst-naked-film-scenesMost-weird-nude-scenes NudeNakedtoplesssex-scenesstrange-sex-scenes.html.

Martin, Liam and Matthew Reynolds. "PlayStation Home Closes Its Doors for Good: A Look Back at Its Best Moments." *Digital Spy.* April 1, 2015. www.digitalspy.com/gaming/feature/a638593/playstation-home-closes-its-doors-for-good-a-look-back-at-its-best-moments/.

Mayer-Schonberger, Viktor, and Lena Wong. "Fan or Foe: Fan Fiction, Authorship, and the Fight for Control." *IDEA: The Intellectual Property Law Review* 54.1 (2013): 1–22.

McCabe, B. *Harry Potter: Page to Screen, the Complete Filmmaking Journey.* New York: Harper Design, 2011.

McCarthy, Amy. "Sorry Privileged White Ladies, But Emma Watson Isn't a 'Game Changer' for Feminism." *XO Jane.* September 24, 2014. www.xojane.com/issues/emma-watson-he-for-she.

McCrumb, Sharyn. *Bimbos of the Death Sun.* New York: Ballantine Books, 1996.

"Mischief Managed." June 2, 2015. http://papertownsy.tumblr.com/post/120485486096.

Moir, Jan. "Where's the Magic in this Tale of Middle-Class Monsters?" *Daily Mail.* September 26, 2012. www.dailymail.co.uk/news/article-2209165/J-K-Rowlings-The-Casual-Vacancy-review-Wheres-magic-tale-middle-class-monsters.html.

Mondello, Bob. "Remembering Hollywood's Hays Code, 40 Years On." *NPR.* August 8, 2008. www.npr.org/templates/story/story.php?storyId=93301189.

Moss, Rachel. "Emma Watson Calls on Men to Fight for Gender Equality in Powerful UN Speech." *The Huffington Post.* September 22, 2014. www.huffingtonpost.co.uk/2014/09/22/emma-watson-un-speech-feminsim-equality_n_5859580.html.

"The Most Interesting Man in the World," *Meme Generator,* September 1, 2016, https://memegenerator.net/instance/66698802.

Mulvey, Laura. "Visual Pleasure and Narrative Cinema." *Screen* 16.3 (1975): 6–18.

Mulvey, Laura. "Afterthoughts on 'Visual Pleasure and Narrative Cinema' Inspired by King Vidor's *Duel in the Sun* (1946)." *Visual and Other Pleasures,* 29–38. Basingstoke: Palgrave Macmillan, 1989.

Neale, Steve. "Masculinity as Spectacle: Reflections on Men and Mainstream Cinema." *Screen* 24.6 (1983): 2–17.

Nel, Phillip. "Lost in Translation?" In *Critical Perspectives on Harry Potter,* ed. Elizabeth E. Heilman, 275–289. London/New York: Routledge, 2003.

Netburn, Deborah. "Seven Clues That 'Potter's' Dumbledore Was Gay." *Los Angeles Times* October 23, 2007. www.latimes.com/entertainment/movies/la-et-showbiz7-23oct23-story.html.

Nexon, Daniel B. and Iver B. Neuman, eds. *Harry Potter and International Relations.* New York: Rowman and Littlefield, 2006.

"Obsessive Thoughts." February 12, 2015. http://snowgall.tumblr.com/post/110854647855/scaredpotter-in-which-draco-and-harry-dress-a.

Olick, Jeffrey K., Vered Vinitzky-Seroussi, and Daniel Levy, eds. *The Collective Memory Reader.* Oxford: Oxford University Press, 2011.

Patterson, Bryan. "Enthusiastic Fans Await New Release." *Melbourne Herald Sun.* November 30, 2008. www.heraldsun.com.au/news/victoria/enthusiastic-fans-await-new-release/story-e6frf92f-1111118176695.

The Perks of Being a Wallflower. Directed by Stephen Chbosky. Summit / Lionsgate, 2013.

Perrier, Ronald. *From Fiction to Film*. St. Cloud, Minn.: Archie Publications, 1992.

"Philosoraptor." *Know Your Meme*. September 1, 2016. http://knowyourmeme .com/memes/philosoraptor.

"Plans, Participation, and Outcomes: Overseas Study at Indiana University Bloomington Indiana University Bloomington." May, 2009. http://overseas. iu.edu/docs/UIRR_Overseas_Study.pdf.

Pogue, David. "The Strange Magic of Micro Movies." *Scientific American*. May 2013: 34.

Pottermore. http://www.pottermore.com.

"Pottermore Launched: J. K. Rowling on New Harry Potter Material." *The Telegraph*. June 23, 2011. YouTube Video. www.youtube.com/watch? feature=player_embedded&v=_NS6fNQMpns.

"Pottermore Prepares for Relaunch to Showcase Wider Wizarding World." *MuggleNet*. July 12, 2016. www.mugglenet.com/2015/09/pottermore-prepares-for-relaunch-to-showcase-wider-wizarding-world/.

"Press Release—11 Sept 2015." *Pottermore*. August 30, 2016. www.pottermore .com/about/press-11-Sept-2015.

Prinzi, Travis. "Don't Occupy Gringotts: *Harry Potter*, Social Upheaval, and the Moral Imagination." *Reason Papers* 34.1 (June 2012): 15–24.

———. *Harry Potter and Imagination: The Between Two Worlds*. Cheshire, CT: Zossima Press, 2008.

———. "The Well-Ordered Mind: How Imagination Can Make Us More Human." *Hog's Head Conversations: Essays on Harry Potter*, ed. Travis Prinzi, 103–23. Allentown: Zossima, 2009.

Pugh, Sheenagh. *The Democratic Genre: Fan Fiction in a Literary Context*. Bridgend, Wales: Seren, 2005.

"Q_A with Pottermore CEO Charlie Redmayne." *Vimeo*. September 15, 2016. https://vimeo.com/145700816.

"Rage Guy." *Know Your Meme*. September 7, 2016. http://knowyourmeme .com/memes/rage-guy-fffffuuuuuuuu.

Reagin, Nancy Ruth, ed. *Harry Potter and History*. Hoboken: Wiley, 2011.

"Reblog Not Repost! A Masterpost." *Reposting Is Stealing*. October 8, 2013. http://repostingisstealing.tumblr.com/post/63482164012/anothermind palace-hello-so-recently-i-found.

Rivière, Joan. "Womanliness as a Masquerade [1928]." *Formations of Fantasy*, ed. V. Burgin, J. Donald and C. Kaplan, 35–44. New York/London: Routledge, 1986.

"Robert Galbraith's Cormoran Strike Novels to be Adapted for Major New BBC Drama Series." *BBC*. December 10, 2014. www.bbc.co.uk/mediacentre/latestnews/2014/cormoran-strike.

Rodowick, David N. "The Difficulty of Difference." *Wide Angle* 5.1 (1982): 4–15.

Rodriguez, Salvador. "Pottermore Launches Competition to Select Beta Users." *The LA Times*. August 1, 2011. http://latimesblogs.latimes.com/technology/2011/08/pottermore-launches-competition-to-select-beta-users-.html.

Rothstein, Edward. "Is Dumbledore Gay? Depends on Definitions of 'Is' and 'Gay.'" *New York Times* October 29, 2007. www.nytimes.com/2007/10/29/arts/29conn.html.

Rowling, J. K., John Tiffany, and Jack Thorne. *Harry Potter and the Cursed Child: Parts One and Two*. New York: Scholastic, 2016.

Rowling, J. K. *Fantastic Beasts and Where to Find Them*. New York: Scholastic, 2000.

———. *Harry Potter and the Chamber of Secrets*. New York: Scholastic, 1998.

———. *Harry Potter and the Deathly Hallows*. New York: Scholastic, 2007.

———. *Harry Potter and the Goblet of Fire*. New York: Scholastic, 2000.

———. *Harry Potter and the Half-Blood Prince*. New York: Scholastic, 2005.

———. *Harry Potter and the Order of the Phoenix*. New York: Scholastic, 2003.

———. *Harry Potter and the Philosopher's Stone*. London: Bloomsbury Publishing, 2014.

———. *Harry Potter and the Prisoner of Azkaban*. New York: Scholastic, 1999.

———. *Harry Potter and the Sorcerer's Stone*. New York: Scholastic, 1997.

———. "Ilvermorny School of Witchcraft and Wizardry. *Pottermore*. www.pottermore.com/writing-by-jk-rowling/ilvermorny.

———. "J. K. Rowling Web Chat Transcript." *The Leaky Cauldron*. July 30, 2007. www.the-leaky-cauldron.org/2007/07/30/j-k-rowling-web-chat-transcript/.

———. *Quidditch Through the Ages*. New York: Scholastic, 2000.

———. *The Tales of Beedle the Bard*. New York: Scholastic, 2008.

———. Twitter post. December 21, 2015, 5:41 a.m. https://twitter.com/jk_rowling/status/678888094339366914?lang=en.

———. *Very Good Lives: The Fringe Benefits of Failure and the Importance of Imagination*. New York: Little, Brown and Company, 2015.

Schoefer, Christine. "Harry Potter's Girl Trouble: The World of Everyone's Favorite Kid Wizard is a Place Where Boys Come First." *Salon*. January 13, 2000. www.salon.com/2000/01/13/potter.

Scott, Suzanne. "Authorized Resistance? Is Fan Production Frakked?" In *Cylons in America: Critical Studies in Battlestar Galactica, ed. C.W. Marshall and Tiffany Potter, 210–223. New York: Continuum, 2008.

"Scottish Fact of the Week: The 'Harry Potter' Café." The Scotsman. April 30, 2013. www.scotsman.com/lifestyle/culture/books/scottish-fact-of-the-week-the-harry-potter-cafe-1-2914364.

"Scumbag Hat." Know Your Meme. September 1, 2016. http://knowyourmeme.com/memes/scumbag-hat.

"Sees brother in marauder map." Quick Meme. September 1, 2016. www.quick-meme.com/meme/3ogpjv.

"Sees brother sleeping with a man named peter every night." Quick Meme. September 1, 2016. www.quickmeme.com/meme/3qwgv8.

"Sees peter pettigrew sleeping next to ron's bed." Quick Meme. September 1, 2016. www.quickmeme.com/meme/3q36rt.

Setoodeh, Ramin. "'Fantastic Beasts' Becomes First 'Harry Potter' Movie to Win an Oscar." Variety. February 26, 2017. http://variety.com/2017/film/news/fantastic-beast-first-harry-potter-oscar-1201997179/.

Shecter, Adam. "Seeking an LGBTQ Middle-Grade Blockbuster." School Library Journal May 14, 2014. www.slj.com/2014/05/diversity/seeking-an-lgbtq-middle-grade-blockbuster/.

Shifman, Limor. Memes in Digital Culture. Cambridge: MIT Press, 2013.

Sieczkowski, Cavan. "Emma Watson Says Nude Photo Leak Threat After Gender Equality Speech a 'Wake-Up Call.'" The Huffington Post. March 9, 2015. www.huffingtonpost.com/2015/03/09/emma-watson-nude-photo-leak-threat_n_6832066.html.

Siegel, Hanna. "Rowling Lets Dumbledore Out of the Closet." ABC News. October 20, 2007. http://abcnews.go.com/Entertainment/story?id=3755544.

Singh, Anita. "JK Rowling Launches Pottermore Website." The Telegraph. June 16, 2011. www.telegraph.co.uk/culture/harry-potter/8579560/JK-Rowling-launches-Pottermore-website.html.

"Snowclone." Know Your Meme. September 1, 2016. http://knowyourmeme.com/memes/snowclone.

Solon, Olivia. "J. K. Rowling's Pottermore Reveal: Harry Potter E-books and More." Arstechnica. June 23, 2011. http://arstechnica.com/gaming/2011/06/jk-rowlings-pottermore-reveal-harry-potter-e-books-and-more/.

Stam, Robert. "Introduction: The Theory and Practice of Adaptation." In Literature and Film: A Guide to the Theory and Practice of Film Adaptation, ed. Robert Stam and Alessandra Raengo (Malden, MA and Oxford: Blackwell Publishing, 2005). 1–52. "Best-Sellers Initially Rejected." Lit Rejections. June 10, 2016. www.litrejections.com/best-sellers-initially-rejected/.

Stanley, Alessandra. "Review: 'The Casual Vacancy,' Based on J. K. Rowling's

Novel, on HBO." *The New York Times*. April 28, 2015. www.nytimes.com/2015/04/29/arts/television/review-the-casual-vacancy-based-on-j-k-rowlings-novel-on-hbo.html.

Stinger, Matt. "Split Decision: How Breaking Movies in Half is Ruining Hollywood Blockbusters." *Screen Crush*. November 21, 2014. http://screencrush.com/splitting-movies-into-parts-1-and-2/.

Sullivan, Andrew. "Dumbledore!" *The Daily Dish*. October 20, 2007. www.theatlantic.com/daily-dish/archive/2007/10/dumbledore/224374/.

Sutton, Eileen. "How Emma Watson Continues to Deal with HeForShe Death Threats." *Racked*. March 9, 2015. www.racked.com/2015/3/9/8175609/emma-watson-heforshe-death-threats.

Swiss Army Man. Directed by The Daniels. A24, 2016.

"Talk: Marauder's Map." *Harry Potter Wiki,* September 1, 2016. http://harry-potter.wikia.com/wiki/Talk:Marauder's_Map;

Tesfaye, Sophia. "Repent that Dumbledore Emerged as a Homosexual Mentor for Harry Potter." *Salon*. November 9, 2015. www.salon.com/2015/11/09/repent_that_dumbledore_emerged_as_a_homosexual_mentor_for_harry_potter_inside_the_bizarre_anti_gay_conference_featuring_ted_cruz_mike_huckabee_bobby_jindal.

This is the End. Directed by Even Goldberg and Seth Rogen. Sony Pictures, 2013.

Thomas, Jeffrey E. and Franklin G. Snyder, eds. *The Law and Harry Potter*. Durham: Carolina Academic Press, 2010.

Thorne, Jack. *Harry Potter and the Cursed Child, Parts I and II*. New York: Scholastic, 2016.

"The Time Turner." *MemeCenter*. September 6, 2016. www.memecenter.com/fun/1555081/time-turner.

"Time Turner Situations I Could Have Been Used For," *WeKnowMemes,* February 1, 2012, http://weknowmemes.com/2012/02/time-turner-situations-i-could-have-been-used-for/.

Trites, Roberta Seelinger. "The Harry Potter Novels as a Test Case for Adolescent Literature." *Style* 35.3 (2001): 472–485.

"True Story." *KnowYourMeme*. September 6, 2016. http://knowyourmeme.com/memes/true-story.

"The Uncle." *Tumblr*. September 7, 2016. http://66.media.tumblr.com/tumblr_lnvqc4zKuH1qk2jwqo3_1280.jpg.

"UN Women announces Emma Watson as Goodwill Ambassador." *UN Women*. July 8, 2014. www.unwomen.org/en/news/stories/2014/7/un-women-announces-emma-watson-as-goodwill-ambassador.

Victoria, Ward, "JK Rowling Unveils Pottermore Website." *The Telegraph*. June

23, 2011. www.telegraph.co.uk/news/uknews/8593930/JK-Rowling-unveils-Pottermore-website.html.

"VS." *Tumblr.* September 7, 2016. http://media.tumblr.com/tumblr_loyeno Cpmf1qh5nc9.jpg.

Walker, Harriet. "First Sight: Pottermore.com, the Internet." *The Independent.* August 16 2011. www.independent.co.uk/arts-entertainment/books/news /first-sight-pottermorecom-the-internet-2338170.html.

"Warner Bros. Studio Tour London—The Making of Harry Potter." *Trip-Advisor.* May 20, 2014. www.tripadvisor.com/Attraction_Review-g2691242-d2147749-Reviews-Warner_Bros_Studio_Tour_London-Leavesden_ Hertfordshire_England.html#REVIEWS.

Watkins, Gwynne. "Portrait of an Influential Fan: Melissa Anelli, Webmistress of Harry Potter's Leaky Cauldron." *Vulture.* October 17, 2012. www.vulture .com/2012/10/influential-fan-harry-potter-melissa-anelli-leaky-cauldron .html.

"Welcome to the Shire." September 30, 2016. http://hobbitsunite.tumblr.com /post/63253859752/life-lessons-with-hagrid.

"Well, Harry?" *Imgur,* April 21, 2013, http://imgur.com/gallery/e7UT02F.

West, Kelly. "Will Harry Potter 8 Ever Happen? Here's What J. K. Rowling Says." *Cinema Blend.* www.cinemablend.com/celebrity/Harry-Potter-8-Ever-Happen-Here-What-J-K-Rowling-Says-71246.html.

"When examining the Marauder's Map." *Quora.* September 1, 2016. www .quora.com/When-examining-the-Marauder%E2%80%99s-Map-how-did-Fred-and-George-fail-to-notice-that-their-brother-Ron-had-another-man-Peter-Pettigrew-in-bed-with-him-every-night-or-that-Voldemort-was-always-beside-Quirrel-in-the-first-book.

"Whirls Snape Out of the Way." *Smash 4 Link Player.* September 7, 2016. http://mycastiel.co.vu/post/99930594303/whirls-snape-out-of-the-way-did-you-shoves.

Whited, Lana A. ed. *The Ivory Tower and Harry Potter: Perspectives on a Literary Phenomenon.* Columbia: University of Missouri Press, 2004.

———. and M. Katherine Grimes. "What Would Harry Do? J. K. Rowling and Lawrence Kohlberg's Theories of Moral Development." In *The Ivory Tower and Harry Potter,* ed. Lana Whited, 182–211. Columbia: University of Missouri Press, 2004.

"Why couldn't Harry or anybody else see Peter Pettigrew," *Science Fiction and Fantasy Stack Exchange,* September 1, 2016, http://scifi.stackexchange .com/questions/11447/why-couldnt-harry-or-anybody-else-see-peter-pettigrew-aka-scabbers-on-the-marau.

"Why Fred and George Didn't See Voldemort and Pettigrew On The Marauder's

Map?" *Potter Plotholes.* September 1, 2016. http://potter-plotholes
.tumblr.com/post/112134776057/fred-george-weasley-marauders-map-
voldemort-pettigrew.

Willemen, Paul. "Anthony Mann: Looking at the Male." *Framework* 15–17
(1981): 16–20.

Williams, Tracy Rundstrom. "Exploring the Impact of Study Abroad on
Students' Intercultural Communication Skills: Adaptability and Sensitivity."
Journal of Studies in International Education 9.4 (2005): 356–71.

Willis, Ika. "Keeping Promises to Queer Children: Making Space (for Mary
Sue) at Hogwarts." *Fan Fiction and Fan Communities in the Age of the
Internet: New Essays*, ed. Kristina Busse and Karen Hellekson, 153–70.
Jefferson: McFarland, 2006.

"Wizard Training for Muggles: Sony Creates New Book of Spells Game to
Keep Harry Potter Fans Happy." *Daily Mail*, June 4 2012. www.dailymail
.co.uk/sciencetech/article-2154725/Calling-Harry-Potter-fans-Sony-
creates-new-Book-Spells-game-Muggles-happy.html.

"The Wizarding World of Harry Potter." May 9, 2013, www.universalorlando
.com/harrypotter.

Wonderbook: Book of Spells. PlayStation.com. May 9, 2013. http://us.play
station.com/games/wonderbook-book-of-spells-ps3.html.

Zelizer, Barbie. (1995). "Reading the Past Against the Grain: The Shape of
Memory Studies." *Critical Studies in Mass Communication* 12.2 (1995):
214–39.

Contributors

Cassandra Bausman graduated from the University of Iowa with a PhD in English literature. Her dissertation focuses on intersections between feminist revisionism and metafiction in a consideration of fantasy literature and its heroines, which helped earn her the International Association for the Fantastic in the Arts' Emerging Scholar Award. She now teaches at Trine University, and her literary criticism can be found in *The Journal of the Fantastic in the Arts*, *The Iowa Journal of Cultural Studies*, and the anthologies *Maps and Mapmaking in Children's Literature* and *Heroines of Film and Television: Portrayals of Women in Popular Culture*.

Michelle Markey Butler is a Lecturer in the College of Information Studies and the Honors College at the University of Maryland College Park, where she teaches medieval literature and modern fantasy. She *will* someday finish that book about the transition from direct address to soliloquy, but is currently obsessed with "amateur" literary criticism on the web. She is also the author of SF/F stories; the historical fantasy *Homegoing* (Pink Narcissus Press, 2014); and the historical fiction *The Last Abbot of Linn Duachaill* (with Jess Barry, S & H Publishing, 2016). She puts research from her day job to good use in her fiction and is absolutely as geeky as you'd expect. http://michellemarkeybutler.com.

Vera Cuntz-Leng is a postdoctoral research fellow at the Department of Media Studies at the Philipps University of Marburg, and the chief editor of the academic journal *MEDIENwissenschaft*. She studied film and theatre science in Mainz, Marburg, and Vienna. Further, she was a visiting researcher at the Berkeley Center for New Media of UC Berkeley. She received her PhD from the Department of Media Studies at the Eberhard Karls university of Tübingen. Her latest book publications are *Harry Potter que(e)r: Eine Filmsaga im Spannungsfeld von Queer Reading, Slash-Fandom und Fantasyfilmgenre*

(Bielefeld: transcript, 2015) and *Creative Crowds: Perspektiven der Fanforschung im deutschsprachigen Raum* (Darmstadt: Büchner, 2014).

Emily Dallaire is an alumnus of Michigan State University, where she studied Professional Writing and Experience Architecture. With an interest in both *Harry Potter* and adaptive fan experiences, Emily was excited to combine these interests in researching the Harry Potter community and their involvement in preserving and sharing memories in multiple forms and spaces.

Maria Dicieanu is an independent new media researcher and blogger. She is equally interested in both theoretical and practical aspects of filmmaking, believing that one does not exclude the other. She sees herself as a "Multimedia in Human Form," as her projects approach so many different fields: she's a film editor, journalist, PR and Social Media mind, researcher, cinephile, book lover, and artistic music videos curator. Her published academic works include "Fanpower and Characters' Migration," "Adaptations: Primitive Transmedia Narratives?" and "The X Factor of Singing Competitions," for volumes published in France, England, and Germany.

Dr. Andrew Howe is Professor of History at La Sierra University (Riverside, CA), where he teaches courses in film studies, popular culture, and American history. Recent scholarship includes book chapters on cultural artifacts associated with the television show *Game of Thrones*, the role of cemeteries and burial rites in the western genre, and portrayals of masculinity in *Star Trek: Deep Space Nine*.

Katharine McCain is a recent graduate of Georgetown University with a Master's in English Literature. She is continuing her studies at The Ohio State University, pursuing a PhD in Television/Media Studies with an emphasis on Fan Studies. She has presented research on queer representation and fanworks at the 2016 Console-ing Passions Conference, as well as a paper on fans' innovative use of GIFs at the 38th annual Southwest Popular/American Culture Association Conference. Other published works include "'Feeling Exposed?': Irene Adler and the Self-Reflective Disguise" in *Gender and the Modern Sherlock Holmes* (McFarland, 2015), as well as a flash fiction titled "Hereditary" in *22 More Quick Shivers* (Cosnomic Multimedia, 2014), and the poem "I Walk a Path of Cyclicality" in *Sherlock's Home: The Empty House* (MX Publishing, 2012).

Liza Potts is a digital humanities scholar working in rhetoric and technical communication, focused on experience architecture. Her research interests include social user experience, participatory culture, and digital rhetoric. She is an associate professor in the Department of Writing, Rhetoric, and American Cultures at Michigan State University, where she is the director of the award-winning WIDE Research Center and the co-founder of the Experience Architecture program. Her work has been published in book form by Routledge, and in journals such as *Participations Journal of Audience and Reception Studies, Kairos, Technical Communication Quarterly, Technical Communication, Programmatic Perspectives*, and the *Journal of Business and Technical Communication*.

Kelly Turner is an alumnus of Michigan State University, where she studied Professional Writing with a concentration in digital and technical writing. As a fan since the first *Harry Potter* book was published, Kelly has enjoyed growing up with the characters and witnessing the growth of the *Harry Potter* fandom. She enjoys exploring how the relationship between fan culture and memory-making changes in various fan spaces.

Index

CPSIA information can be obtained
at www.ICGtesting.com
Printed in the USA
BVOW08s0152060218
507351BV00001B/2/P

9 780814 342862